Voluntary health insurance in Europe: country experience

The European Observatory on Health Systems and Policies supports and promotes evidence-based health policy-making through comprehensive and rigorous analysis of health systems in Europe. It brings together a wide range of policy-makers, academics and practitioners to analyse trends in health reform, drawing on experience from across Europe to illuminate policy issues.

The Observatory is a partnership hosted by the WHO Regional Office for Europe, which includes the governments of Austria, Belgium, Finland, Ireland, Norway, Slovenia, Sweden, the United Kingdom and the Veneto Region of Italy; the European Commission; the World Bank; UNCAM (French National Union of Health Insurance Funds); the London School of Economics and Political Science; and the London School of Hygiene & Tropical Medicine. The Observatory has a secretariat in Brussels and it has hubs in London (at LSE and LSHTM) and at the Technical University of Berlin.

Voluntary health insurance in Europe

Country experience

Edited by:

Anna Sagan

Sarah Thomson

World Health Organization
REGIONAL OFFICE FOR Europe

European Observatory on Health Systems and Policies
a partnership hosted by WHO

Keywords:
INSURANCE, HEALTH
HEALTHCARE FINANCING
HEALTH SERVICES ACCESSIBILITY
EUROPE

Please address requests about the publication to:
Publications, WHO Regional Office for Europe, UN City, Marmorvej 51, DK-2100 Copenhagen Ø, Denmark

Alternatively, complete an online request form for documentation, health information, or for permission to quote or translate, on the Regional Office web site (http://www.euro.who.int/en/what-we-publish/publication-request-forms).

ISBN 978 92 890 5037 1

Printed in the United Kingdom

Typeset by Peter Powell

Cover design by M2M

Contents

Acknowledgements

We are indebted to the many country experts who contributed to the study by writing the chapters in this book and reviewing parts of its companion volume. We are also grateful to Anna Maresso (European Observatory on Health Systems and Policies) and Sherry Merkur (European Observatory on Health Systems and Policies) for their help with earlier drafts of the 34 country profiles. We thank Erica Richardson (European Observatory on Health Systems and Policies) for translating the Ukrainian profile into English, Champa Heidbrink (LSE Health) for financial management of the study and our colleagues at the European Observatory on Health Systems and Policies and the WHO Barcelona Office for Health Systems Strengthening for vital project and production support. The production and copy-editing process for this book was coordinated by Jonathan North with the support of Caroline White. Additional support came from Aki Hedigan and Sonia Cutler (copy-editing) and Peter Powell (typesetting).

List of tables and figures

Tables

Figures

List of abbreviations

ACPR	Prudential Supervisory Authority (*Autorité de contrôle prudentiel et de résolution*) (France)
ALD	long-term illness (*affection de longue durée*) (France)
AMD	Armenian dram
ASVG	General Social Security Act (*Allgemeines Sozialversicherungsgesetz*) (Austria)
ATS	Austrian schilling
AVB	general conditions of insurance (*Allgemeine Versicherungsbedingungen*) (Austria)
BGN	Bulgarian lev
BVB	specific insurance conditions (Austria)
CBA	Central Bank of Armenia
CHIF	Croatian Health Insurance Fund
CHSC	Child Health State Certificate (Armenia)
CMU-C	complementary universal health coverage (*couverture maladie universelle complémentaire*) (France)
CT	computerized tomography
CZK	Czech koruna
DECO	Portuguese Association for Consumer Protection (*Associação Portuguesa para a Defesa de Consumidores*)
DKK	Danish krone
DPS	Drugs Payment Scheme (Ireland)
DRG	diagnosis-related group
ECJ	European Court of Justice
EEA	European Economic Area
EEC	European Economic Community
EHIF	Estonian Health Insurance Fund
EOPYY	National Organization for Health Care Provision (Greece)
ESY	National Health System (*Ethniko Systima Ygeias*) (Greece)
EU	European Union
FFS	fee-for-service
FMA	Austrian Financial Market Authority
FSC	Financial Supervision Commission (Bulgaria)
GBP	Pound sterling
GDP	gross domestic product
GEL	Georgian lari
GP	general practitioner
HANFA	Croatian Financial Services Supervisory Authority (*Hrvatska agencija za nadzor financijskih usluga*)
HIA	Health Insurance Authority (Ireland and the Netherlands)
HIIS	Health Insurance Institute of Slovenia
HRK	Croatian kuna
HSE	Health Service Executive (Ireland)
HTD	High Tech Drugs Scheme (Ireland)
HUF	Hungarian forint
IHI	Icelandic Health Insurance
ISC	Insurance Supervision Commission (Lithuania)
KCE	Health Care Knowledge Centre (Belgium)
LTC	long-term care
LTI	Long-Term Illness Scheme (Ireland)
MFSA	Malta Financial Services Authority
MIP	Medical Insurance Programme (Georgia)
MRI	magnetic resonance imaging
MSA	medical savings account
NHF	National Health Fund
NHI	National Health Insurance
NHIF	National Health Insurance Fund (Bulgaria and Romania)
NHIFA	National Health Insurance Fund Administration (Hungary)
NHS	National Health Service

NTPF	National Treatment Purchase Fund (Ireland)
OCM-CDZ	Control Office of the Mutual Health Funds and the National Unions of Mental Health Funds (*Office de contrôle des mutualités et des unions nationales de mutualités/Controledienst voor de ziekenfondsen en de landsbonden van ziekenfondsen*) (Belgium)
OCSC	Obstetric Care State Certificate (Armenia)
OECD	Organisation for Economic Cooperation and Development
OOP	out-of-pocket
PET	positron emission tomography
PPN	preferred provider network
RUB	Russian ruble
SIMES	self-insured medical expenses scheme
SNS	Spanish national health system (*Sistema Nacional de la Salud*)
SSN	National Health Service (*Servizio Sanitario Nazionale*) (Italy)
TB	Tuberculosis
UAH	Ukrainian hryvnia
Ukrstat	State Statistics Service of Ukraine
UNOCAM	National Union of Complementary Health Insurers (*Union nationale des organismes d'assurance maladie complémentaire*) (France)
VAG	Insurance Supervision Act (*Versicherungsaufsichtsgesetz*), later called Law on the Supervision of Insurance Undertakings (Austria)
VHI	voluntary health insurance
VMSA	voluntary medical savings account
VšZP	General Health Insurance Company (*Všeobecná zdravotná poisťovňa*) (Slovakia)
VVG	Insurance Contract Act (Austria)
VVO	Austrian Insurance Association (*Versicherungsverband Österreich*)
ZLD	Pharmacies Activity Act (Slovenia)
ZUJF	Fiscal Balance Act (*Zakon za uravnoteženje javnih finance*) (Slovenia)
Zvw	Health Insurance Act (*Zorgverzekeringswet*) (the Netherlands)
ZZavar	Health Insurance Act (*Zakon o zavarovalništvu*) (Slovenia)
ZZavar-UPB	Health Insurance Act – Official Consolidated Text (*Zakon o zavarovalništvu – uradno in prečiščeno besedilo* (Slovenia)
ZZDej	Health Care Activity Act (*Zakon o zdravstveni dejavnosti*) (Slovenia)
ZZVZZ	Health Care and Health Insurance Act (*Zakon o zdravstvenem varstvu in zdravstvenem zavarovanju*) (Slovenia)
ZZVZZ-H	Act on Changes and Supplementation of the Health Care and Health Insurance Act (*Zakon o spremembah in dopolnitvah Zakona o zdravstvenem varstvu in zdravstvenem zavarovanju*) (Slovenia)

Contributors

Editors

Anna Sagan
Research Fellow at the European Observatory on Health Systems and Policies, London School of Economics and Political Science

Sarah Thomson
Senior Health Financing Specialist at the WHO Barcelona Office for Health Systems Strengthening, Division of Health Systems and Public Health, WHO Regional Office for Europe and Senior Research Associate at the European Observatory on Health Systems and Policies

Country profile authors

Natasha Azzopardi-Muscat University of Malta, Msida

Peter Balik Health Policy Institute, Bratislava

Konstantin Beck Institute for Empirical Health Economics, Lucerne and University of Zurich

Karen Berg Brigham URC Eco (Paris Health Services and Health Economics Research Unit, AP-HP)

Girts Brigis Riga Stradins University

Karine Chevreul URC Eco (Paris Health Services and Health Economics Research Unit, AP-HP)

Joan Costa-i-Font London School of Economics and Political Science

Thomas Czypionka Institute for Advanced Studies, Vienna

Antoniya Dimova Medical University of Varna

Martin Dlouhy University of Economics, Prague

Mónica Duarte Oliveira Centre for Management Studies of Instituto Superior Técnico, University of Lisbon

Charalampos Economou Panteion University of Social and Political Sciences, Athens

Antonis Farmakas Open University of Cyprus, Nicosia

Francesca Ferré Centre for Research on Health and Social Care Management (CERGAS), Università Bocconi, Milan

Thomas Foubister London School of Economics and Political Science

Péter Gaál Semmelweis University, Budapest

Sophie Gerkens Belgian Health Care Knowledge Centre, Brussels

Stefan Greß University of Applied Sciences, Fulda

Nana Gugeshashvili Independent scholar, London and Tbilisi

Triin Habicht Ministry of Social Affairs, Tallinn

Jan Roth Johnsen Health economist, Oslo

Gintaras Kacevicius National Health Insurance Fund, Vilnius

Valery Lekhan Dnipropetrovsk Medical Academy

Ferenc Lindeisz Independent scholar, Budapest

Karmen Lončarek University of Rijeka

Hans Maarse Maastricht University

Hripsime Martirosyan American University of Armenia, Yerevan

Anja Milenkovic Kramer University of Ljubljana

Sofia Nogueira da Silva Universidade Católica Portuguesa, Porto

Victor Olsavszky WHO Country Office, Romania

Peter Pazitny Health Policy Institute, Bratislava

Marc Perronnin Institute for research and information in health economics (IRDES), Paris

Varduhi Petrosyan American University of Armenia, Yerevan

Elena Potapchik National Research University, Higher School of Economics, Moscow

Erica Richardson European Observatory on Health Systems and Policies

Clemens Sigl Federation of Austrian Social Security Organisations, Vienna

Sigurbjörg Sigurgeirsdóttir University of Iceland, Reykjavik

Caj Skoglund Independent scholar, Lulea

Alicja Sobczak University of Ecology and Management, Warsaw

Szabolcs Szigeti WHO Country Office, Hungary

Mamas Theodorou Open University of Cyprus, Nicosia

Brian Turner University College Cork

Viktor von Wyl University of Zurich

Karsten Vrangbæk University of Copenhagen

Lauri Vuorenkoski Finnish Medical Association, Helsinki

Note

This study on voluntary health insurance (VHI) in Europe has been prepared by the European Observatory on Health Systems and Policies and the WHO Regional Office for Europe.

The study is published in three separate volumes:

- Short profiles of VHI in 34 countries in Europe, including 27 European Union Member States (this book)
- An analytical overview of markets for VHI across the 34 countries (a companion book)
- A review of VHI's impact on health system performance and implications for policy (a policy summary)

The views expressed in this volume are those of the authors and do not necessarily reflect the views of the organizations with which they are affiliated.

Introduction

Anna Sagan and Sarah Thomson

This book is part of a larger study on voluntary health insurance (VHI) in Europe. Building on earlier work,[1] the study presents an up to date overview of the size, operation, regulation and policy implications of markets for VHI in countries across the WHO European Region. Its main aim is to provide analysis and evidence for policymakers interested in knowing whether and how VHI can contribute to stronger health system performance through improvements in financial protection, responsiveness, equity, efficiency, quality, transparency and accountability.

International analysis of VHI clearly demonstrates the importance of national contexts. No two markets for VHI are the same. All differ in some way, not least because they are heavily shaped by the nature and performance of publicly financed health systems and by the historical contexts in which they have evolved. To understand how VHI affects the attainment of health system goals – its usefulness as a policy instrument – therefore requires an understanding of how a given market developed, how it operates in practice and how it interacts with the health system as a whole.

This volume contains short profiles of markets for VHI in 34 countries: 27 of the 28 European Union Member States, 3 European Free Trade Association countries (Iceland, Norway and Switzerland), and Armenia, Georgia, the Russian Federation and Ukraine. The profiles place VHI within a national context, providing an opportunity to discuss national policy goals, challenges and debates. Each one covers the following areas: health system context – a short summary of the

1 Colombo & Tapay (2004), Mossialos & Thomson (2004), Thomson & Mossialos (2009), Thomson (2010)

health financing mix, entitlement to publicly financed health care and gaps in coverage; an overview of the VHI market; public policy towards VHI; and debates and challenges.

A companion volume analyses markets for VHI across all of these countries.[2] It focuses on why people buy VHI, how VHI markets work, public policy towards VHI and implications for health system performance.

The subject of both volumes is health insurance that is voluntary. We define this as health insurance that is taken up and paid for at the discretion of individuals or employers on behalf of employees (including group policies sponsored by employers that "come with the job" and are thus not strictly voluntary). VHI can be offered by public and quasi-public bodies and by profit-making (commercial) and non-profit-making private organizations. Throughout, we distinguish between VHI markets that play a substitutive, complementary and supplementary role in relation to publicly financed health coverage, as set out in Table 0.1. Table 0.2 shows how the countries covered in this volume fit into this classification. It also indicates the size of different VHI markets in terms of spending on health and population coverage.

2 Sagan & Thomson (2016).

Table 0.1 *VHI market roles*

Market role	Driver of market development	Nature of VHI coverage
Supplementary	Perceptions about the quality and timeliness of publicly financed health services	Offers faster access to services, greater choice of health care provider or enhanced amenities
Complementary (services)	The scope of the publicly financed benefits package	Services excluded from the publicly financed benefits package
Complementary (user charges)	The existence of user charges for publicly financed health services	User charges for goods and services in the publicly financed benefits package
Substitutive	The share of the population entitled to publicly financed health services	People excluded from or allowed to opt out of publicly financed coverage

Source: Adapted from Foubister et al. (2006).

Table 0.2 *Summary of VHI markets in Europe, 2014*

VHI role	VHI share (%) of total spending on health (2014)			
	≤1%	≤5%	≤10%	>10%
Supplementary	Bulgaria Hungary Italy Lithuania Norway Romania Slovakia Sweden Ukraine	**Austria** **Belgium** Finland Greece **Latvia** **Malta** Poland Russian Federation Spain United Kingdom	Georgia **Portugal** **Switzerland**	**Ireland**
Complementary (services)		Armenia **Denmark**	**Netherlands**	Georgia
Complementary (user charges)		**Denmark** Finland	**Croatia**	**France** **Slovenia**
Substitutive	Czech Republic Estonia Iceland	**Cyprus**	Germany	

Source: Country profiles in this volume.

Note: Only the main role of VHI is considered here. For Denmark, Finland and Georgia, it was not possible to determine which role was dominant. In countries marked in bold, VHI covers over 20% of the population.

References

Colombo F, Tapay N (2004). *Private health insurance in OECD countries.* Paris, Organisation for Economic Co-operation and Development.

Foubister T et al. (2006). *Private medical insurance in the United Kingdom.* Copenhagen, WHO Regional Office for Europe on behalf of the European Observatory on Health Systems and Policies.

Mossialos E, Thomson S (2004). *Voluntary health insurance in the European Union.* Copenhagen, WHO Regional Office for Europe.

Sagan A, Thomson S (2016). *Voluntary health insurance in Europe: role and regulation.* Copenhagen, WHO Regional Office for Europe on behalf of the European Observatory on Health Systems and Policies.

Thomson S (2010). What role for voluntary health insurance? In Kutzin J, Cashin C and Jakab M (eds.), *Implementing health financing reform: lessons from countries in transition.* Copenhagen, WHO Regional Office for Europe on behalf of the European Observatory on Health Policies and Systems.

Thomson S, Mossialos E (2009). *Private health insurance in the European Union.* Final report prepared for the European Commission, Directorate General for Employment, Social Affairs and Equal Opportunities. London and Brussels, LSE Health and Social Care, London School of Economics and Political Science and European Commission.

1 Armenia

Varduhi Petrosyan and Hripsime Martirosyan

Health system context

The health financing mix

Private expenditure accounts for the largest share of health financing in Armenia (WHO, 2016). It is followed by government expenditure and international grants (Ministry of Health of the Republic of Armenia, 2012). In 2014, out-of-pocket (OOP) payments accounted for 53.5% of total spending on health and VHI for 3.5%. The government plans to gradually lower public spending on health from an already very low level of 1.93% of gross domestic product (GDP) in 2014 (WHO, 2016) to 1.69% of GDP in 2015, 1.68% in 2016, 1.57% in 2017 and 1.47% in 2018 (Government of the Republic of Armenia, 2015). As a result, the burden of OOP payments is likely to increase.

Entitlement to publicly financed health care and gaps in coverage

Public funds cover a basic benefits package that includes a broad range of public health services, basic primary care, obstetric and postnatal care for all women and neonates, hospital services for children under seven years of age, emergency resuscitation services, medical services for selected socially significant conditions, including tuberculosis (TB) and HIV/AIDS and partial coverage of other conditions, for example, cancer (Government of the Republic of Armenia, 2004; Ministry of Health of the Republic of Armenia, 2015; Richardson, 2013). Socially vulnerable and special groups (for example, people with a disability) are eligible to receive additional health services (Government of the Republic of Armenia, 2004; Ministry of Health of the Republic of Armenia, 2015).

Formal entitlements are not always guaranteed in practice, however. Because of the very low level of public funding for health, the real cost of services is not compensated and, to cover the shortfall in financing, providers seek informal payments from patients, which encourages people to delay seeking care or forego care to avoid having to pay (Richardson, 2013; Sekhri, Kutzin & Tsaturyan, 2007).

To improve the quality of publicly financed health care and address issues of informal payments and access barriers, the government introduced the Obstetric Care State Certificate (OCSC) programme in 2008 and the Child Health State Certificate (CHSC) programme in 2011 (Crape et al., 2011). These initiatives were successful in increasing state budget allocations for the health sector, improving provider payment mechanisms, assuring affordable obstetric and inpatient paediatric care, significantly reducing OOP payments and increasing patient satisfaction (Crape et al., 2011; Truzyan et al., 2010). In 2011 and 2012, the government introduced official user charges for emergency services, gynaecological services (except maternity services), treatment of sexually transmitted infections and oncological services (Government of the Republic of Armenia, 2010). This reform reduced informal payments but also made services less affordable for households (Economic Development and Research Center & Oxfam Armenia, 2013).

Overview of the VHI market

Market origins, aims and role

Although the first Law on Insurance dates from 1996 (Hakobyan et al., 2006), most VHI developments have happened since 2007, when the new Law on Insurance and Insurance Activities came into force. VHI plays both a *complementary* (covering services excluded from the publicly financed basic benefits package) and a *supplementary* role. Supplementary cover may offer protection against informal payments and access to perceived higher-quality care.

Types of plan available

Insurers offer VHI plans for individuals and families and corporate plans for employers (INGO Armenia Insurance, 2015; Martirosyan H, Research Associate and Project Coordinator, in-depth interviews with administrative staff of major insurance companies in Armenia, 2012; Nairi Insurance, 2015). However, to limit adverse selection, insurers avoid selling individual plans (Martirosyan H, Research Associate and Project Coordinator, in-depth interviews with administrative staff of major insurance companies in Armenia, 2012; Nairi Insurance, 2015). VHI cover ranges from basic to comprehensive and can be tailored to meet corporate needs.

VHI plans are not well defined (for example, the list of benefits can include items such as oncological disease – one time coverage), which may cause problems when the insured try to claim benefits. VHI cover may include immunization, emergency care and care in the acute stages of certain chronic diseases. It may also include inpatient care, diagnostics, cost of medicines and other medical supplies, dental care, eye care and cardiac and neural surgery – these services are not available for the general population under the publicly financed benefits package but may be covered for certain vulnerable populations (defined by the Ministry of Health), such as young children, people with low incomes, war veterans and people with certain disabilities (Martirosyan H, Research Associate and Project Coordinator, in-depth interviews with administrative staff of major insurance companies in Armenia, 2012). VHI may also cover the cost of prescribed medicines.

VHI plans usually do not cover older people (> 65 years old) and exclude many conditions, including pre-existing conditions and most noncommunicable and communicable diseases (Martirosyan H, Research Associate and Project Coordinator, in-depth interviews with administrative staff of major insurance companies in Armenia, 2012; Nairi Insurance, 2015). Premiums are linked to health risk and benefits are capped (but do not involve deductibles or other forms of user charges).

Why do people buy VHI?

Insurers target their products at relatively large employers (mainly companies that have international partners or are branches of international companies) and the majority of people with VHI obtain cover via employers as an employment benefit (Martirosyan H, Research Associate and Project Coordinator, in-depth interviews with administrative staff of major insurance companies in Armenia, 2012). Corporate VHI is encouraged through tax relief. The introduction of mandatory car insurance in 2011 further raised interest in VHI as it contained a health insurance component.

In 2012, the government introduced a new initiative called the Social Package for the Government, covering civil servants and public employees working in education, culture and social protection (Government of the Republic of Armenia, 2011). The Social Package was introduced to boost the attractiveness of government employment, address the social needs of government employees and increase their motivation and productivity. Each employee received a voucher (paid for entirely by the Government) worth Armenian dram (AMD) 132 000 annually (approximately €256; the average exchange rate in 2012 was €1= AMD 516), out of which AMD 52 000 (approximately €101) had to be mandatorily spent on buying health insurance (a basic package) and the remaining AMD 80 000 (approximately €155) could be spent on buying a more generous VHI plan, a VHI plan for one other family member or another social programme (for example, paying for a holiday, children's education or a mortgage). Buying additional VHI cover was the most popular choice and as a result, this new initiative significantly increased demand for VHI. While in 2010 VHI accounted for 0.7% of total spending on health, this share increased to 3.5% in 2013 (Ministry of Health of the Republic of Armenia, 2012; WHO, 2016). In 2012, the Central Bank of Armenia (CBA) projected that VHI premium income from the mandatory and voluntary components of the Social Package would increase 4.5-fold and that the average VHI claims ratio (that is, the share of VHI revenue spent on health services) would drop from 70.7% in 2011 to 41.4% in 2012 (CBA, 2012). In fact, the claims ratio was 33% one year after the implementation of the health insurance component of the Social Package, which is very low by international standards (Ministry of Finance of the Republic of Armenia, 2013).

Who buys VHI?

People with VHI cover are younger (the average age is 35–40 years old), better educated, on average earning more than the general population and are employed in the capital, Yerevan (almost 80% of those with VHI cover).

Who sells VHI?

All insurers are limited joint-stock companies operating on a commercial basis. In 2011, the administrative costs of insurers amounted to 35% of total premium income, which is high by international standards (CBA, 2012). The number of insurers has fallen since 1996 (Hakobyan et al., 2006; Insurance Armenia, 2012). Five offered VHI in 2011 and had the following market shares: Garant-Limens: 32%; Cascade Insurance: 25%; INGO Armenia: 25%; Rosgosstrakh-Armenia: 16%; and RESO Insurance: 2% (CBA, 2007, 2008, 2009, 2011, 2013). In 2012, INGO Armenia and Cascade Insurance merged and Nairi Insurance and Rasco Insurance (now called Armenia Insurance) started offering VHI. In 2014 Rosgosstrakh-Armenia and Garant- Limens merged (Armbanks, 2014; Armenia Insurance, 2015; Martirosyan H, Research Associate and Project Coordinator, in-depth interviews with administrative staff of major insurance companies in Armenia, 2012). Some insurers are Armenian and others are owned by foreign companies; all of them have foreign reinsurers. The CBA projected that the market would concentrate more on the benefit of bigger insurers following the introduction of the Social Package (CBA, 2012).

Insurer relations with providers

Most insurers operate their own medical facilities, but their clients are not constrained to using those facilities and may also use contracted public and private facilities. Staff working in contracted facilities can simultaneously work in both private and public sectors. Usually, the same facilities serve both publicly financed and VHI patients. The same service can be covered by both public financing and VHI, and health care providers can receive payments for the same service from both the government and insurers, leading to inefficiencies.

Insurers reimburse providers according to negotiated tariffs, which can differ from provider to provider; big hospitals, for example, often dictate reimbursement mechanisms to insurers, which means insurers are passive price-takers and do not engage in active purchasing. Insurers' capacity to engage in active purchasing is limited for several reasons: (1) they do not have specialists with skills in active purchasing; (2) the lack of standard treatment guidelines makes it more difficult for insurers to negotiate terms with providers; and (3) some providers have monopoly power (Martirosyan H, Research Associate and Project Coordinator, in-depth interviews with administrative staff of major insurance companies in Armenia, 2012).

Public policy towards VHI

Since 2006, the CBA has regulated the insurance market, including VHI. The government began to encourage the development of VHI in 2010 by amending the Law on Income Tax to encourage employers to purchase VHI plans for employees (Table 1.1). Employers who provide VHI cover for employees are exempt from paying income tax for up to AMD 120 000 (approximately €233) per employee per year. This amendment increased the number of employers buying VHI for employees (Martirosyan H, Research Associate and Project Coordinator, in-depth interviews with administrative staff of major insurance companies in Armenia, 2012).

Table 1.1 *Public policy promoting VHI in Armenia, 1996–2012*

Year	Policy
1996	Law on Insurance comes into force
2007	Law on Insurance and Insurance Activities comes into force
2010	Amendment to the Law on Income Tax comes into force, establishing tax incentives for employers to purchase VHI for employees
2011	Mandatory car insurance containing a health insurance component is introduced
2012	Social Package for government employees is introduced

Source: Authors.

Debates and challenges

Health financing debates in the 2000s included the possibility of introducing some form of mandatory coverage financed through earmarked contributions to complement financing from the general government budget and the strengthening of VHI as a transitional mechanism for moving to a health system predominantly financed from public sources (Hayrapetyan & Khanjian, 2004; Sekhri, Kutzin & Tsaturyan, 2007).

In 2012, there was active discussion about introducing mandatory employment-based coverage through commercial insurers by 2014. However, in 2013, analysis published by the Ministry of Finance (Ministry of Finance of the Republic of Armenia, 2013) and independent studies (Tumasyan, 2013) revealed multiple inefficiencies in the implementation of the (mandatory and voluntary) health insurance component of the Social Package. For example, the claims ratio was extremely low (33%, see earlier), which meant that commercial insurers were the key beneficiaries of the scheme. This made policymakers reconsider the idea. The presence of the State Health Agency of the Ministry of Health in its role as an active purchaser for publicly financed services on behalf of the government and the recent successes of the OCSC and CHSC programmes (Crape et al., 2011; Truzyan et al., 2010) suggest that, with stronger capacity, the State Health Agency can be an active purchaser of health services financed through general taxes and mandatory contributions.

The government amended how the health component of the Social Package is administered in 2014 and designated the State Health Agency as the sole purchaser of health services included in the mandatory component (basic package) of the Social Package. Beneficiaries of the Social Package can still buy more generous coverage and/or coverage for one other family member through private insurers (Government of the Republic of Armenia, 2014).

The future of VHI

The results of the implementation of the mandatory and voluntary components of the Social Package for civil servants and public employees since 2012 have significantly influenced the policy debate on health financing in Armenia. The disadvantages of relying too heavily on VHI have been acknowledged and are confirmed by international experience, which shows how the most vulnerable people (older, disabled, chronically ill, unemployed or poorer people and workers in the informal sector or agricultural workers) are often excluded from VHI or employment-based coverage, particularly in low- and middle-income countries (Chanturidze et al., 2009; Hsiao, 1995). Now the government is exploring plans to introduce mandatory health coverage through a single payer system. The challenge facing the government is to develop a health financing system that can address existing fragmentation and inefficiencies and promote equity and efficiency. This suggests a more limited role for VHI, complementing publicly financed coverage.

References

Armbanks (2014). Armenia's insurance companies posted 2,350.4 mln drams in net profit in nice months. Published on 6 November 2014 at Armbanks Armenian Banks (http://www.armbanks.am/en/2014/11/06/81124/, accessed 22 November 2015).

Armenia Insurance (2014) [website]. Yerevan, Armenia Insurance (http://armeniainsurance.am/, accessed 22 November 2015).

CBA (2012). *ՀՀ ԱՊԱՀՈՎԱԳՐԱԿԱՆ ՀԱՄԱԿԱՐԳԻ ՀՆԱՐԱՎՈՐ ԶԱՐԳԱՑՈՒՄՆԵՐԸ 2012–14 ԹԹ. ԸՍՏ ԱՊԱՀՈՎԱԳՐԱԿԱՆ ԸՆԿԵՐՈՒԹՅՈՒՆՆԵՐԻ 2012–14 ԹԹ. ԳՈՐԾԱՐԱՐ ԾՐԱԳՐԵՐԻ [Possible developments of insurance system in the Republic of Armenia in 2012–2014 – according to the business plans of insurers]*. Yerevan, Agency for Stability and Development of the Financial System, Department of Financial Developments, CBA (https://www.cba.am/AM/panalyticalmaterialsresearches/INSURANCE%20STRATEGY%202012-2014.pdf, accessed 22 November 2015).

CBA (2007, 2008, 2009, 2011, 2013). *Central Bank of Armenia's regulations for the insurance market*. Yerevan, CBA (https://www.cba.am/en/SitePages/reginsurance.aspx, accessed 22 November 2015).

Chanturidze T et al. (2009). Georgia: health system review. *Health Systems in Transition*, 11(8):1–116.

Crape B et al. (2011). *Evaluation of the Child Health State Certificate Program*. Yerevan, Center for Health Services Research and Development, American University of Armenia (http://chsr.aua.am/materials-reports-2011, accessed 22 November 2015).

Economic Development and Research Center & Oxfam Armenia (2013). *Budget financing and copayment system: public policy assessment in healthcare system*. Economic Development and Research Center, Oxfam Armenia Branch (May 2013) (http://mchealth.am/wp-content/uploads/2013/06/Policy-Paper_Eng.pdf, accessed 22 November 2015).

Government of the Republic of Armenia (2004). *Decree No. 318-N from March 3, 2004 on "State Guaranteed Free Delivery of Medical Aid and Services"*. Yerevan, Government of the Republic of Armenia.

Government of the Republic of Armenia (2010). *Decision No. 1762-N on making amendments and additions to Decree No. 318-N from March 3, 2004 on "State Guaranteed Free Delivery of Medical Aid and Services"*. Yerevan, Government of the Republic of Armenia.

Government of the Republic of Armenia (2011). *ՀԱՅԱՍՏԱՆԻ ՀԱՆՐԱՊԵՏՈՒԹՅԱՆ ԿԱՌԱՎԱՐՈՒԹՅՈՒՆ Ո Ր Ո Շ ՈՒ Մ 29 դեկտեմբերի 2011 թվականի N 1923-Ն ՍՈՑԻԱԼԱԿԱՆ ՓԱԹԵԹԻ ԲՈՎԱՆԴԱԿՈՒԹՅՈՒՆԸ, ԾԱՌԱՅՈՒԹՅՈՒՆՆԵՐԻ ՑԱՆԿԸ, ԾԱՌԱՅՈՒԹՅՈՒՆՆԵՐԸ ՄԱՏՈՒՑՈՂ ԿԱԶՄԱԿԵՐՊՈՒԹՅՈՒՆՆԵՐԻ ՑԱՆԿԵՐԸ ԵՎ (ԿԱՄ) ԶԱՓՈՐՈՇԻՉՆԵՐԸ ՀԱՍՏԱՏԵԼՈՒ ՄԱՍԻՆ [Government of the Republic of Armenia Decision Number N 1923-N (December 29, 2011) on the Content of the Social Package, List of Services, List of Service Provider Companies]*. Yerevan, Government of the Republic of Armenia (http://www.arlis.am/DocumentView.aspx?docID=73526, accessed 22 November 2015).

Government of the Republic of Armenia (2014). *ՀԱՅԱՍՏԱՆԻ ՀԱՆՐԱՊԵՏՈՒԹՅԱՆ ԿԱՌԱՎԱՐՈՒԹՅՈՒՆ Ո Ր Ո Շ ՈՒ Մ 25 դեկտեմբերի 2014 թվականի N 1483-Ն*

ՀԱՅԱՍՏԱՆԻ ՀԱՆՐԱՊԵՏՈՒԹՅԱՆ ԿԱՌԱՎԱՐՈՒԹՅԱՆ 2012 ԹՎԱԿԱՆԻ ԴԵԿՏԵՄԲԵՐԻ 27-Ի N 1691-Ն ԵՎ 2014 ԹՎԱԿԱՆԻ ՄԱՐՏԻ 27-Ի N 375-Ն ՈՐՈՇՈՒՄՆԵՐՈՒՄ ԼՐԱՑՈՒՄՆԵՐ ԵՎ ՓՈՓՈԽՈՒԹՅՈՒՆՆԵՐ ԿԱՏԱՐԵԼՈՒ ՄԱՍԻՆ [Government of the Republic of Armenia Decision Number N 1483-N (December 25, 2014) on Making Amendments to the Government of the Republic of Armenia Decision 1691-N (December 27, 2012) and Decision 375-N (March 27, 2014)]. Yerevan, Government of the Republic of Armenia (http://www.arlis.am/documentview.aspx?docid=94918, accessed 22 November 2015).

Government of the Republic of Armenia (2015). *ՀԱՅԱՍՏԱՆԻ ՀԱՆՐԱՊԵՏՈՒԹՅԱՆ 2016-2018 ԹԹ. ՊԵՏԱԿԱՆ ՄԻՋՆԱԺԱՄԿԵՏ ԾԱԽՍԵՐԻ ԾՐԱԳԻՐ [Medium-Term State Expenditure Framework for 2016–2018 of the Republic of Armenia]*. Yerevan, Government of the Republic of Armenia (http://www.gov.am/files/docs/1603.pdf, accessed 22 November 2015).

Hakobyan T et al. (2006). Armenia: health system review. *Health Systems in Transition*, 8(6):1–178.

Hayrapetyan S, Khanjian A (2004). *Health care in Armenia: challenges and prospects*. Working Paper No. 04/13. Washington, DC, Armenian International Policy Research Group.

Hsiao WC (1995). Abnormal economics in the health sector. *Health Policy*, 32(1–3):125–139.

INGO Armenia Insurance (2015) [website]. Yerevan, INGO Armenia Insurance (http://www.ingoarmenia.am/index/index/lang/en, accessed 22 November 2015).

Ministry of Finance of the Republic of Armenia (2013). *Statement for the Government of Armenia on the 2012 results of the Social Package. July 29, 2013*. Yerevan, Ministry of Finance.

Ministry of Health of the Republic of Armenia (2012). *ՀԱՅԱՍՏԱՆԻ ՀԱՆՐԱՊԵՏՈՒԹՅԱՆ ԱՌՈՂՋԱՊԱՀՈՒԹՅԱՆ ԱԶԳԱՅԻՆ ՀԱՇԻՎՆԵՐ 2010 [Armenia National Health Accounts 2010]*. Yerevan, Ministry of Health.

Ministry of Health of the Republic of Armenia (2015). *ԻՐԱՎԱԿԱՆ ԱԿՏԵՐ / ՉԱՓՈՐՈՇԻՉՆԵՐ / ՊԵՏՈՒԹՅԱՆ ԿՈՂՄԻՑ ԵՐԱՇԽԱՎՈՐՎԱԾ ԱՆՎՃԱՐ ԲԺՇԿԱԿԱՆ ՕԳՆՈՒԹՅԱՆ ԵՎ [Orders and decrees on provision of state guaranteed free medical services included in the Basic Benefit Package]*. Yerevan, Ministry of Health (http://moh.am/?section=static_pages/index&id=588&subID=648, accessed 22 November 2015).

Nairi Insurance (2015) [website]. Yerevan, Nairi Insurance (http://www.nairi-insurance.am/?id=1&lang=en, accessed 22 November 2015).

Richardson E (2013). Armenia: Health system review. *Health Systems in Transition*, 15(4): 1– 99.

Sekhri N, Kutzin J, Tsaturyan S (2007). *Voluntary health insurance in Armenia: issues and options*. Health Financing Policy Paper 2007/3. Copenhagen, WHO Regional Office for Europe.

Truzyan N et al. (2010). *Protecting the right of women to affordable and quality health care in Armenia: analysis of the Obstetric Care State Certificate Program*. Yerevan, Center for Health Services Research and Development, American University of Armenia (http://chsr.aua.am/materials-reports-2010, accessed 22 November 2015).

Tumasyan A (2013). *Health insurance component of the social package: a qualitative assessment*. Yerevan, School of Public Health, American University of Armenia (http://auachsr.com/UserFiles/File/new%20/Thesis%202013/Armine%20Tumasyan.pdf, accessed 22 November 2015).

WHO (2016). Global Health Expenditure Database (GHED) [online database]. Geneva, WHO (http://www.who.int/health-accounts/ghed/en/, accessed 5 April 2016).

2
Austria

Thomas Czypionka and Clemens Sigl

Health system context

The health financing mix

In 2014, public spending accounted for 77.9% of total spending on health, while OOP payments and VHI accounted for 16.1 and 4.6% respectively (WHO, 2016).

Entitlement to publicly financed health care and gaps in coverage

Publicly financed coverage is virtually universal, covering over 99% of the population. A very small part of the population (0.2% in 2011; VVO, 2012) is not publicly covered because, since 2000, some self-employed occupational groups (such as physicians, chemists, architects, lawyers and notaries) have been allowed to opt out of the statutory scheme as long as they purchase substitutive private health insurance instead.

The publicly financed benefits package is comprehensive and includes basic dental services. The extent of user charges is small. The most common user charge is the *Rezeptgebühr* (prescription charge), a flat-rate (annually valorized) copayment of €5.55 (2015) for each package of a reimbursable drug. People with low incomes are exempt, as are some other patient groups such as asylum seekers, and an overall cap is generally in effect at 1% of annual income (*Rezeptgebührenobergrenze*). Civil servants and the self-employed must pay 20% coinsurance for outpatient services (reduced to 10% for self-employed people who enter a prevention programme). Deductibles are applied to some forms of dental care.

Overview of the VHI market

Market origins, aims and role

VHI did not play an important role in the health system before the Second World War. After 1945, the market expanded rapidly, with premium income rising from Austrian schilling (ATS) 58.5 million in 1950 to ATS 3.5 billion in 1975. From the mid-1970s, the VHI market began to shrink and then stagnated as publicly financed health coverage grew (Eckhart, 2009:78).

In recent years, the VHI market has been growing continuously (Table 2.1). In 2014, approximately 36% of the population had some form of VHI cover (Table 2.2). VHI mainly plays a *supplementary* role, offering more choice via private providers, faster access to elective care in public hospitals or better hospital accommodation. It also plays a *complementary* role, providing access to services that are not publicly financed, and a *substitutive* role for those who opt out of the publicly financed scheme.

Table 2.1 *Premiums and claims in the Austrian VHI market, 2014*

	All VHI plans	Individual	Group
Premiums (€, in billions)	1.880	1358	0.522
Average annual growth rate since 2011 (%)	3.5	3.53	3.38
Claims (€, in billions)	1 219	0.853	0.367
Average annual growth rate since 2011 (%)	2.95	3.15	2.6
Number of claims	3 052 948	2 532 369	520 579
Average annual growth rate since 2011 (%)	1.02	2.15	1.37

Source: VVO (2014).

Types of plans available

Supplementary VHI plans may cover benefits ranging from fees for noncontracted ambulatory care physicians, additional check-ups, choice of hospital doctor and better hospital amenities (for example, double or single rooms, additional choice of food) to daily cash benefits for inpatient care. Although it is illegal to prioritize patients with VHI, it has long been rumoured, and has been shown empirically (Czypionka, Kraus & Röhrling, 2013), that those who have supplementary VHI can obtain faster access to elective care in public hospitals. Services provided by noncontracted physicians are only partly publicly financed and the 20% that is not publicly covered can be partially covered by VHI (VVO, 2012).

Complementary VHI plans are usually not offered independently but sold as an addition to supplementary cover (special eye and dental care, physiotherapy, home visits, psychotherapy or care in health resorts).

The basic level of cover offered by substitutive VHI plans is nearly identical to the publicly financed benefits package.

Why do people buy VHI?

Because of the broad scope of publicly financed coverage, people mostly purchase VHI for better amenities in hospital (*Sonderklasse*, special class) or to choose the physician who treats them in hospital or among noncontracted physicians (who are thought to spend more time with their patients and provide better care than contracted physicians). Moreover, there is anecdotal evidence that waiting times for elective surgery, albeit not very long, are shorter for people with VHI.

Claims data suggest that VHI mainly covers hospital costs (67.3% of total VHI claims in 2014; VVO, 2014). Just under a fifth of the population (19.8%) has a VHI plan covering hospital costs (Table 2.2). VHI is also used to provide cash benefits during hospital stays (7.8% of total VHI claims in 2014) and reimbursement of physician services (7.9%), dental treatments (2.9%), spa treatments (2.9%) and medicines (2.1%) (VVO, 2014).

Who buys VHI?

Individual plans dominate in the VHI market; group policies account for only 27.7% of total premium income (Table 2.2). Over half of those with VHI are aged between 20 and 50 years old. About 20% of policyholders are children under the age of one. No information is available on the socioeconomic characteristics of people with VHI. VHI take-up varies geographically (Table 2.2), ranging from 53.4% of the population in Carinthia to 25.1% in Lower Austria. Although self-employed people and white-collar workers are more likely to take out VHI, this factor alone cannot account for the marked geographical differences in VHI take-up. Three quarters of people who opt out of publicly financed health coverage purchase supplementary VHI cover in addition to substitutive cover (VVO, 2012).

Who sells VHI?

The VHI market is highly concentrated and dominated by four commercial insurers: UNIQA, Wiener Städtische,

Table 2.2 *Number of VHI policyholders in Austria by state, 2014*

Persons holding any VHI plan								
Austria	Vienna	Lower Austria	Upper Austria	Styria	Tyrol	Carinthia	Salzburg	Burgenland
Number (in millions)								
3.053	0.689	0.409	0.436	0.261	0.257	0.297	0.151	0.077
% of population								
35.8	38.7	25.1	30.5	42	35.4	53.4	48.7	26.7
Persons holding a VHI plan covering hospital costs								
Austria	Vienna	Lower Austria	Upper Austria	Styria	Tyrol	Carinthia	Salzburg	Burgenland
Number (in millions)								
1.687	0.389	0.203	0.250	0.288	0.164	0.125	0.151	0.040
% of population								
19.8	21.9	12.4	17.5	2.7	22.7	22.4	28.2	13.8

Source: VVO (2014).

Merkur and Generali. Together they account for 95% of the VHI market, with the biggest insurer UNIQA covering 47% of the market (Figure 2.1).

Figure 2.1 *Market share of VHI insurers in Austria (%), 2014*

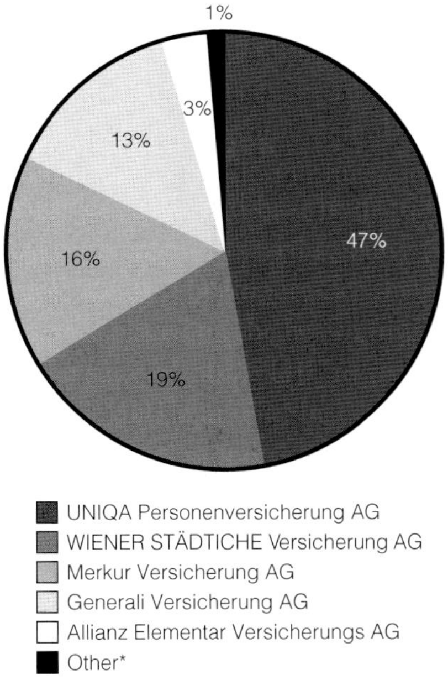

Source: VVO (2014).

Note: *MuKi Versicherungsverein AG, CALL DIRECT Versicherung AG, Wüstenrot Versicherungs-AG, Donau Versicherung AG Vienna Insurance Group.

The average VHI claims ratio (expenditure on health services as a percentage of total premium income) was approximately 60% in 2014 (Table 2.1). Operating expenses accounted for approximately 5.4% of net premium income in 2010 (GuV der Krankenversicherung, 2010).

Insurer relations with providers

The Austrian Insurance Association (VVO) negotiates fees with inpatient services providers, hospital doctors and regional medical associations on behalf of insurers. Providers are paid on a fee-for-service (FFS) basis. Some insurers partly own private medical facilities, but subscribers are not obliged to use them. Contractual agreements with hospitals, including a cost guarantee commitment, enable electronic direct billing of insurers. For outpatient care, patients are generally required to pay providers and seek reimbursement from their insurer. To improve efficiency, quality criteria and requirement profiles for providers are embedded in agreements.

Public policy towards VHI

VHI falls under the same regulations as the broader insurance market: the Insurance Contract Act (VVG), the Law on General and Specific Insurance conditions (AVB, BVB) and the Law on the Supervision of Insurance Undertakings (VAG); there are no VHI-specific regulations. The Austrian Financial Market Authority (FMA) supervises all forms of insurance. The development and regulation of the VHI market is shown in Table 2.3.

Debates and challenges

Publicly financed health coverage is generous and, regardless of whether people have or do not have VHI, all patients must be treated equally in inpatient and outpatient settings. Nevertheless, the fear of two-tier medicine – for those with and those without VHI – is strong and fuelled by frequent anecdotal evidence

Table 2.3 *Development and regulation of the VHI market in Austria, 1889–2012*

Year	Policy
1889	Health Insurance Law (*Krankenversicherungsgesetz*): in case of illness all workers and trainees from industry, independent of their actual salary, get 60% of the daily wage that is customary at their place of work; the warranted medical treatment is restricted to 20 weeks
1917	Wage bracket system is applied
1956	General Social Security Act (*Allgemeines Sozialversicherungsgesetz*, ASVG): consistent rules for self-employed persons and essential increase of service range are established
1939–1979	German Insurance Supervision Act (VAG) 1931 is adopted, regulating the interests of insurers in general (concessions, investment rules, own resources, insurance coverage funds, insurance supervision)
1979	VAG becomes effective
1986	Opportunities for capital investment are extended, reporting requirements standardized and four-eyes-principle for boards and management is introduced
1991	Accounting rules are adapted to EU law
1992	General adaptation to EU law takes place
1994	Regulatory provisions and required adjustments are adapted in the course of Austrian EU accession
1994	Insurance Contract Law determining health insurance as lifelong contractual relationship (with the exception of group insurance, income replacement insurance and dental insurance) is adapted
1996	Provisions for strengthening the supervision of financial institutions are made, and regulations on the use of derivative financial instruments are introduced
1999	Consolidated financial statements and capital participation are amended
2000	Coverage value lists and detailed provisions for monitoring after concession loss are introduced
2002	Structure of investment provisions is changed and minimum capital requirements and guarantee funds are raised
2004	Capital requirements and supervision are changed; EU directives concerning insurance broking and balancing provisions (Solvency I) are implemented
2005	Regulations on risk management are introduced
2006	Consolidated financial statements to international accounting standards are adopted
2008	EU's reinsurance directives are adopted
2010	Implementation process of Solvency II directives begins
2012	29 March (effective from 1 July): Insurance Contract Law is amended (*Versicherungsrechts-Änderungsgesetz*) – main changes concern the approval requirements and the right of objection in health data collection (policyholders must give separate consent for insurers to collect their health data), the electronic communication of insurance contracts (a separate agreement is required) and the general right of withdrawal for the insured (the insured were granted this right)
2012	Judgement of the European Court of Justice (ECJ) – differentiation of VHI premiums by gender prohibited from the end of 2012

Source: Holzer & Stickler (2012).

of people with VHI having shorter waiting times (also confirmed by Czypionka, Kraus & Röhrling, 2013). Insurers use this fear as a marketing tool for VHI. For example, lists of the *best doctors* that can be accessed through VHI have attracted media attention in recent years. VHI covers treatment methods (such as homeopathy and phytotherapy) that do not pass the cost–effectiveness test for inclusion in the publicly financed benefits package (for example, homeopathy and phytotherapy), making access to these services easier for people with VHI.

Debates about waiting times, informal payments and VHI as a *door opener* became especially heated in the summer of 2011, as the Ministry of Health was preparing an amendment to the Hospital Act imposing an obligation on the hospitals to publish waiting lists, including the VHI status of each patient. At the forum held in Alpbach, the Minister of Health expressed his contempt towards preferential treatment of patients with VHI, while other participants, for example, the Chambers of Physicians, took an opposing view and emphasized the importance of VHI in hospital financing. The amendment was carried, but the implementation did not improve transparency significantly as most states introduced laws that do not make public transparency of waiting lists mandatory (Czypionka, Kraus & Röhrling, 2013).

Another issue concerns the financing of long-term care (LTC). Some insurers offer plans with LTC coverage. However, these plans have had little success, as the public system is thought to be unable to deny care when the need arises in the future; if federal attendance allowance is not sufficient to cover LTC costs, recipients will have to draw on their income and assets up to a certain amount, after which the federal state covers residual expenses.

The future of VHI

More than a third of the population has some form of VHI, even though publicly financed health coverage is comprehensive. This may be an indication of the high value people attach to health care and choice of provider. It may also reflect fears about the potential for cuts to public spending in the future. Although the financial and economic crisis had no obvious effects on the VHI market (measured in premium income; Table 2.1), the health care reform of 2013 puts more emphasis on closer monitoring of budgets and budget caps, which may limit the ability of the statutory scheme to offer additional health benefits. It is unlikely, however, that user charges will increase, as they are extremely unpopular in the policy arena. An ageing population, rising health care costs (including the rising costs of LTC) and spending constraints are likely to open up opportunities for VHI, because people fear a decrease in service quality, a fear that is constantly fuelled by some physician representatives. This may increase VHI's share of health financing. However, the industry will also be faced with sharp increases in costs due to population ageing and the rising costs of new technologies. If this is the case, actuarially calculated premiums might rise above the willingness to pay of many households.

References

Czypionka T, Kraus M, Röhrling G (2013). Wartezeiten auf Elektivoperationen: Neues zur Frage der Transparenz? [Waiting times for elective surgery: What's new?]. *Health System Watch* 2/2013. Supplement to *Fachzeitschrift Soziale Sicherheit [Journal of Social Security]*, 66(10): 1–16 (https://www.ihs.ac.at/departments/fin/HealthEcon/watch/hsw13_2d.pdf, accessed 22 November 2015).

Eckhart E (2009). *Krankenversicherung in Österreich – Struktur, Finanzierungsprobleme und Reformansätze.* Vienna, University of Vienna.

GuV der Krankenversicherung (2010). *Aggregated profit and loss account of the health insurance 2010.* Vienna, Verband der Versicherungsunternehmen Österreichs.

Holzer E, Stickler R (2011). *Die österreichische Versicherungswirtschaft: Struktur, Wirtschaftlichkeit und Entwicklung.* Vienna, BFI WIEN.

VVO (2012). *Expert Interview with representative of Association of Austrian Insurers.* Vienna, Versicherungsverband Österreich.

VVO (2014). *Association of Austrian Insurers annual report 2014.* Vienna, Versicherungsverband Österreich.

WHO (2016). Global Health Expenditure Database (GHED) [online database]. Geneva, WHO (http://www.who.int/health-accounts/ghed/en/, accessed 5 April 2016).

3
Belgium

Sophie Gerkens

Health system context

The health financing mix

In 2014, public spending accounted for around 77.9% of total spending on health, with OOP payments and VHI accounting for 17.8% and 4.1% respectively (WHO, 2016).

Entitlement to publicly financed health care and gaps in coverage

Publicly financed health care covers almost the whole population (>99%) and offers a very broad benefits package. User charges in the form of coinsurance are applied at a rate of around 25% for general practitioner (GP) consultations, 35% for GP home visits and 40% for specialist consultations, physiotherapy, speech therapy, podiatry and dietetics (Gerkens & Merkur, 2010). Low-income households pay lower user charges. For inpatient care, patients must pay the following user charges: a copayment per day in hospital; additional room and physician charges for a single room in hospital (extra billing); the costs of some non-reimbursable medicines and medical products; copayments for medicines, laboratory tests, radiology and other interventions (Gerkens & Merkur, 2010).

Overview of the VHI market

Market origins, aims and role

VHI has traditionally played a substitutive, complementary and supplementary role. Publicly financed health coverage has been progressively extended (Table 3.1). When it was extended to cover outpatient care for self-employed people in 2008, the *substitutive* VHI market was effectively abolished.

Sickness funds – the entities responsible for the reimbursement of publicly financed health services – provide two types of additional cover for their members: mandatory *complementary* cover of services like orthodontics, homeopathy and osteopathy, which are not publicly financed, and voluntary *supplementary* cover of extra billing for a single room in hospital. This complementary cover became legally mandatory for all members of a sickness fund in 2012 (Table 3.3), although it was already widespread before this. Sickness fund members pay an additional flat-rate contribution (a community-rated premium) directly to their sickness fund in return for mandatory complementary cover; dependants are covered for free (Assuralia, 2012; Moniteur Belge, 2010a). Those who do not want this form of additional cover have to leave their sickness fund and enrol with a special sickness fund that does not provide complementary cover. However, very few people choose to do this. As a result, almost the whole population benefits from mandatory complementary cover provided by sickness funds.

The focus of this chapter is on supplementary VHI, which is offered by sickness funds (through mutual health insurance funds, see following sections) and by commercial private insurers (Assuralia, 2012).

Types of plan available

Initially, the voluntary hospital plans offered by sickness funds mainly guaranteed subscribers a fixed payment per day in hospital. As extra billing increased, sickness funds began to offer limited or full coverage of all OOP payments for hospital stays (similar to the plans offered by private insurers). Sickness funds also offer other VHI plans (for example, cover of dental care) but, in contrast to private insurers, they are not allowed to offer group plans (Brisson, Steylemans & Brenez, 2011; Gerkens & Merkur, 2010). Over two thirds of VHI plans sold by private insurers are group policies (71% in 2010) (Assuralia, 2012).

Why do people buy VHI?

VHI mainly covers extra billing for people who choose a single room in hospital (Gerkens & Merkur, 2010) and has been fuelled in recent years by increases in extra billing. Expenditure covered by the VHI offered by sickness funds grew from €190 million in 1995 to €228 million in 2010 (OCM, 2011). Expenditure covered by hospital plans sold by private insurers grew from €277 million in 2003 to €422 million in 2010 (Assuralia, 2012).

Who buys VHI?

According to Assuralia, 5 469 000 people had VHI cover from a private insurer in 2013 (Assuralia, 2014). Additionally, the OCM-CDZ (Control Office of the Mutual Health Funds and the National Unions of Mutual Health Funds) (*Office de contrôle des mutualités et des unions nationales de mutualités/Controledienst voor de ziekenfondsen en de landsbonden van ziekenfondsen*) estimates that 3 466 788 had VHI in a mutual fund in 2013 (Verschoren R, Advisor, OCM-CDZ, personal communication, 2015). This means that up to 80% of the population may have VHI cover. However, this figure

Table 3.1 *Development of publicly financed health coverage in Belgium, 1944–2012*

1944	Social security system with compulsory membership for all salaried workers is established
1964	Self-employed people are made to insure themselves against major medical risks (Assuralia, 2012)
1965	Health insurance coverage is extended to public sector workers for both major and minor risks (Moniteur Belge, 2010a)
1967	Health insurance coverage is extended to those physically incapable of working
1968	Health insurance coverage is extended to those with a mental illness
1969	Health insurance coverage is extended to everyone not yet protected
1998	All beneficiaries of compulsory health insurance are covered either under the general scheme (for minor and major risks) or the scheme for self-employed workers (for major risks). Major risks include hospital care, delivery of babies, major surgery, dialysis functional rehabilitation care, implantable medical devices and specialist care, among others. Minor risks include physicians' visits, dental care, minor surgery, home care and outpatient medicines, among others
2008	All beneficiaries are covered for both minor and major risks
2012	Complementary services offered by sickness funds becomes mandatory for all members and premiums paid for these services must be equal for all members

Source: Gerkens & Merkur (2010), additional research.

is likely to overestimate the actual share of population with VHI, as some people may be insured by both a private insurer and a mutual fund and thus be double counted. A 2011 survey (*n*=762) found that 60% of respondents had hospital VHI. Thirty-six per cent were covered through their employer (19% through a non-profit-making mutual health insurance fund and 17% through a private insurer). Some had double VHI cover. The survey showed that, in Wallonia, the unemployed and self-employed were significantly less likely to have hospital VHI. The main reasons for not having hospital VHI were already being covered through their employers, their sickness funds or other (67%), or finding cover too expensive (21%) (Van de Voorde, Kohn & Vinck, 2011). Another 2011 survey (*n*=801) found that only 16% of respondents were not covered by hospital VHI and that the following groups were more likely to be uninsured: people of a lower social class, people over 65 years old, single persons and households with a monthly income below €1600. The following reasons were cited for the lack of coverage: no need (28%), too expensive (22%) and other (in 50% of cases the reasons were exclusion, denial of a claim and waiting to receive VHI cover from the employer) (Assuralia, 2012; Van de Voorde, Kohn & Vinck, 2011).

Who sells VHI?

Supplementary VHI is sold by sickness funds and commercial private insurers. Since 2010, VHI offered by sickness funds can no longer be managed by the sickness funds themselves but must be managed by a separate legal entity, a mutual health insurance fund (*société mutualiste*) (Moniteur Belge, 2010a). In 2010, there were 13 mutual and 26 private health insurers. Mutual health insurers are strictly specialized in health insurance, while almost all private health insurers provide a range of insurance products (Assuralia, 2012; OCM, 2011). Table 3.2 shows the market shares of the leading 15 private insurers.

Insurer relations with providers

Insurers are not integrated with providers. About 70% of hospitals are private non-profit-making organizations and hospital specialists are mainly paid on a FFS basis. Since patients are free to choose their health care provider (physician and hospital), insurers are reluctant to limit reimbursement to selected hospitals (Gerkens & Merkur, 2010).

Table 3.2 *Market shares of the leading 15 private insurers in Belgium, 2010*

Companies	Market share (%)
DKV Belgium	31.56
AG Insurance	18.25
Ethias	12.75
AXA Belgium	12.35
Allianz Belgium	4.66
Vivium	4.31
KBC Assurances SA	4.11
Argenta Assurances	3.49
Dexia Insurance Belgium SA	1.71
Delta Lloyd Life	1.10
Inter Partner Assistance	0.88
Justitia	0.78
Fidea NV	0.75
Mercator Assurances	0.63
Chartis Europe SA	0.48
Cumulative market share	**97.81**

Source: Adapted from Assuralia (2012).

Public policy towards VHI

Private health insurers are supervised by the Financial Services and Markets Authority and the National Bank of Belgium. Mutual health providers are supervised by the OCM-CDZ. Both are subject to identical rules. By law, they must all offer open enrolment and lifetime cover; they are not allowed to refuse cover to people under 65 years old with a disability or chronic illness (but they can exclude costs linked to these pre-existing conditions from cover – private health insurers – or limit the cover to a flat rate with a minimum legally fixed level of cover –mutual health insurers); they are restricted in changing policy conditions (premiums and benefits); and they cannot invoke unintentional concealment of a pre-existing condition if it has not been diagnosed within two years of taking up VHI (Moniteur Belge, 2007a, 2007b, 2010a, 2010b, 2010c). Table 3.3 summarizes the development and regulation of the VHI market since 1990.

In recent years, several measures have been taken to promote access to publicly financed health care for people in lower socioeconomic groups, including the abolition of extra billing for two-person rooms and day cases from 2009. This measure was subsequently extended to the whole population in 2010 and 2013 (Table 3.3).

Regulation of VHI has also intensified to make VHI more accessible and affordable in the context of rising

Table 3.3 *Development and regulation of the VHI market in Belgium, 1990–2012*

Year	Policy
Act of 6 August 1990	Act on sickness funds and national unions of sickness funds confirming the role of sickness funds as administrators of compulsory insurance. Increased control of sickness funds is implemented
Act of 25 June 1992	Act on insurance regulating health and other forms of private insurance
Act of 11 May 2007	Act amending the Act of 6 August 1990 on sickness funds and national unions of sickness funds strengthening the social nature of services provided by sickness funds
Act of 20 July 2007	Act amending issues related to private health insurance contracts in the Act of 25 June 1992 on insurance, strengthening the protection of the insured and limiting risk selection (for example, protection of chronically ill people)
Act of 21 December 2007	Act forbidding differences in premiums between men and women
Act of 23 December 2009	Room supplements for hospitalizations in double rooms (for the financing of operating costs) are abolished
Royal Decree of 2 February 2010	Decree on the medical index determining how to calculate specific indexes; this allows private insurers to adapt premiums and coverage. (Premium and coverage can be adapted either based on the consumer price index or based on one of the specific indexes, called medical indices, calculated by the Federal Public Service Economy in the manner described by this Royal Decree.)
Act of 26 April and 2 June 2010	Act containing various provisions for the organization of complementary health insurance. (For example, from 1 January 2012 complementary cover offered by sickness funds must be mandatory for all their members, premiums must be the same for all members and pre-existing diseases must be covered; hospital plans must be offered through separate legal entities that must comply with the same rules as private insurers.)
Act of 27 December 2012	Physician fee supplements for hospitalization in double rooms is abolished (except for day cases)

Source: Author.

premiums. Changes introduced in 2007 aimed to strengthen the social nature of services provided by sickness funds, including VHI, and to limit risk selection and the exclusion of people with disabilities and chronic illnesses by private insurers. However, the 2007 legislation did not define disability or chronic disease and was only a temporary measure. A report on VHI in Belgium showed that few people were aware that patients with chronic conditions had access to hospital VHI. It also noted the lack of transparency with regard to VHI premiums, benefits and general conditions, which may lead to double insurance of the same risk. At the same time, the study showed that few people encountered problems when subscribing to VHI or when using their policy following hospitalization (Van de Voorde, Kohn & Vinck, 2011). The report recommended that the minimum conditions that hospital VHI plans must satisfy should be established (Van de Voorde, Kohn & Vinck, 2011). Since the 2007 Act, private insurers can only change the premiums and benefits of individual policies in specific cases defined by the Act, for example, changes can be linked to changes in the index of consumer prices or the medical index as described in the Royal Decree of 2 February 2010 (Moniteur Belge, 2010b). The fall in the number of complaints about VHI premium increases (down by 15% in 2011) could perhaps be attributed to this development, although the number of complaints about premium increases also fell for group policies, which are not subject to these rules (Assuralia, 2012).

Debates and challenges

Extensive changes in VHI regulation have provoked tension between different types of insurers. In 2010, a private insurer (Assuralia) complained to the European Commission (EC) about differences in the treatment of insurers and sickness funds (unfair competition). This complaint resulted in legislation requiring complementary plans sold by sickness funds to be mandatory for all members of a sickness fund; complementary premiums to be community rated; and sickness fund and VHI business to be separated (from 2012). It also required the newly established mutual funds to be subject to the same rules as private insurers (Moniteur Belge, 2010b, 2010c).

Some sickness funds have criticized this development as unfair: they now face the same constraints as private insurers in addition to specific constraints that do not apply to private insurers. For example, they can only offer VHI to their members, not to the population as a whole, and they can only offer insurance- and assistance-related health services and cannot sell other products (Brisson, Steylemans & Brenez, 2011).

The future of VHI

As government interest in controlling health spending grows, the role of VHI in health financing could increase. A key challenge, however, will be to preserve the principle of solidarity between rich and poor and healthy and sick, and avoid risk selection. The new constraints imposed on sickness funds from 2012 mean that the VHI plans they offer may decline or even disappear, which could have negative effects on the accessibility of VHI (Brisson, Steylemans & Brenez, 2011).

References

Assuralia (2012). *Infos, publications et chiffres*. Brussels, Assuralia (http://www.assuralia.be/index.php?id=11&L=1, accessed 22 November 2015).

Assuralia (2014). *Infos, publications et chiffres*. Brussels, Assuralia http://www.assuralia.be/index.php?id=379&L=1, accessed 26 November 2015).

Brisson S, Steylemans T, Brenez X (2011). L'assurance mutualiste change de visage. *Health Forum, Le magazine de l'Union Nationale des Mutualités Libres*, 8:6–11.

Gerkens S, Merkur S. (2010). Belgium: health system review. *Health Systems in Transition*, 12(5):1–266.

Moniteur Belge (2007a). Loi du 11 mai 2007 modifiant la loi du 6 août 1990 relative aux mutualités et aux unions nationales de mutualités. *Moniteur Belge*, 31 mai 2007.

Moniteur Belge (2007b). Loi du 20 juillet 2007 modifiant, en ce qui concerne les contrats privés dassurance maladie, la loi du 25 juin 1992 sur le contrat d'assurance terrestre. *Moniteur Belge*, 10 août 2007.

Moniteur Belge (2010a). Loi du 26 avril 2010 portant des dispositions diverses en matière de l'organisation de l'assurance maladie complémentaire. *Moniteur Belge*, 28 mai 2010.

Moniteur Belge (2010b). Arrêté royal du 2 février 2010 déterminant les indices spécifiques visés à l'article 138bis-4, § 3, de la loi du 25 juin 1992 sur le contrat d'assurance terrestre. *Moniteur Belge*, 8 février 2010.

Moniteur Belge (2010c). Loi du 2 juin 2010 portant des dispositions diverses en matière de l'organisation de l'assurance maladie complémentaire (II). *Moniteur Belge*, 1 juillet 2010.

OCM (2011). Rapport annuel 2010. Brussels, Office de contrôle des mutualités et des unions nationales de mutualités.

Van de Voorde C, Kohn L, Vinck I (2011). Droit à une assurance hospitalisation pour les personnes malades chroniques ou handicapées. KCE Reports 166B. Brussels, Centre fédéral d'expertise des soins de santé (KCE).

WHO (2016). Global Health Expenditure Database [online database]. Geneva, WHO (http://www.who.int/health-accounts/ghed/en/, accessed 5 April 2016).

4 Bulgaria

Antoniya Dimova

Health system context

The health financing mix

In 2014, public spending accounted for 54.6% of total spending on health, while OOP payments and VHI accounted for 44.2% and 0.3% respectively (WHO, 2016).

Entitlement to publicly financed health care and gaps in coverage

According to the Health Insurance Act (1998), all Bulgarian citizens and permanent residents are publicly covered by the National Health Insurance Fund (NHIF), although in 2011 over 1.7 million people (23% of the population, mainly the unemployed) did not pay their mandatory contributions and were effectively not covered (Dimova et al., 2012). People who fail to pay their contributions, or are not covered by the NHIF for other reasons, are only entitled to receive publicly financed emergency care in life-threatening situations; this is financed through the government budget.

Overview of the VHI market

Market origins, aims and role

VHI was established through the 1998 Health Insurance Act that introduced the current system of publicly financed health coverage through the NHIF. The aim was to diversify sources of revenue for the health system. However, the VHI market is very limited and covers only a small share (2.4%) of the population (2013 data; FSC, 2013a).

VHI plays a *supplementary* role, giving people direct and faster access to specialist visits and inpatient care, free choice of hospital physician and accommodation in a single room. Most hospitals and diagnostic centres have contracts with the NHIF and private insurers. VHI also plays a *complementary* role covering services not covered by the NHIF (for example, some laboratory tests and medicines).

Types of plan available

Until 2013, VHI plans offered the following benefits packages covering: prevention; outpatient care; inpatient care; dental care; supplementary services related to the provision of medical care (such as a private room, choice of physician, transportation); reimbursement of costs; and other plans, which combined two or more benefits packages. In 2013, combined plans accounted for the biggest share of VHI premium income (Figure 4.1) and claims (Figure 4.2). Each package was offered with two options, a minimum/basic option and an extended/luxury (or full) option, differing by the number of services covered. Individual policies have risk-rated premiums.

Figure 4.1 *Premiums in the Bulgarian VHI market by type of benefits package (%), 2013*

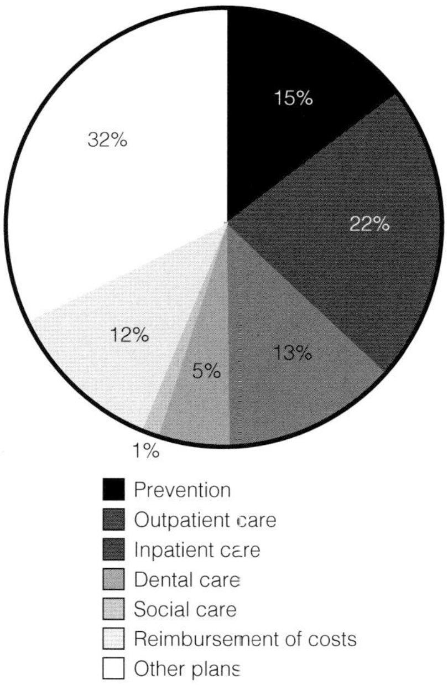

Source: FSC (2013b).

Following legislative changes introduced in 2012 with effect from 2013 (see further on), private insurers

Figure 4.2 *Claims in the Bulgarian VHI market by type of benefits package (%), 2013*

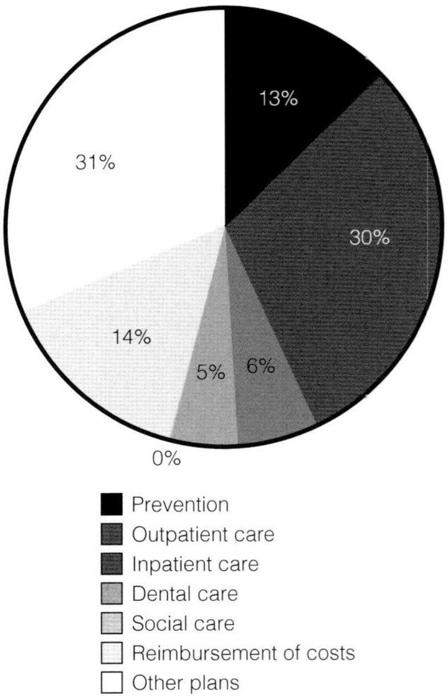

Source: FSC (2013b).

no longer specialize in health. They continue to offer the same plans as before but now provide less detailed information in their reporting to the FSC. (Information is now grouped under sickness and/or accidents (injury or illness) whereas previously it distinguished among various types of VHI plan.)

Why do people buy VHI?

People usually buy VHI to obtain faster access to health care and better quality of services. The main factors hampering the development of the VHI market are the broad range of services covered by the NHIF (even though the population does not seem to be satisfied with the NHIF) and the low income of most households (Dimova et al., 2012).

Who buys VHI?

Most VHI policies (98%) are bought by businesses on a group basis (CPC, 2009). Employers purchase VHI policies to enhance employee satisfaction and limit the costs of sickness and absenteeism. Tax relief is not substantial and does not constitute an important factor driving demand for VHI. VHI is beyond the reach of poorer, older people and people with chronic conditions (Dimova et al., 2012).

Who sells VHI?

All VHI plans are sold by commercial joint-stock companies. Before 2013, these companies sold VHI only (that is, they specialized in health), but a change in the law allowed all insurers to offer VHI and all former specialist health insurers had to be relicensed. They either joined an insurance conglomerate (about two thirds of insurers were part of an insurance conglomerate before 2013) or extended their activity to include sickness insurance. Since 2013, there have been no specialist health insurers and all VHI companies sell insurance plans covering sickness and/or medical incidents. In 2013, the premium income of these general insurance companies rose by 126.1% compared to 2012 and an increase of more than 100% was registered in the first half of 2014. Sickness insurance accounted for the biggest share of these increases (FSC, 2013c, 2014).

The number of insurers selling VHI has increased gradually over time, from 2 in 2001 to 20 in 2011. In 2012, the market share of the largest insurer operating in the market was 20.1% and the three largest insurers had a market share of 58.0% (FSC, 2012).

The profitability of the VHI market varies widely year on year. Administrative costs have shown a declining trend from 2007 to 2012, but remain high (Table 4.1). Three of the six largest insurers made a total profit of approximately €733 000 in the first half of 2013, while the other three registered a total loss of almost €259 000 in the same period.

Insurer relations with providers

Insurers selectively contract with private and public health care providers. They can also own health care providers and pharmacies. In both cases, the level of provider remuneration is determined by the market.

Public policy towards VHI

Due to changes to the 1998 Health Insurance Act (in force since 7 August 2012) all insurers had to be relicensed under the terms of the 2003 Insurance Code and start operating as general insurers no later than 7 August 2013. The purpose of these changes was to harmonize Bulgarian VHI legislation with the EU's general insurance legislation.

As part of the general insurance market, the VHI market is regulated and supervised by the FSC, an independent governmental commission under the National Assembly.

VHI activities are not subject to value added tax. Employers benefit from tax breaks in the form of a fixed amount per month for each insured person. In 2008, the government increased these tax breaks from Bulgarian lev (BGN) 40 (approximately €20; the average exchange rate in 2008 was €1=BGN 1.95) to up to BGN 60 (approximately €31) per month for each insured person. Individuals with VHI can also reduce their taxable income by up to 10% (National Revenue Agency, 2015; Nikolaeva, 2013). However, the level of this discount, together with the wide scope of NHIF benefits, has not significantly motivated employers and individuals to buy VHI so far.

Debates and challenges

The development of the VHI market has caused a great deal of debate among political and professional groups. Policymakers would like to strengthen the role of VHI in health financing but there is no clear vision of how to do this. Ideas under consideration include the establishment of a so-called third pillar for compulsory complementary health insurance (with people paying premiums into individual accounts) or the introduction of free choice of health insurance fund for publicly financed coverage (Dimova et al., 2012). However, there are serious concerns about the feasibility of introducing this third pillar and its potentially negative effect on risk pooling and solidarity. There are also valid concerns about whether a pension-like savings mechanism would work for health care; whereas the need for income replacement on retirement is known and distant (allowing resources to accumulate in individual accounts), there is a great

Table 4.1 *Financial indicators of Bulgarian VHI companies, 2007–2013*

Indicators	2007	2008	2009	2010	2011	2012	30 June 2013
Administrative costs (% of premium income)	32.5	31.2	30.5	25.7	23.5	18.4	19.4
Loss/profit (€, in thousands)	–1 277	–3 975	112	–678	–262	407	474
Claims ratio (claims paid as % of premium income)	60.4	69.6	56.8	58.2	58.9	59.9	68.7

Source: FSC (2013b).

deal of uncertainty around the timing and severity of ill-health and the costs of health care (Dimova et al., 2012).

The future of VHI

The most recent amendments to the Health Insurance Law (August 2015) introduced significant changes to the basic benefits package offered within the statutory health insurance system. The benefits package was divided into basic and complementary parts. Services included in the complementary part will continue to be offered by the NHIF but will require some waiting time for patients. The precise scope of both parts will be defined by the Ministry of Health in an Ordinance expected to come into force in January 2016. The intention is to give people the right to choose to buy VHI to cover services in the complementary part of the benefits package, if they so wish. This may increase the role of VHI in the future.

References

CPC (2009). *Анализ на конкурентната среда на националния пазар при доброволното здравно осигуряване [Analysis of the voluntary health insurance competitive environment]*. Sofia, Commission on Protection of Competition (http://reg.cpc.bg/DepartmentDecisions.aspx?vp=4, accessed 22 November 2015).

Dimova A et al. (2012). Bulgaria: health system review. *Health Systems in Transition*, 14(3):1–186.

FSC (2013a). *Обзор на небанковия финансов сектор в България към края на първото тримесечие на 2013 г. [An overview of non-bank financial sector in Bulgaria]*. Sofia, FSC (http://www.fsc.bg/d.php?id=262, accessed 22 November 2015).

FSC (2013b). *Статистика на пазара на доброволно здравно осигуряване [Statistic on voluntary health insurance market]*. Sofia, FSC (http://www.fsc.bg/bg/podnadzorni-litsa/statistika/pazar-po-dobrovolno-zdravno-osiguryavane/http-www-fsc-bg-2013-bg-881/, accessed 18 September 2015).

FSC (2013c). *Обзор на небанковия финансов сектор в България към края на третото тримесечие на 2013 [An overview of non-bank financial sector in Bulgaria]*. Sofia, FSC (http://www.fsc.bg/d.php?id=256, accessed 18 September 2015).

FSC (2014). *Обзор на небанковия финансов сектор в България през първото тримесечие на 2014 г [An overview of non-bank financial sector in Bulgaria]*. Sofia, FSC www.fsc.bg/d.php?id=253, accessed 22 November 2015)

National Revenue Agency (2015). *Данъчни облекчения за 2014 [Taxation discounts for 2014]*. Sofia, NRA (http://www.nap.bg/page?id=336, accessed 22 November 2015).

Nikolaeva, V. (2013). *Данъчно облагаче според случая [Taxation depending on the case]*. Capital Daily (http://www.capital.bg/biznes/finansi/2013/03/25/2029194_danuchno_oblagane_spored_sluchaia/, accessed 22 November 2015).

WHO (2016). Global Health Expenditure Database (GHED) [online database]. Geneva, WHO (http://www.who.int/health-accounts/ghed/en/, accessed 5 April 2016).

5 Croatia

Karmen Lončarek

Health system context

The health financing mix

In 2014, public spending accounted for 81.9% of total spending on health in Croatia, while OOP payments and VHI accounted for 11.2 and 6.9% respectively (WHO, 2016).

Entitlement to publicly financed health care and gaps in coverage

All permanent residents must be enrolled with the Croatian Health Insurance Fund (CHIF). Groups such as students, war veterans, soldiers, asylum seekers and the unemployed are exempt from paying CHIF contributions and the government pays contributions on their behalf (Vončina et al., 2007). The scope of publicly financed coverage is broad. However, access to services is subject to user charges: 20% of the price for inpatient and outpatient hospital services and dentistry; Croatian kuna (HRK) 15 (approximately €2; the average exchange rate in the first half of 2015 was €1=HRK 7.6) per visit for primary care and gynaecology; and HRK 15 (€2) per prescription. User charges are capped at HRK 3000 (approximately €395) per episode of illness. A substantial part of the population is exempt from user charges.

Overview of the VHI market

Market origins, aims and role

The VHI market emerged following the passing of the 1993 Law on Health Insurance. Initially, VHI could play two roles, offering *complementary* cover of user charges (offered exclusively by the CHIF until 2001 and known as supplemental insurance) and *substitutive* cover for people not enrolled in the CHIF (called private insurance). Since 2004, *supplementary* health insurance covering higher standard of care has slowly emerged. It has developed on a very modest scale because the VHI market continues to be dominated by the CHIF. *Substitutive* VHI is not offered in practice. It existed on a very small scale but declined after amendments to the Law in 2001 and 2008.

In 2012, 1 555 876 people (approximately 36% of the population) purchased and paid for their own complementary VHI from the CHIF. In addition, 944 301 people (approximately 22% of the population) benefited from complementary VHI from the CHIF paid for by the government. These are people who also have their mandatory CHIF contributions paid by the government: people with a physical or mental disability; people unable to perform age-appropriate activities independently; organ donors; blood donors with more than 35 (men) or 25 (women) donations; regular students over 18 years old; and people whose total annual income (calculated per family member per month) does not exceed 45.59% of the budgetary salary base defined every year by the government (about HRK 2000 in 2012, €262) (Džakula et al., 2014).

The commercial VHI market is much smaller, covering only 91 609 persons (approximately 2% of the population) in 2011. It had been growing until 2009 but since then gross premium income has consistently declined (Croatian Insurance Bureau, 2012).

Types of plan available

Complementary VHI plans cover all user charges for publicly financed health care. Those sold by the CHIF have community-rated premiums. Only people covered by the CHIF for publicly financed health care are entitled to purchase VHI from the CHIF. Anyone can buy VHI from private insurers. Supplementary VHI provides services targeted at active people in good health (preventive systematic and cardiovascular exams; direct access to specialists; diagnostic imaging; laboratory tests; physiotherapy; and a better standard of hospital accommodation). Supplementary group plans are available to employees at the managerial level (antistress programmes; preventive cardiovascular exams, for example, cardiac ultrasound).

Why do people buy VHI?

People who buy supplementary VHI do so to jump waiting lists for diagnostic tests and physiotherapy and to obtain a higher standard of hospital accommodation. People who buy complementary VHI do so to benefit from coverage of all user charges. As nobody can be excluded from complementary VHI cover based on pre-existing conditions, people purchase such plans mainly when they fall ill and need to pay user charges.

Who buys VHI?

VHI plans offered by commercial insurers are bought mainly by people from higher socioeconomic groups, with better education and living in urban areas. Complementary VHI offered by the CHIF tends to be bought by persons who have recently fallen ill or have a high risk of illness (for example, due to age or hereditary factors). The CHIF provides VHI to over 2.5 million people out of the total number of 4.3 million people (almost 60% of the population) it covers for publicly financed health care.

Who sells VHI?

VHI is sold by six commercial insurers (supplementary and complementary VHI) and the CHIF (complementary VHI only). While the number of people purchasing VHI from the CHIF has steadily increased, the opposite trend has been observed for commercial insurers. The CHIF dominates the overall VHI market. The commercial market is highly concentrated. In 2010, the two largest insurers accounted for over 90% of total premium income (Croatian Insurance Bureau, 2011).

Insurer relations with providers

Insurers typically reimburse VHI policyholders. Services are provided by individually contracted providers or in facilities owned by the insurer (vertical integration). The renewal of contracts with providers depends on customer satisfaction, which is measured by telephone surveys.

Public policy towards VHI

The development and regulation of the VHI market is shown in Table 5.1. Provision of VHI, both by the CHIF and private insurers, is regulated by the Voluntary Health Insurance Act of 2006 (and its amendments). The CHIF must keep the funds for supplementary health insurance

Table 5.1 *Development and regulation of the VHI market in Croatia, 1993–2012*

Year	Policy
1993	Law on Health Insurance allows for complementary (referred to in Croatia as supplemental) or private (substitutive) VHI based on market principles; complementary VHI could only be provided by the CHIF
2001	New Law on Health Insurance that allows insurers other than the CHIF to offer complementary VHI as part of a continuous process of health system privatization; opting out from the CHIF is prohibited to protect the financial stability of the health insurance model (Džakula et al., 2014). Opting out was previously available for the highest earners, that is, those with annual incomes over approximately HRK 30 000 (approximately €6200 according to the 2001 exchange rate), but not many people chose to opt out (only about 2000 people) (Langenbrunner, 2002); complementary and supplementary VHI premiums are tax deductible
2006	Law on Voluntary Health Insurance is passed permitting any insurer licensed by the HANFA, the supervisory authority for all insurers, to offer VHI if it has permission from the Ministry of Health
2008	New law on Mandatory Health Insurance is passed: CHIF financing is diversified to include contributions and general tax revenues
2010	Amendments to the Voluntary Health Insurance Act deprive many people of state coverage of complementary VHI offered by the CHIF
2011	Complementary and supplementary VHI premiums are no longer tax-deductible
2012	Mandatory contributions to finance the CHIF are lowered from 15 to 13%

Source: Author.

separate from the funds of the mandatory scheme. All private health insurers must be approved by the Ministry of Health and are supervised by the Croatian Financial Services Supervisory Authority (HANFA) (Džakula et al., 2014).

Debates and challenges

For many decades social and health insurance schemes were seen as key to ensuring social stability (Mastilica & Babić-Bosanac, 2002). The importance that all Croatian governments have placed on the health insurance system has allowed the state-owned CHIF to retain virtually a monopoly in the VHI market. Since commercial VHI accounts for a marginal proportion of total spending on health, it draws little public attention. The key issue is the fear among the general public that the emergence of the commercial insurance market would seriously threaten the social welfare system (Mastilica & Kušec, 2005; Radin, Džakula & Benković, 2011).

Several factors limit the development of the VHI market: frequent changes in regulations and business conditions make long-term planning difficult; boundaries between compulsory and voluntary health insurance are blurred (with the CHIF providing both mandatory cover and complementary voluntary cover); there is no tax relief; and insufficient information about VHI is available to the general public. Demand for VHI is also likely to have been driven down by the economic crisis.

The limited availability of private health care provision may be a further limiting factor. Public hospitals have almost no excess capacity. In addition, the CHIF covers the cost of all medical services that are not available in Croatia but are available in other countries and are expected to be reasonably successful. Private provision is limited to services such as medical imaging, laboratory diagnostics and simple medical services that have very low risk of malpractice lawsuits. In addition, the number of physicians practising privately is relatively small – of the 16 500 licensed physicians only 2700 do not have contracts with the CHIF and provide their services in the commercial market (Bagat et al., 2008). As a result, it is hard for commercial insurers to offer complex medical coverage that is better than that offered by the CHIF.

The economic crisis has seriously affected the government's ability to generate additional funds for the health system. It also seems to have had a negative effect on the commercial VHI market, which has seen a decrease in premium revenues. The reform of health care financing pursued since 2008 has involved changes that have led to a substantial increase in private funding to match the levels observed in other central European countries (Vončina et al., 2012).

The future of VHI

Attempts to stimulate the development of the VHI market have so far been received with scepticism by the public. If the economic situation forces the government to limit the scope of the CHIF benefits package, which could expand the VHI market, public opposition is to be expected (Škaričić, 2011). Likewise, if the recession drives down the level and quality of services provided in public hospitals, demand for privately provided services and VHI could increase. Since VHI is oriented towards prevention and diagnostics, the influx of more seriously ill patients requiring complex and expensive treatments would cause a rise in VHI premiums.

References

Bagat M et al. (2008). Influence of urbanization level and gross domestic product of counties in Croatia on access to health care. *Croat Med J*, 49(3):384–391.

Croatian Insurance Bureau (2011). Croatian Insurance Market 2011. Zagreb, Croatian Insurance Bureau. (https://www.huo.hr/download_file.php?file=annual-report-20111.pdf&docID=470&seID=f7548944ed927e43b1b4db4d70ef06c8, accessed 22 November 2015).

Croatian Insurance Bureau (2012). *Hrvatski ured za osiguranje. Izvješće o tržištu obveznih osiguranja u prometu s posebnim osvrtom na osiguranje od automobilske odgovornosti [Report on the market of compulsory insurance in traffic with a special focus on motor insurance]*. Zagreb, Croatian Insurance Bureau (https://www.huo.hr/download_file.php?file=huo-izvjesce-ao2012.pdf&docID=496&seID=564e0d5e218f666553fecd2f2fa712b4, accessed 22 November 2015).

Džakula A et al. (2014). Croatia: health system review. *Health Systems in Transition*, 16(3):1–162.

Langenbrunner JC (2002). Supplemental health insurance: did Croatia miss an opportunity? *Croatian Med J*, 43(4):403-407.

Mastilica M, Kušec S (2005). Croatian healthcare system in transition, from the perspective of users. *BMJ*, 331(7510):223–226.

Mastilica M, Babić-Bosanac S (2002). Citizens' views on health insurance in Croatia. *Croatian Medical Journal*, 43(4):417–424.

Radin D, Džakula A, Benković V (2011). Health care issues in Croatian elections 2005–2010: series of public opinion surveys. *Croatian Medical Journal*, 52(5):585–592.

Škaričić N (2011). The future of health care in Croatia. *Croatian Medical Journal*, 52(3):433–435.

Vončina L et al. (2007). Use of preventive health care services among unemployed in Croatia. *Croatian Medical Journal*, 48(5):667–674.

Vončina L et al. (2012). Croatian 2008–2010 health insurance reform: hard choices toward financial sustainability and efficiency. *Croatian Medical Journal*, 53(1):66–76.

WHO (2016). Global health expenditure database [online database]. Geneva, WHO (http://www.who.int/health-accounts/ghed/en/, accessed 5 April 2016).

6
Cyprus

Mamas Theodorou and Antonis Farmakas

Health system context

The health financing mix

In 2014, OOP payments accounted for 48.7% of total spending on health in Cyprus, followed by funding from the government budget (45.2%) and VHI (4.1%) (WHO, 2016).

Entitlement to publicly financed health care and gaps in coverage

Publicly financed health coverage does not extend to the whole population. The legal basis for entitlement to publicly financed health services is citizenship and gross annual earnings below a certain level. Up to August 2013, there were three groups of beneficiaries:

- Beneficiaries A (83% of the population) are entitled to almost free-of-charge health care, including medicines, in public facilities.
- Beneficiaries B (2% of the population) have access to the same package of services as A but must pay user charges when using public facilities, which amount to 50% of the service price set by the Ministry of Health.
- Non-beneficiaries (15% of the population) include high-income citizens and people from non-EU countries. These people have to pay 100% of the service price in public facilities.

Following an agreement between the Government of Cyprus, the EU and the International Monetary Fund signed in August 2013, beneficiaries B lost the right to access public facilities at reduced cost and were transferred to the group of non-beneficiaries; new user charges were introduced for almost all beneficiaries A for visits, medicines and diagnostic tests and service prices for all public facilities were increased by 30%.

The high share of OOP payments can be explained by the absence of universal entitlement to publicly financed health care, limited public sector capacity and long waiting lists for certain services, which leads many to seek care from private providers (Andreou, Pashardes & Pashourtidou, 2010).

Overview of the VHI market

Market origins, aims and role

General insurers first came to Cyprus in the 1980s and health insurance was established in the mid-1990s, mainly because of rapid economic development and rising incomes. VHI can be seen to play a *substitutive* role as the main source of coverage for non-beneficiaries. It also plays a *supplementary* role, offering greater choice, faster access and better conditions for elective treatment in private clinics and hospitals. In 2012, VHI covered around 21.5% of the population (Theodorou et al., 2012).

Types of plan available

Individual and group policies cover outpatient and inpatient care. They usually provide access to private and public providers and treatment abroad (mainly for planned treatment abroad). Plans vary widely in terms of user charges and coverage ceilings.

Why do people buy VHI?

There are no survey results to explain why people buy VHI, but demand may be stimulated by uncertainty about health care costs among non-beneficiaries and by deficiencies in public provision, such as long waiting lists. The economic crisis, the abolition of beneficiaries B and growing difficulties in financing publicly provided health care have had a positive effect on the demand for VHI.

Who buys VHI?

Group VHI is mainly purchased by medium-sized and large private companies and semi-state organizations for their employees, while individual policies are usually purchased by people with higher incomes. Most VHI policyholders (60% in 2009) are individuals (Table 6.1).

Table 6.1 *Overview of the VHI market in Cyprus, 2008 and 2009*

	Individual schemes		Group schemes	
	2008	2009	2008	2009
Number of people covered by VHI	102 764	103 097	65 065	69 779
Gross premiums (€, in millions)	35.6	30.3	41.3	30.1
Claims (€, in millions)	13.9	11.4	13.4	12.8

Source: Insurance Association of Cyprus (2011).

VHI take-up is concentrated in people with higher incomes and a median age of 43 years. It is equally distributed by gender. It is more common for people who have VHI to be working in companies with employment VHI schemes, usually in the private sector in both small and large enterprises.

Who sells VHI?

In the early 1980s, the only insurer in the VHI market was Universal Life. Today, there are 17 commercial insurers offering VHI. The four leading insurers have >60% of the market share (Table 6.2).

Table 6.2 *Overview of VHI insurers in Cyprus, 2010*

Insurer	Market share (%)*
Universal Life	27.00
CNP Cyprialife	12.40
MetLife Alico	12.27
Eurolife	11.70

Source: Insurance Association of Cyprus (2011).

Note: *The market shares refer to both health and accident insurance.

Insurer relations with providers

Insurers are not usually integrated with providers. Only one company has established its own preferred provider network (PPN); the rest provide unlimited choice of provider. The law does not allow doctors to work in both public and private facilities. Insurers usually pay providers on a FFS basis with market-determined prices. Providers of ambulatory care are paid directly by patients, who are subsequently reimbursed by their insurer, while hospitals are paid by the insurers. To promote efficiency and quality in care provision, insurers audit all claims.

Public policy towards VHI

All insurers are supervised by the Insurance Companies Control Service in the Ministry of Finance (Insurance Companies Control Service, 2012). The Insurance

Association of Cyprus is the official representative body of insurers in Cyprus, and is charged with maintaining good relations between the insurance industry and the government. See Table 6.3 for an overview of the development and regulation of the VHI market.

Table 6.3 *Development and regulation of the VHI market in Cyprus, 1967–2002*

Year	Policy
1967	Insurance Companies Laws of 1967–1980; the 1967 Law is the first to refer to insurers in Cyprus in general
1984	Insurance Companies Laws of 1984–1990
2002	Insurance Services and Other Related Issues Law; this law is fully harmonized with all EU Insurance Directives and regulates the insurance sector including VHI

Source: Insurance Companies Control Service (2012).

Debates and challenges

Although VHI covers a fifth of the population, its relatively small contribution to total spending on health may be due to differences in risk profile between people with and without VHI and the fact that a significant share of those with VHI are also entitled to publicly financed health care; they mainly purchase VHI to avoid long waiting times for public provision and to benefit from the more personalized care offered by private providers. Under present conditions, without VHI, waiting lists in the public sector would almost certainly be longer.

Health policy issues are often the topic of public debate, particularly in relation to the planned introduction of the National Health System (NHS). In spite of this, VHI is rarely discussed. Insurers frequently raise the issue of introducing tax incentives to encourage demand for VHI, but the government argues that direct or indirect public subsidies for VHI would distort the allocation of already stretched public resources in favour of VHI policyholders, who tend to be higher-income households, increasing inequalities in financing the health system.

The two major factors that may influence the market for VHI in the future are the planned implementation of the NHS and the ongoing economic crisis and its negative impact on fiscal revenues and economic growth.

The future of VHI

Uncertainty regarding the implementation of the NHS and the impact of the economic crisis on both public spending on health and on households makes it difficult to say how the VHI market will develop over the next few years. The introduction of the NHS could have negative consequences for VHI if it successfully moves Cyprus towards universal health coverage. However, if the new system fails to address the problem of long waiting times, demand for VHI may continue to grow. The flexibility and readiness of insurers to respond to new challenges in a new environment and under adverse economic conditions will also play a role in determining the size of the VHI market in future.

References

Andreou M, Pashardes P, Pashourtidou N (2010). Cost and value of health care in Cyprus. *Cyprus Economic Policy Review*, 4(1):3–24.

Insurance Association of Cyprus (2011). Insurance in Cyprus 2010: directory and statistical information. Nicosia, Insurance Association of Cyprus.

Insurance Companies Control Service (2012) [website]. Nicosia, Ministry of Finance (http://www.mof.gov.cy, accessed 22 November 2012).

Theodorou M et al. (2012). Cyprus: health system review. *Health Systems in Transition*, 14(6):1–128.

WHO (2016). Global Health Expenditure Database (GHED) [online database]. Geneva, WHO (http://www.who.int/health-accounts/ghed/en/, accessed 5 April 2016).

7
Czech Republic

Martin Dlouhy

Health system context

The health financing mix

In 2014, public spending accounted for 84.5% of total spending on health, with OOP payments and VHI accounting for 14.3% and 0.2%, respectively (WHO, 2016).

Entitlement to publicly financed health care and gaps in coverage

Participation in publicly financed health coverage is compulsory for all permanent residents and people working in the Czech Republic. Health insurance funds are autonomous public organizations that collect contributions from their members and purchase health services on their behalf. The largest public insurer is the General Health Insurance Fund of the Czech Republic, which enrols about half of the population. Seven other health insurance funds cover the rest of the population. The government pays contributions on behalf of economically inactive people (children, students, unemployed people and pensioners).

Migrants from outside the EU who are not employed (children, pensioners, students or the self-employed) are excluded from publicly financed health coverage. The law requires that they are covered by their home country or purchase private health insurance covering basic health care benefits.

Before 2008, people only paid user charges for prescription medicines. In 2008, the government introduced the following user charges: Czech koruna (CZK) 30 (about €1.2; the average exchange rate in 2008 was €1=CZK 25) for each outpatient visit; CZK 30 (€1.2) for each item on a prescription (changed to CZK 30 per prescription in 2012); CZK 60 (€2.4) per inpatient day (raised to CZK 100 in 2011); and CZK 90 (€3.6) for emergency services. There is a yearly cap on some user charges.

Overview of the VHI market

Market origins, aims and role

VHI plays two roles: a *substitutive* role for nonemployed foreigners (migrants) from non-EU countries and a *supplementary* role providing access to above-standard hospital rooms and dental services. In addition, insurers offer (under the misleading name of private health insurance) policies that cover cash benefits in case of illness or hospital admission. There are also insurance policies that cover the costs of acute care abroad for people travelling outside the EU. These types of policies are not described here.

The role of substitutive private health insurance for foreigners has increased as the number of migrant workers from non-EU countries has grown – for example, in October 2012, there were 104 438 migrants from Ukraine and 56 623 from Vietnam (Ministry of the Interior of the Czech Republic, 2015) – and with stricter control of the possession of health insurance by immigration police. A valid health insurance policy is a legal requirement for a long-term residence permit. The number of migrants with private health insurance is not known and there are many foreigners who do not have either public or private health insurance. These people usually work without a formal job contract.

Types of plan available

Two types of substitutive private health insurance policies for foreigners are usually available: an urgent care (short-term) plan and a complex (long-term) plan. Long-term policies offer relatively comprehensive benefits, comparable to those offered under publicly financed coverage, but some services, especially services related to chronic conditions, are excluded (Pojistovna VZP, 2015). The benefits are provided in kind and user charges may be required. An initial medical examination may be required. Premiums are usually in the form of a fixed price for the agreed period (from one month to two years). Age is the main factor influencing premium prices. Officially, there is no restriction on purchasing private health insurance for disabled or older people. However, anecdotal evidence suggests that high-risk migrants and migrants over 65 years of age may have problems in obtaining private cover.

Supplementary VHI products are sold in combination with other insurance products or on a stand-alone basis.

Why do people buy VHI?

The main reason for purchasing private health insurance is the legal requirement for migrants from outside the EU to purchase private cover.

Who buys VHI?

The majority of people purchasing private health insurance are non-EU migrants who are economically inactive.

Who sells VHI?

Private health insurance is sold by commercial insurers and public health insurance funds. The latter sell private insurance through subsidiaries or sell policies on behalf of commercial insurers, keeping the flow of public and private money separate. Only two companies are specialized health insurers: Pojistovna VZP and Vitalitas – both subsidiaries of public health insurance funds. Information about market concentration is not available.

Insurer relations with providers

Private health insurers do not engage in active purchasing. In theory, they may selectively contract with providers, but because of the small size of the market, it is not cost–effective to do so. In practice, insurers simply reimburse providers (on a FFS basis) or policyholders for expenses incurred. People with private health insurance policies can obtain care from any provider, private or public. To date, there have been no cases of vertical integration between insurers and providers.

Public policy towards VHI

All types of insurance are regulated by the Czech National Bank, which authorizes market entry and monitors solvency. There is no tax incentive for purchasing private health insurance.

Debates and challenges

Private health insurance provides financial protection for those excluded from publicly financed coverage. The exclusion of children or other dependants of foreigners without employment from publicly financed coverage is seen to be in conflict with the health system's goal of equity of access to health services. Measures aimed at increasing the inclusion of migrants, for example, extending publicly financed coverage to the dependants of an employed migrant after 90 days of stay, may be introduced in the future.

The small contribution private health insurance makes to total spending on health reflects the generosity of the publicly financed benefits package and, until recently, the near absence of user charges. User charges introduced in 2008 opened up opportunities for complementary VHI covering user charges, but so far, the role of complementary VHI does not seem to be growing.

The future of VHI

The generosity of publicly financed health coverage leaves little space for VHI and the possible extension of this coverage to foreigners may undermine the substitutive VHI market. However, if user charges grow in future, complementary VHI covering user charges may increase slowly among wealthier segments of the population. This could have negative effects on equitable access to health care.

References

Ministry of the Interior of the Czech Republic (2015). Foreigners with legal stay on the territory of the Czech Republic. 30 June 2015. Prague, Ministry of the Interior of the Czech Republic (http://www.mvcr.cz/soubor/06-2015-tab-internet-stav-k-30-6-2015-xls.aspx, accessed 22 November 2015).

Pojistovna VZP (2012). *Translation of insurance terms and conditions – foreigner's comprehensive medical insurance, effective as of 1 July, 2015*. Prague, Pojistovna VZP (https://cizinci.pvzp.cz//Data/PdfTemplates/_Static/KZPC_PP_1_15_EN.pdf, accessed 22 November 2015).

WHO (2016). Global Health Expenditure Database (GHED) [online database]. Geneva, WHO (http://www.who.int/health-accounts/ghed/en/, accessed 5 April 2016).

8 Denmark

Karsten Vrangbæk

Health system context

The health financing mix

In 2014, public spending accounted for 84.8% of total spending on health, with OOP payments and VHI accounting for 13.4 and 1.8% respectively (WHO, 2016).

Entitlement to publicly financed health care and gaps in coverage

Publicly financed health coverage is universal and all primary and secondary health services are provided free of charge on referral. User charges are mainly applied to prescription medicines, dental care and glasses obtained out of hospital. Patients also pay for a number of other outpatient services, such as physiotherapy or psychological treatment. Waiting times for hospital treatment and access to private specialists have been a concern, but a waiting time guarantee of one month introduced in 2007 (now a diagnosis guarantee) has contributed to reducing waiting times.

Overview of the VHI market

Market origins, aims and role

The market for *complementary* VHI has existed for several decades. The number of people covered has grown from about 270 000 in 1973 to 2.3 million (41% of all Danes) in 2014 ("danmark", 2014; Olejaz et al., 2012). The market for *supplementary* VHI has developed rapidly since the government introduced a tax exemption for this type of employee benefit in 2002 as part of a deliberate attempt to boost the private health care sector. In 2001, only 50 000 persons had supplementary VHI cover. In 2010, the figure was around 1 million (Forsikring & Pension, 2012; Kjellberg, Andreasen & Søgaard, 2010).

Types of plan available

Complementary VHI provides full or partial coverage for services that are only partially or not at all publicly covered. The non-profit-making insurer "danmark", which dominates the complementary VHI market, offers four plans (Olejaz et al., 2012):

- *Group 1* covers expenses related to private hospital care, medicines, medical aids, chiropractic services, chiropody, physiotherapy, dental treatment, eye care, glasses, contact lenses, funeral aid and sanatorium visits.
- *Group 2* is designed for people who choose to pay a greater amount of their health expenses in exchange for greater freedom in choice of GPs and specialists. Group 2 members are reimbursed for expenses relating to GPs and specialists, in addition to receiving Group 1 coverage.
- *Group 5* covers medicines, dental care, glasses and contact lenses. This group is mainly aimed at young people and offers lower premiums. Group 5 is by far the most popular plan.
- *The Basic Insurance Scheme* is designed for people with no current need for cover. It does not cover costs but allows members to switch to one of the other plans when necessary without having to requalify for membership.

Complementary cover provides cash benefits on an annual or long-term basis. Applications for cover may be rejected and children are usually covered by their parents' policies (Olejaz et al., 2012).

Supplementary plans cover the following (Olejaz et al., 2012):

- *Treatment plans* cover treatment costs in private hospitals (excluding cosmetic surgery, preventive interventions, dental care or treatments related to pregnancy or sexuality). In 2009, this kind of plan accounted for 88% of supplementary plans.
- *Preventive plans* (10.5% of the supplementary market) cover the costs of preventive services by physiotherapists and chiropractors and aims to reduce the risk of premature retirement.
- *Health and prevention plans* (1.7% of the supplementary market) cover costs associated with general health check-ups (but not any subsequent treatment).

Why do people buy VHI?

Complementary VHI is purchased to cover user charges and other OOP payments. Supplementary VHI is mostly provided as a fringe benefit in the workplace because of tax exemption. Many employees are covered by collective agreements, and have not made a conscious, individual decision to purchase VHI (Kiil, 2012a; Kjellberg, Andreasen & Søgaard, 2010). Quality and waiting times are perceived as problems in Denmark and providers of supplementary VHI have been able to benefit from these concerns (Olejaz et al., 2012).

Who buys VHI?

There is no information on who buys complementary VHI. Nine out of 10 people with supplementary VHI are covered by their employer (mainly private companies (Olejaz et al., 2012)). Employment status is therefore the most important determinant of supplementary VHI coverage (Kiil, 2012b; Sundhedsstyrelsen, 2011). A special condition attached to tax exemption – that the insurance should be offered to all employees in the company to qualify for tax exemption – has succeeded in preventing companies from offering employer-paid VHI exclusively to employees at managerial level (Kiil, 2012a). Employer-paid VHI generates some horizontal inequity in access to health services along the dimensions of income, occupational status and age (Kiil, 2012a).

Who sells VHI?

Complementary VHI is almost exclusively offered by the non-profit-making mutual health insurance organization "danmark". The market for supplementary VHI is dominated by five commercial insurers (the top five in Table 8.1).

Insurer relations with providers

Insurers and providers are not vertically integrated. Insurers buy services from private providers (specialists and hospitals) in Denmark or abroad. Large insurers

Table 8.1 *Premium levels and market shares of insurers selling supplementary VHI in Denmark, 2013*

Company	Premium income (Danish krone (DKK))	Market shares (%)
PFA Pension	351 295	22.4
Tryg	266 336	17.0
Danica Pension	224 558	14.3
Codan A/S	189 201	12.1
Skandia	179 177	11.4
Topdanmark	126 608	8.1
PensionDanmark	123 271	7.9
If …	107 274	6.8
Alka	1230	0.1
PenSam	563	0.0
Total	**1 569 513**	**100.0**

Source: Forsikring & Pension (2015).

negotiate contracts with providers and presumably have some leverage over them.

Public policy towards VHI

Insurers are regulated by the Danish Financial Services Authority. Private health care was explicitly promoted during the 2000s through tax exemptions (2002–2011) and favourable payments to private providers for services delivered to the public sector. In 2012, the Social Democratic government removed the tax exemption, except for policies covering preventive services and employment-related health needs. This is likely to reduce demand for VHI.

Debates and challenges

Proponents of tax exemption for employer-paid VHI argue that supplementary VHI benefits the health system because it increases the diversity of providers, relieves pressure on public providers and contributes to reducing waiting times (Kjellberg, Andreasen & Søgaard, 2010; Næss-Schmidt, 2008). Critics argue that VHI-funded services do not relieve pressure on public health services because VHI increases financial rather than human resources, leading to price inflation as opposed to boosting capacity (Olejaz et al., 2012). Public providers also incur financial risk, as they often end up covering complicated cases and errors made in the private sector. In addition, VHI covers treatments that are not publicly covered (for example, obesity treatment and cosmetic surgery) and has contributed to lowering indication levels for treatment, so that more people are now treated at an earlier stage than previously (Kjellberg, Andreasen & Søgaard, 2010).

Critics also point to the loss of tax revenue associated with VHI, the social bias in the take-up of VHI and the fact that publicly employed health staff working part-time in the private sector may favour private patients. For example, under certain conditions, office-based specialists receive higher payments for treating patients with VHI. When a specialist physician's public income exceeds a certain level, they receive a smaller payment for each extra intervention provided; the specialist therefore faces a financial incentive to treat patients paid for by VHI rather than patients paid for by the government (Olejaz et al., 2012).

The future of VHI

The market for employer-paid VHI is likely to contract now that tax incentives have been largely removed, although it is not clear by how much. The future of the supplementary market will also depend on how well the public sector is able to maintain quality and relatively short waiting times. So far, the government has been willing to let health care expenditure grow in contrast to other sectors, where cuts have been introduced. The market for complementary VHI is expected to continue to increase slightly ("danmark", 2014). Increases in user charges are being discussed in the wake of the economic downturn, but so far politicians have been reluctant to move in that direction. An increase in user charges would probably further strengthen the market for complementary VHI.

References

"danmark" (2014). Årsrapport [*Annual report*]. (http://www.sygeforsikring.dk/Default.aspx?ID=23, accessed 22 November 2015).

Forsikring & Pension (2012). *Sundhedsforsikring – Antal forsikrede, præmier og erstatninger [Health insurance – number of insured, premiums and claims]*. Hellerup, Forsikring and Pension (http://www.forsikringogpension.dk/presse/Statistik_og_Analyse/statistik/forsikring/antal/Sider/Sundhedsforsikring_Antal_forsikrede_praemier_erstatninger.aspx, accessed 29 June 2012).

Forsikring & Pension (2015). *Sundhedsforsikring – Kvartalsvise markedsandele [Health insurance – quarterly market shares]*. Hellerup, Forsikring & Pension. (http://www.forsikringogpension.dk/presse/Statistik_og_Analyse/statistik/forsikring/markedsandele/Sider/Sundhedsforsikring_Kvartalsvise_markedsandele.aspx, accessed 22 November 2015).

Kiil A (2012a). Determinants of employment-based private health insurance coverage in Denmark. *Nordic Journal of Health Economics*, 1(1):29–60.

Kiil A (2012b). What characterises the privately insured in universal health care systems? A review of the empirical evidence. *Health Policy*, 106(1):60–75.

Kjellberg J, Andreasen MN, Søgaard J (2010). *Private sundhedsforsikringer: notat udarbejdet for LO [Private health insurance: memo prepared for the TUC]*. Copenhagen, Dansk Sundhedsinstitut [Danish Institute of Health Services Research] (http://projekt.dsi.dk/uploads/upload_4d3e940b968b7.pdf, accessed 22 November 2012).

Næss-Schmidt HS (2008). *Sundhedsforsikringer – en løsning på fremtidens velfærd? [Health insurance – a solution to the future welfare?]*. Copenhagen Economics. Forsikring & Pension Analyserapport 2008:4. Copenhagen, Forsikring & Pension (http://www.forsikringogpension.dk/presse/Statistik_og_Analyse/analyser/Documents/Sundhedsforsikringer%20final%20version%20101008%20(2).pdf, accessed 22 November 2012).

Olejaz M et al. (2012). Denmark: health system review. *Health Systems in Transition*, 14(2):1–192.

Sundhedsstyrelsen (2011). *Ulighed i sundhed – årsager og indsatser [Inequality in health – causes and stakes]*. Copenhagen, Sundhedsstyrelsen (http://www.sst.dk/publ/Publ2011/SURA/Ulighed_i_sundhed/UlighedSundhedAarsagerIndsatser.pdf, accessed 22 November 2012).

WHO (2016). Global Health Expenditure Database (GHED) [online database]. Geneva, WHO (http://www.who.int/health-accounts/ghed/en/, accessed 5 April 2016).

9 Estonia

Triin Habicht

Health system context

The health financing mix

In 2014, public spending accounted for 78.8% of total spending on health, with OOP payments and VHI accounting for 20.7% and 0.2% respectively (WHO, 2016).

Entitlement to publicly financed health care and gaps in coverage

At the end of 2011, the Estonian Health Insurance Fund (EHIF) covered 94.5% of the population (around 1.25 million people). Those not covered by the EHIF have access to emergency care and the State budget covers their expenses. The EHIF's benefits can be divided into two groups: cash benefits (15% of EHIF expenditure on health benefits) for temporary health-related incapacity for work, adult dental care and additional reimbursement for prescription medicines; and in-kind benefits (85%), which may be subject to user charges. Overall, the range of health care benefits covered by the EHIF is broad and only a few services, such as cosmetic surgery, alternative therapies and optician services, are excluded. At the end of 2002, the list of benefits provided in kind did not include dental care for adults. The EHIF sets maximum waiting time limits for outpatient specialist care (six weeks), elective inpatient care (eight months), family physician visits for acute conditions (same day) and chronic conditions (within five days).

OOP payments consist of user charges for EHIF benefits (for example, outpatient medicines and dental care) and direct payments to providers of services outside the EHIF benefits package or to non-EHIF providers. Following claims of underfunding by providers, since 2002 providers can introduce capped user charges (copayments) for specific benefits.

Overview of the VHI market

Market origins, aims and role

Prior to 2002, a commercial market for VHI had not really been established due to the comprehensiveness of EHIF benefits, the absence of substantial waiting times for treatment and the absence of tax incentives for VHI. (In fact, supplementary VHI offered to employees by employers – with the exception of insurance related to international business travel – is subject to a 33% tax on benefits in-kind.) VHI cover available then mainly consisted of medical travel insurance; some foreign insurers also provided *supplementary* VHI for their employees to enable them to obtain faster access to specialist services (Koppel et al., 2008).

In 2002, the EHIF began to offer limited voluntary coverage for those not otherwise eligible for EHIF coverage (for example, the non-working spouses of the EHIF-insured) – that is, *substitutive* VHI. At the end of 2011, such policies covered only 264 persons (EHIF, 2011) and this number has not changed much over time.

Today VHI mainly plays a substitutive role. Only one company offers complementary and supplementary VHI. The number of people with VHI cover has remained stable over time and is fewer than 1000 persons in total. Medical travel insurance or schemes related to injuries and accidents exist, but are beyond the scope of this study and are not described here.

Types of plan available

The EHIF is the only provider of substitutive VHI. Only one insurer (ERGO) offers supplementary and complementary VHI through a range of schemes (Table 9.1).

Why do people buy VHI?

Supplementary and complementary VHI schemes offered by ERGO target people who want to have faster access to EHIF services or cover for services not reimbursed by the EHIF, including people not eligible for statutory cover (for example, Estonians working abroad, diplomats).

Who buys VHI?

No information is available on subscriber characteristics.

Who sells VHI?

Substitutive VHI is offered by the EHIF only. One commercial insurer offers supplementary and complementary VHI.

Insurer relations with providers

ERGO contracts selected providers and uses EHIF's prices when setting tariffs. ERGO's tariffs are set at a higher rate to ensure attractiveness of the contracts to providers.

Table 9.1 *Overview of the schemes offered by ERGO in Estonia, 2013*

Scheme	MIDI-care: maximum benefit covered per year/ coinsurance rate (%)	MAXI-care: maximum benefit covered per year/ coinsurance rate (%)
Scheme 1 – Outpatient care (primary/specialist consultations and diagnostics; five-day waiting time guarantee)	€750/25%	€750/25%
Scheme 2 – Inpatient care (including operations, medicines, accommodation in a private ward)	€1000/0%	€1000/0%
Scheme 3 – Dental care	€50/50%	€50/50%
Scheme 4 – Post-accident rehabilitation and medical aids not covered by the EHIF	€1000/0%	€1000/0%
Scheme 5 – Post-accident dental care	€1000/0%	€1000/0%
Scheme 6 – Critical care (inpatient and outpatient care in case of, for example, cancer, myocardial infarction, stroke)	–	€7000/0%

Source: ERGO (2013).

Public policy towards VHI

Private health insurers fall under the legal framework for private insurance and are not supervised by health authorities (Koppel et al., 2008). The Financial Services Authority provides financial supervision of the insurance industry. A government action plan published in 2011 identified extending supplementary VHI as a priority (Estonian Government, 2011), but no steps have been taken so far.

Debates and challenges

VHI has been the subject of public discussion since the early 1990s, when the EHIF was established. Substitutive VHI was proposed as an option, but it was not widely supported as VHI was seen more as an addition to public financing. The priority then shifted to developing the publicly financed system and the VHI issue became less important.

In 2002, when the new Health Insurance Act was enforced, the role of VHI was discussed once again. The Health Insurance Act defined clearly the role of publicly financed coverage and it was expected that VHI would offer cover for things like adult dental care and user charges for outpatient prescription medicines. However, the role of VHI remained marginal (WHO, 2016). Adult dental care and user charges were not attractive areas for private insurers to cover due to the high administrative costs involved and the absence of tax incentives. The small size of the Estonian population (1.3 million people) was an additional obstacle.

In 2009, the EHIF, the Ministry of Social Affairs and the WHO Regional Office for Europe conducted an in-depth analysis of the mid- and long-term sustainability of the health financing system (Thomson et al., 2010). The study was based not only on technical assessment but also on interviews with political and other actors in the health system. About half of all interviewees did not think it would be appropriate to expand the role of VHI, mainly because of its potential to undermine solidarity and equality of access. Others were broadly in favour of expanding VHI as a means of providing patients with faster access to care and a greater range of services. However, most of those in favour of an increased role for VHI noted how small the market was and acknowledged it would be difficult to stimulate demand. Those interviewed also emphasized that the people most likely to buy VHI would either be rich enough to pay for care on an OOP basis or have access to an informal network that guaranteed faster access to care. One idea put forward by some stakeholders was to develop VHI cover for LTC for older people. Overall, the analysis did not recommend expanding the role of VHI in Estonia.

In 2011, the Ministry of Finance commissioned a study on the financial sustainability of the social insurance system (including pensions, unemployment and incapacity to work benefits and health insurance). The study discussed VHI and medical savings accounts (MSAs) as potential options for ensuring the long-term sustainability of health system financing (Praxis Center for Policy Studies, 2011). It concluded that MSAs diminish solidarity, increase the risk borne by individuals and widen inequalities. With regard to VHI, three different roles were considered: substitutive, complementary and supplementary. The study concluded that substitutive VHI was likely to decrease overall financial sustainability. For complementary VHI (the focus was on providing insurance for dental care and user charges) the conclusion was that it would improve access to care but could also lead to an increase in service prices or volumes, which might increase the costs of publicly financed care. For supplementary VHI, while it might improve access to care for richer people, it would reduce access for poorer people. In addition, it could lead to price increases that might increase costs and lead to less cost-effective use of resources in the public system.

The future of VHI

In the future, VHI could play a complementary role covering user charges for medicines or dental care costs or a supplementary role ensuring faster access to care or better non-clinical standards of care, for example, in the area of LTC for older people. Higher incomes, long-term fiscal sustainability issues and rising expectations would drive the demand for VHI. Having said that, private insurers show little interest in entering the market. There is no scope for an increased role for substitutive VHI as EHIF coverage is mandatory and the number of uninsured people is very low. However, supplementary VHI seems likely to stay on the policy agenda.

References

EHIF (2011). *Estonian Health Insurance Fund annual report 2011.* Tallinn, EHIF (http://www.haigekassa.ee/

uploads/userfiles/EHK_Aastaaruanne2011_ENG_web.pdf, accessed 22 November 2015).

ERGO (2013). *Ravikindlustus. Eesti kodanikule [Terms of health care insurance contract]*. Tallinn, ERGO Insurance SE (http://www.ergo.ee/erakliendile/ravikindlustus/kodanikule, accessed 22 November 2015).

Estonian Government (2011). *Erakonna isamaa ja res publica liit ning eesti reformierakonna valitsusliidu programm konkurentsivõimeline majanduskeskkond [Pro Patria and Res Publica Union and Estonian Reform Party, Union Government Program, Competitive Business Environment]*. Tallinn, Republic of Estonia Government Office (https://valitsus.ee/UserFiles/valitsus/et/valitsus/tegevusprogramm/valitsuse-tegevusprogramm/Valitsusliidu%20programm%202011-2015.pdf, accessed 22 November 2015).

Koppel A et al. (2008). Estonia: health system review. *Health Systems in Transition*, 10(1):1–230.

Praxis Center for Policy Studies (2011). *Eesti sotsiaalkindlustussüsteemi jätkusuutliku rahastamise võimalused [The financial sustainability of the social insurance system in Estonia]*. Tallinn, Praxis (http://www.praxis.ee/fileadmin/tarmo/Projektid/Tervishoid/Eesti_tervishoiu_rahastamise_jatkusuutlikkus/Eesti_sotsiaalkindlustussuesteemi_jaetkusuutliku_rahastamise_voimalused_taeisversioon.pdf, accessed 22 November 2015).

Thomson S et al. (2010). *Responding to the challenge of financial sustainability in Estonia's health system*. Copenhagen, WHO Regional Office for Europe (http://www.haigekassa.ee/uploads/userfiles/E93542.pdf, accessed 22 November 2015).

WHO (2016). Global Health Expenditure Database (GHED) [online database]. Geneva, WHO (http://www.who.int/health-accounts/ghed/en/, accessed 5 April 2016).

10
Finland

Lauri Vuorenkoski

Health system context

The health financing mix

In 2014, public spending accounted for 75.3% of total spending on health, with OOP payments and VHI accounting for 18.2% and 2% respectively (WHO, 2016).

Entitlement to publicly financed health care and gaps in coverage

Municipal health services and National Health Insurance (NHI) cover all permanent residents. Municipalities cover all necessary health services. While user charges are relatively low (accounting for around 7% of municipal health expenses), waiting times can be long. NHI covers part of the costs of outpatient medicines, travel expenses, rehabilitation services and sickness allowances. It also covers part of the costs of private spending on health services and on occupational health services organized by employers for employees only (usually only basic GP services). NHI cover is subject to high user charges. On average, it only covers 65% of the cost of outpatient medicines and 25% of the cost of private spending.

Overview of the VHI market

Market origins, aims and role

VHI has always played a marginal role in the health system, offering *complementary* cover of NHI user charges (especially for medicines) and playing a *supplementary* role in relation to municipal health care, ensuring more choice and faster access to health services. About 18% of the population (930 000 people) had VHI in 2012, of which 150 000 were covered by employers; the number of people with VHI increased by 13% between 2009 and 2012 (Federation of Finnish Financial Services, 2013).

Types of plan available

VHI plans cover children (430 000 insured children at the end of 2012), adults (350 000) or employees (150 000) (Federation of Finnish Financial Services, 2013). In general, VHI plans do not cover services that are not covered by NHI. Insurers are free to decide on eligibility criteria, premiums and benefit design. A wide range of options is therefore available and consumers can find it difficult to compare plans. The age limit for most plans is 60–65 years. Deductibles and maximum annual benefit limits usually apply (Vuorenkoski, 2008). Not all VHI plans cover NHI user charges.

Why do people buy VHI?

People purchase VHI to reduce OOP payments for outpatient medicines (for which NHI user charges are high) and for privately provided health care. Although most people tend to use publicly provided health services, where user charges are low, especially for specialist outpatient and inpatient care and for occupational health services, the use of private providers is increasing, leading to higher demand for VHI. Demand for VHI is mainly driven by an increase in waiting times for municipal care. Other reasons for buying VHI are to have greater choice of provider (including physicians) in the private sector and the perception that quality of care is higher in the private sector than in the municipal sector.

Who buys VHI?

The most commonly purchased policies are for children, mainly because adults can use occupational health services to avoid long waiting times for municipal primary care, and occupational services are not available for children. Richer people are also more likely to have VHI.

Who sells VHI?

The VHI market is highly concentrated: the three largest insurers cover about two thirds of the market. All three are general insurers; one is owned by its members (a kind of cooperative) and the other two are commercial firms.

Insurer relations with providers

Insurers are not vertically integrated with providers and do not normally contract providers. Instead, people are free to go to any health care provider, including in the municipal sector, and are reimbursed afterwards. Insurers cover only those expenses not covered by the municipal system or by NHI. In 2013, an insurer opened its own hospital focusing on orthopaedic surgery.

Private providers are free to set their own fees. Many insurers state in their insurance contracts that prices that are much higher than the normal rate will not be reimbursed; in practice, official normal rates do not exist.

Public policy towards VHI

The legislative framework for VHI is set out in the Insurance Contracts Act, which covers all types of insurance. There is no special legislation for VHI.

Debates and challenges

There is not much public debate about VHI. The increasing use of VHI is seen by some as an indicator of the poor quality of municipal health services and a reflection of high user charges for NHI services. The absolute share of service cost that NHI covers has not risen since the late 1980s and the actual average share it covers has fallen from 40 to 25% as service prices have increased. This could lead to a situation where the municipal system is catering for poorer people, while middle-class people rely more and more on NHI, privately provided services and VHI to finance (faster) access to private providers. The increasing popularity of VHI has therefore been an argument for reducing NHI user charges.

VHI covers OOP payments for municipal and privately provided health services. However, VHI is mainly purchased to cover privately provided services because the patient share of expenses is greater when private providers are used. VHI is likely to increase the use of private services, as people who have purchased VHI have an incentive to use health services more, although this factor does not seem to attract much public attention.

The view that municipal services supplemented by NHI-covered privately provided services should provide people with a sufficient degree of financial protection is strongly held in Finland. A larger role for VHI does not easily fit with this perspective.

The future of VHI

VHI market growth should continue in the near future. Due to economic pressures, NHI reimbursement rates are unlikely to be increased and the municipal sector is unlikely to receive additional resources. Rather, there is pressure to lower public spending on health care. The current government plans to cut half of NHI spending on private services, which would significantly decrease reimbursement rates. Although the government plans to improve publicly financed health services by reforming the municipal health system, which would affect demand for VHI, this has proven to be much more difficult than anticipated.

References

Federation of Finnish Financial Services (2013). *Sairauskuluvakuutus [Information on the number of persons with medical expenses insurance between 2009 and 2012].* Helsinki, Federation of Finnish Financial Services (http://www.fkl.fi/tilastot/Tilastot/Sairauskuluvakuutuksen_lukumaaratilasto_2009-2012.pdf, accessed 22 November 2015).

Vuorenkoski L (2008). Finland: health system review. *Health Systems in Transition*, 10(4):1–168.

WHO (2016). Global Health Expenditure Database (GHED) [online database]. Geneva, WHO (http://www.who.int/health-accounts/ghed/en/, accessed 5 April 2016).

11
France

Karine Chevreul, Karen Berg Brigham and Marc Perronnin

Health system context

The health financing mix

In 2014, public spending accounted for over three-quarters of total spending on health (78.2%), while VHI accounted for 13.3% and OOP payments for 6.3% of total spending on health – making France one of the three largest VHI markets in Europe (WHO, 2016).

Entitlement to publicly financed health care and gaps in coverage

The health system provides near universal coverage through a publicly financed statutory health insurance scheme. The publicly financed benefits package is considered generous in terms of the scope of its coverage, but user charges are applied to most services, mainly in the form of coinsurance (except for treatment for chronic conditions covered by the *affections de longue durée* (ALD) scheme).

Patients have access to public and private hospitals. Hospital treatment requires 20% coinsurance from patients. Coinsurance is not needed for costly surgeries. Patients also pay a lump sum per day in hospital for food. Outpatient care involves three types of user charges: coinsurance, extra-billing and deductibles. Coinsurance rates are 30% for physician and dentist care and 40% for ancillary services and laboratory tests. For most medicines, coinsurance amounts to either 70 or 35%, but ranges from 0% for non-substitutable or expensive medicines, to 85% for so-called convenience medicines. Some outpatient specialists use extra-billing.

New user charges were introduced in 2005 and extended in 2008. These flat-rate user charges (see Chevreul et al., 2010:63) are referred to as deductibles and are generally applied to all outpatient care: €1 for physician services and laboratory procedures (limited to €50 per year); €0.50 per prescription drug package or ancillary service; and €2 per medical transport (limited to €50 per year). Patients also pay €18 for treatments for which the statutory scheme tariff is over a certain amount (€120). These deductibles are intended to lower use.

Overview of the VHI market

Market origins, aims and role

Private health insurance offered by mutual benefit associations (*mutuelles de santé*) has existed in France since the 19th century and covered two thirds of the population by 1939 (Chevreul et al., 2010). The 1945 law that established the social security system redefined the role of *mutuelles* as complementary to the statutory health insurance scheme; by the early 1960s, their coverage had declined to one third of the population. VHI coverage began to grow again, however, and by 2010 VHI covered 90% of the population (Figure 11.1).

Figure 11.1 *VHI population coverage in France (%), 1960–2010*

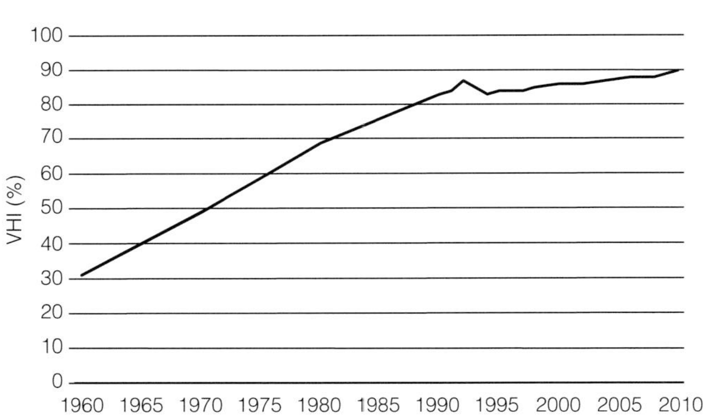

Sources: Insee (1960–2010), Insee-IRDES (1960–1991), IRDES (1992–2010).

VHI's main role is *complementary*, covering most user charges (but not the so-called deductibles; see further on). VHI policies also offer enhanced coverage of things not well covered by the statutory scheme, such as dental and optical care, and *supplementary* coverage for private amenities, such as the cost of a single room up to a daily limit. With the saturation of the VHI market, some insurers now offer services not covered by the statutory scheme. However, VHI is generally not used to jump public sector waiting lists or to obtain access to elite providers.

In 2000, the government introduced a system of free VHI covering user charges (*couverture maladie universelle* (CMU-C)) for the poorest households. By 2010, CMU-C covered nearly 6% of the population (Dourgnon, Guillaume & Rochereau, 2012).

Types of plan available

All VHI plans offer complementary cover of user charges; many cover supplementary amenities (hospital accommodation in a single room) and a few cover services not covered by the statutory scheme. Policies differ in the extent of user charges and extra billing they cover. Most cover coinsurance (based on statutory tariffs) for most services fully, but the VHI coverage of the costs of convenience medicines, medical devices and extra-billing varies. In 2010, the largest share of VHI expenditure (41%) was on fees paid to health professionals (Figure 11.2).

Figure 11.2 *Breakdown of VHI expenditure in France by type of care (%), 2010*

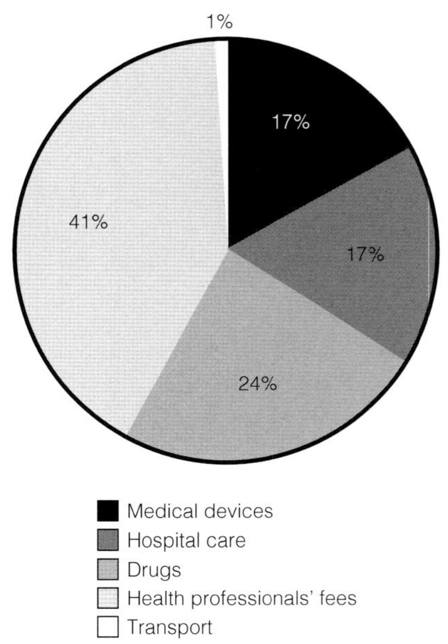

Source: Fenina, Le Garrec & Koubi (2011).

VHI may be purchased by individuals or by businesses for their employees. A survey showed that, in 2009, 44% of privately insured individuals were covered by group contracts (Garnero, 2012). While most individual VHI contracts are voluntary (56%), group contracts are usually mandatory for all employees and offer broader coverage.

Why do people buy VHI?

People mainly buy VHI for protection against widespread user charges for publicly financed health services. Since the early 1990s, over 90% of hospital expenditure has been financed publicly. However, public financing of outpatient care fell from 77% in 1980 to 63% in 2010 (Fenina, Le Garrec & Koubi, 2011). Between 1980 and 2008, the annual OOP payment per person grew from €217 to €547 in constant prices (Perronnin, Pierre & Rochereau, 2011). With the shifting of outpatient costs from the statutory scheme to households, VHI's role in financing and ensuring access to care has grown.

Rising incomes have also contributed to the growth in VHI coverage, and insurers have broadened their range of contracts to attract younger and healthier people. At the same time, the government has implemented significant demand-side measures to increase VHI take-up, including free VHI (CMU-C) for the poorest households (since 2000), vouchers subsidizing VHI for the near poor (since 2006) and favourable tax treatment for businesses paying for group contracts (since 2009).

Who buys VHI?

In spite of government efforts to make VHI more affordable, and although a large share of low-income individuals are enrolled in CMU-C, social disparities in access to VHI remain. Among the 5% of the population with no complementary VHI coverage in 2010, 43% attributed it to financial constraints (Dourgnon, Guillaume & Rochereau, 2012). These people are unlikely to be eligible for CMU-C and are probably not eligible for employer group contracts, which are often mandatory and less expensive than individual contracts. The share of household income spent on VHI varies from 3% for the wealthiest households to 10% for the poorest (Perronnin, Pierre & Rochereau, 2011). VHI coverage increases with age, ranging from 87% of those under 16 years old to 95% of those over 65. Lower coverage among younger people may be the result of lower health care needs, lower income and reduced access to group contracts.

Who sells VHI?

The VHI market is characterized by a large number of insurers: 711 in 2010 (DREES, 2011). This number has decreased by more than half since 2001, as many insurers merged or left the market due to heavy competition in a saturated market and stricter underwriting rules.

Insurers belong to one of three families (Table 11.1 shows their relative market shares): mutual, commercial and provident. Mutual insurers (known as *mutuelles*) operate on a non-profit-making basis and their aim is to achieve solidarity and mutual aid among their members by avoiding, to the extent permitted by competition, differentiation in premiums for a given level of coverage. They use limited risk rating of premiums and some even offer income-related premiums. Health insurance contracts represent 89% of their turnover (ACPR, 2010). They mainly offer individual contracts, and the majority of their group contracts are voluntary.

Table 11.1 *Types of French VHI providers and their market shares, 2010*

	Mutual insurers	Commercial insurers	Provident institutions
Number	587	92	34
% of total number	82	13	5
% of VHI turnover	55	29	16
% of VHI health care funding	56	26	18
% premiums from health insurance contracts	89	Mixed: 6 Non-life: 14	48
% individual VHI contracts	74	Mixed: 23 Non-life: 76	16

Sources: DREES (2011) for information on the number, turnover, health insurance premiums and share of individual contracts; Fenina, Le Garrec & Koubi (2011) for information on health care funding.

Note: Mixed companies insure both life and non-life risks.

Commercial insurers entered the VHI market in the early 1980s when other branches of the non-life insurance market became saturated. They often use a large set of characteristics, including health status, to rate premiums. In 2010, health insurance represented 14% of turnover for non-life companies and 6% for businesses offering mixed contracts.

Provident institutions were created after the Second World War to manage the supplementary retiree pensions of executives; they later expanded to cover heavy risks and VHI. They account for the smallest share of the VHI market and specialize in mandatory group contracts for companies (84% of their health insurance turnover) (DREES, 2011). Since 1993, a single provident institution cannot manage retiree pensions and heavy risks, such as health insurance. In 2010, 48% of the provident turnover came from health insurance activity (ACPR, 2010).

Insurer relations with providers

VHI does not generally involve purchasing and most insurers do not therefore have much contact with providers. Some insurers have agreements with selected health care providers (preferred providers), to cap costs and limit patient user charges. The National Union of Complementary Health Insurers (UNOCAM) participates in the negotiation of national agreements with health care professionals.

Public policy towards VHI

Mutual and provident institutions are regulated by the Department of Social Security within the Ministry of Health; the Ministry for the Economy and Finance regulates commercial insurers. All three are subject to oversight by the Prudential Supervisory Authority (*Autorité de contrôle prudentiel et de résolution*, ACPR).

In the 1980s, the entrance of commercial insurers and provident institutions (Mauroy, 1996) significantly affected the individual contract market. Previously, mutuals had been the only insurers in the individual VHI market, offering a uniform level of coverage and community-rated premiums. The entrance of new competitors offering multiple levels of coverage and using risk rating strategies subjected them to adverse selection. Facing the risk of a death spiral, mutuals adopted more commercially oriented strategies, starting with risk rating. In 2001, the permissible rating practices were codified (in the *Code de la Mutualité*) to include income, age, contract duration, the insured's statutory health insurance fund, place of residence and number of beneficiaries. The use of health status to rate premiums continued to be prohibited. By 2005, community rating based on age was used in two thirds of mutual contracts (Arnould, Pichetti & Rattier, 2007), compared to nearly 100% for commercial contracts. Mutuals also started to offer tailored contracts, in which coverage is adapted to health care consumption. In addition, a 1985 reform allowed mutuals to sell group contracts.

The government has also intervened in the VHI market by implementing measures to support solidarity and other public sector objectives. In 2002, the concept of solidarity-based VHI policies, with no limitations on pre-existing conditions or health questionnaires, was introduced. VHI policies not meeting these standards were subject to a 7% tax on premiums.

In 2004, tax exemption from the 7% tax on premiums was extended to so-called responsible VHI policies. These are policies that do not cover deductibles or the increased coinsurance amounts patients must pay if they do not follow a coordinated care pathway with gatekeeping; however, they do cover at least 95% of the most important medicines and laboratory tests and a minimum of 2 preventive services. By 2006 almost all VHI policies met the criteria for responsible policies (Arnould & Rattier, 2008). However, recent austerity measures introduced by the government have resulted in the reimposition of taxes on such contracts, starting at 3.5% in 2010 and rising to 7% in 2011. Contracts not meeting the so-called responsible criteria are now subject to a 9% tax.

The growing role of VHI in the funding of the health system has been recognized by giving insurers a greater role in system's governance. In 2004, UNOCAM was established to represent insurers selling VHI. UNOCAM is consulted prior to the introduction of new products to the publicly financed benefits package. It is also part of the pricing committee for publicly financed medicines and medical devices and participates in the negotiation of national agreements with health care professionals.

Debates and challenges

VHI coverage has tripled in the last 50 years and VHI plays an important role in ensuring access to health care and financial protection in the context of widespread and increased user charges and in improving equity of access via responsible policies. However, increases in user charges in the statutory scheme, leading to an increase in VHI's role in health financing, has reduced equity in financing because statutory health insurance contributions are income-related while VHI premiums are usually not. Thus, wealthier people spend a much lower share of their income on VHI compared to poorer people. Moreover, certain population groups, such as the unemployed and the retired, are unable to benefit from the favourable premiums and terms associated with group VHI policies.

The role of VHI in ensuring the sustainability of the current system is subject to growing debate. Despite policies to expand VHI coverage, including premium tax exemptions for insurers and substantial subsidies for households, inequities in access and levels of coverage remain. There is a need for better understanding of why some people have no VHI coverage and of the impact of lack of VHI on access to care and health outcomes (Perronnin, Pierre & Rochereau, 2011).

In addition, competition in the VHI market must be strengthened to contain premium costs. One way to improve competition is by increasing transparency. In the context of a market with many insurers and no standardized format of presenting VHI benefits, consumers struggle to compare the scope and depth of VHI coverage. A provision in the 2012 Social Security Financing Act, effective from January 2014, requires VHI companies to report the amount and composition of administrative costs as a percentage of premiums to enhance the transparency and comparability of VHI contracts.

The future of VHI

The growing role of VHI in the health system is partly because of its historically established role as a complementary source of health care financing and partly because of more recent fiscal constraints within the statutory scheme. In spite of measures introduced to enhance the efficiency of the statutory scheme, a growing share of health care costs has been slowly shifted to VHI. To minimize the negative effects of increased reliance on VHI on equity of access to health care, the government has applied stricter controls on the content of VHI contracts – for example, through tax incentives linked to responsible contracts. However, these restrictions on the content of VHI contracts have resulted in higher premiums.

An expanded role for VHI has not led to a decrease in the costs of the statutory scheme. A growing number of chronically ill patients are now fully covered under the ALD scheme (within the statutory scheme), which exempts them from user charges for chronic illness. This has reduced the share of the sickest patients covered by VHI and increased the profitability of the VHI sector. In the context of the economic crisis and public budget constraints, the government has taken several measures to offset this windfall. In 2009, a one-off contribution of €1 billion was imposed on insurers selling VHI to reduce the deficit of the statutory scheme. In 2011, the tax on turnover that these insurers pay to fund the CMU-C programme was increased dramatically from 1.75 (since 2007) to 6.27%.

Nevertheless, in recognition of its increasing role in health financing, VHI has been given a greater role in the governance of the health system, including participation in negotiations with providers and providing input into annual legislative proposals for the financing of the statutory scheme.

References

ACPR (2010). *Les chiffres du marché français de la banque et de l'assurance 2010*. Paris, Autorité de contrôle prudentiel (http://www.acp.banque-france.fr/fileadmin/user_upload/acp/publications/rapports-annuels/2010-ACP-chiffres-du-marche-francais-banque-et-assurance.pdf, accessed 22 November 2015).

Arnould M-L, Rattier M-O (2008). *Les contrats les plus souscrits auprès des organismes complémentaires santé en 2006*. Etudes et résultats No. 635. Paris, Direction de la recherche, des études, de l'évaluation et des statistiques (DREES) (http://www.drees.sante.gouv.fr/les-contrats-les-plus-souscrits-aupres-des-organismes-complementaires-sante-en-2006,4324.html, accessed 22 November 2015).

Arnould M-L, Pichetti S, Rattier M-O (2007). *Les contrats les plus souscrits auprès des organismes complémentaires santé en 2005*. Etudes et résultats No. 575. Paris, DREES (http://www.drees.sante.gouv.fr/les-contrats-les-plus-souscrits-aupres-des-organismes-complementaires-sante-en-2005,4392.html, accessed 22 November 2015).

Chevreul K et al. (2010). France: health system review. *Health Systems in Transition*, 12(6):1–291.

Dourgnon P, Guillaume S, Rochereau T (2012). *Enquête sur la santé* et la protection sociale 2010. Paris, Institut de Recherche et Documentation en Economie de la Santé (IRDES) (http://www.irdes.fr/Publications/Rapports2012/rap1886.pdf, accessed 22 November 2015).

DREES (2011). *La situation financière des organismes complémentaires assurant une couverture santé*. Paris, DREES (http://www.drees.sante.gouv.fr/IMG/pdf/rapport_oc_2011.pdf, accessed 22 November 2015).

Fenina A, Le Garrec M-A, Koubi M (2011). *Comptes nationaux de la santé 2010. Document de travail*. Paris, DREES (http://www.drees.sante.gouv.fr/IMG/pdf/seriestat161.pdf?bcsi_scan_628cd39dca2568d2=Gdwb

Bdb1rZphikq0D3rCKwiP+xcCAAAAVvOJCQ==&bcsi_scan_filename=seriestat161.pdf, accessed 22 November 2015).

Garnero M (2012). *Les contrats les plus souscrits auprès des complémentaires santé en 2009*. Etudes et résultats No 789. Paris, DREES (http://www.drees.sante.gouv.fr/IMG/pdf/er789.pdf, accessed 22 November 2015).

Insee (1960–2010). *Population au premier janvier*. Institut national de la statistique et des études économiques (Insee) (http://www.insee.fr/fr/themes/series-longues.asp?indicateur=pop-debut-annee, accessed 22 November 2015).

Insee-IRDES (1960–1991). *Enquête sur la santé et les soins médicaux, Insee-Irdes (anciennement Credes) (ESSM)*. Institut national de la statistique et des études économiques (Insee) and Institut de la recherche et documentation en économie de la santé (IRDES) (http://www.ecosante.fr/DEPAFRA/4002.html; accessed 22 November 2015).

IRDES (1992–2010). *Enquête sur la santé et la protection sociale (ESPS)*. Institut de la recherche et documentation en économie de la santé (IRDES) (http://www.irdes.fr/recherche/enquetes/esps-enquete-sur-la-sante-et-la-protection-sociale/actualites.html, accessed 22 November 2015).

Mauroy H (1996). *La Mutualité en mutation: les pratiques solidaristes en question*. Paris, L'Harmattan.

Perronnin M, Pierre A, Rochereau T (2011). *La complémentaire santé en France en 2008: une large diffusion mais des inégalités d'accès*. Paris, Institut de Recherche et IRDES (http://www.irdes.fr/Publications/2011/Qes161.pdf, accessed 22 November 2015).

WHO (2016). Global Health Expenditure Database (GHED) [online database]. Geneva, WHO (http://www.who.int/health-accounts/ghed/en/, accessed 5 April 2016).

12
Georgia

Erica Richardson and Nana Gugeshashvili

Health system context

The health financing mix

The Georgian health system relies heavily on OOP payments. In 2014, OOP payments accounted for 58.6% of total spending on health, while public spending on health accounted for 20.9% and VHI for 19.2% (WHO, 2016).

Entitlement to publicly financed health care and gaps in coverage

In 2006, the government changed from using the government budget to finance health care for the whole population to using budgetary funds to cover the poorest households only. It also handed over responsibility for purchasing health services to private insurers – that is, the government purchased coverage for the poorest households from private insurers. The Medical Insurance Programme (MIP) was rolled out nationwide in 2008, targeting households registered as living below the poverty line. It was accompanied by a number of state-funded programmes covering specific services, such as psychiatric care or TB treatment. The government also purchased private cover for other groups (children in care, government workers, teachers and recent internally displaced persons), and some people obtained private cover by buying it themselves or through employment. However, most people had no health coverage at all.

Prior to elections held at the end of 2012, the MIP was broadened to include pensioners, children under six years old, students and people with registered disabilities (an extra 800 000 people), extending coverage to around 45% of the population. In February 2013, the new government introduced a new publicly financed *basic package* of benefits for those without any coverage – the Universal Health Care Programme. This included primary care and some diagnostic services (with 20–30% coinsurance) and emergency care up to Georgian lari (GEL) 15 000 (about €6600). From July 2013, the basic package for the uninsured was expanded to cover elective surgery, oncological services and obstetric care, which had previously been covered under separate state-funded programmes. The basic package is administered through the Social Services Agency under the Ministry of Health rather than private insurers. Publicly financed coverage now covers over 90% of the population, although it remains relatively limited in its coverage of medicines. It also requires substantial user charges, especially for medicines and outpatient care, but also for other health services for people who were previously uninsured.

Overview of the VHI market

Market origins, aims and role

VHI initially developed to play a *substitutive* role. The market emerged in 2007/2008 because of government policy to reduce the role of the state in public life through the targeting of social benefits, including health. The introduction of the MIP was a key policy for achieving both of these goals and the result was a rapid expansion of the private health insurance industry; prior to this, the VHI market had been extremely small. Under the MIP, eligible vulnerable households were initially given a voucher with which they could purchase a comprehensive annual health insurance policy from their choice of private insurer. In 2010, the system was changed so that one company only would cover each region; private insurers competed for a tender to be the exclusive insurer for the MIP in each region for three years. Those not eligible for MIP cover had to purchase their own insurance. The government supported a number of initiatives to encourage uninsured citizens to purchase cover and thereby grow the VHI market. However, following the introduction of the Universal Health Care programme in 2013, VHI plays a largely *supplementary* and *complementary* role, providing benefits for people who want greater coverage than the state provides.

Types of plan available

There is a wide range of plans available on the market. Under the MIP, benefits were defined by the government and covered inpatient and outpatient care but excluded most outpatient medicines, dental care and optical care.

Why do people buy VHI?

Before 2013, people bought VHI for protection against OOP payments. VHI was really the only form of coverage available for the vast majority of health services. For part of the population, this voluntary coverage was financed by the state.

Who buys VHI?

Before 2013, the government was by far the largest purchaser of VHI, purchasing VHI on behalf of the poorest households covered by the MIP and some other groups. Coverage not funded by the government was mainly bought by professionals living in urban areas, on a group basis. Post 2013, VHI continues to be the preserve of professionals living in urban areas. Because of fears about adverse selection, insurers have never been keen to sell individual policies and pre-existing conditions are not usually covered (Gabrichidze, Kechinashvili & Baker, 2011). Table 12.1 shows the distribution of different types of health coverage in 2011.

Who sells VHI?

In 2012, there were 14 general insurers active in the market. The MIP encouraged rapid growth in the insurance sector, as well as consolidation. In the same year, Aldagi BCI was the biggest insurer in the country with a 26% market share (most of the company's portfolio is health insurance) and Imedi L (in which Aldagi BCI are the majority shareholders) had an 11% share.

Insurer relations with providers

Insurers generally retrospectively reimburse providers. However, as part of a hospital privatization programme launched in 2011, insurers were encouraged to purchase from hospitals in a given region as part of an exclusive contract to provide health insurance to the local population eligible for government-funded VHI. As a result, some integration of insurers and health care providers took place.

Table 12.1 *Distribution of types of individual health insurance in Georgia (n=14 837) by per adult equivalent consumption quintile of household, 2011*

Type of health insurance	% individuals by consumption quintile of household					Total
	1 (poorest)	2	3	4	5 (richest)	
No health insurance	54.6	68.3	73.8	77.9	75.1	69.9
MIP (with or without non-MIP state-subsidized or private)	40.3	24.7	16.5	10.9	5.2	19.5
Non-MIP state-subsidized (with or without private)	3.5	3.1	3.8	2.5	2.4	3.1
Private only (self-financed or sponsored by employer)	1.6	3.6	5.9	8.7	17.4	7.5

Source: UNICEF Georgia, University of York (2012).

Public policy towards VHI

From 2007 to 2012, public policy towards VHI was very supportive because the government wanted to develop private insurance as the backbone of health financing (Table 12.2). Consequently, regulation of the insurance sector in general and the VHI market was very light touch. It focused on setting financial standards for entry and operation in the market and did not require open enrolment or guaranteed renewal of contracts, although under the MIP insurers had to provide a standard benefits package defined by the government for MIP subscribers.

Debates and challenges

The decision to embrace VHI as a means of providing publicly financed health coverage had two main aims: to limit public budget commitments by reducing the role of the state; and to target health spending so that those most in need benefited the most from public spending (Chanturidze et al., 2009). The changes also sought to improve transparency in the health system and to formalize informal payments by drastically cutting and simplifying the publicly financed package of benefits. The approach was in keeping with the prevailing political climate, which saw marketization and deregulation as essential for economic development and for addressing corruption.

Developments in the run up to the elections in 2012 made it clear that better financial access to health care was an important political issue. It was under these circumstances that the More Benefit to the People strategy was announced, which was to significantly broaden the MIP, from 1 September 2012, to cover all children aged under 6 years, all pensioners and all full-time students, thereby extending state-financed cover to 1.9 million people (with 0.5 million purchasing their own cover). The scope of cover was also to be broader for these groups as preventive services and palliative care were covered (Transparency International Georgia, 2012). The high cost of outpatient medicines was recognized as a central concern for people, so expanding cover to include essential medicines was also included, albeit with a low cap.

Following the election of a new government, public policy took a very different approach, largely in response to the limitations of the VHI and MIP system. An evaluation of the impact of the MIP reform identified a range of concerns, including the very narrow breadth, scope and depth of coverage, the technical efficiency of the system, the weak regulation of private insurance providers and the quality of care provided (Smith, 2013). During the time the MIP was in operation, the VHI market expanded from covering less than 1% of the population in 2006 to around 30% in 2011 and 45% in late 2012. However, while the MIP was well targeted to the poorest households, and had a positive impact on financial

Table 12.2 *Development and regulation of the VHI market, 1997–2013*

Year	Policy
1997	Medical Insurance Act (amended 2007, 2009) provides the legislative base for compulsory and VHI
2008	MIP: health insurance cover for the poorest is purchased by the state from private insurance companies
2009	Government Decree No. 218 of 9 December 2009 defines the terms and conditions of cover available under the MIP
2011	Hospital Privatization Programme: private insurers are encouraged to become regional integrated purchaser–providers
2012	More Benefit to the People strategy: in the run up to the election, MIP is extended to other groups
2013	The Universal Health Care Programme is introduced and all publicly financed health coverage is now administered by the Social Services Agency rather than private insurers

Source: Authors.

protection for its beneficiaries, this did not translate into greater financial protection for the population as a whole (Smith, 2013). In fact, health care costs continued to drive significant numbers of households into poverty and to impose a catastrophic financial burden on many other households. Analysis of Household Budget Survey data has shown that the share of households facing catastrophic levels of OOP payments for health care rose from 6.1% in 2006 to 8.5% in 2010, with the poorest fifth of households most likely to face catastrophic health spending (Rukhadze & Goginashvili, 2011). The MIP did not lead to greater use of health care among its beneficiaries, better health outcomes or greater provider responsiveness to patients (Smith, 2013). A combination of lack of awareness of eligibility for the programme, low quality of care and the absence of good coverage of medicines may have reduced people's motivation to seek care (Smith, 2013).

In addition, the efficiency gains expected from increasing competition in the health insurance sector did not materialize, particularly as transaction costs appeared to be extremely high (Zoidze et al., 2012). In 2012, the two largest insurers spent only a tiny share of their gross premium revenue on claims (2.6% for Aldagi BCI and 4.4% for Imedi L). A system in which 14 insurers covered fewer than a million people was also inevitably fragmented.

Finally, weak regulation of the VHI market led to adverse selection and so-called cream-skimming by private insurers. There were reported cases where MIP beneficiaries were denied services, particularly expensive diagnostic procedures, even when all the correct administrative procedures were followed and the interventions clinically indicated (Zoidze et al., 2012). In this regulatory environment, the integration of private insurers (many owned by pharmaceutical companies) with hospitals as the main means of privatizing the inpatient network is also potentially fraught with conflicts of interest (Transparency International Georgia, 2012).

The future of VHI

The change in political balance following parliamentary and presidential elections in 2012 has changed the focus of public policy from developing the VHI market to extending publicly financed health coverage to the whole population and shifting responsibility for administering coverage from private insurers to the government. As a result, the VHI market has declined dramatically and its role has changed from substitutive to supplementary and complementary. How the market develops in the next few years will depend on public satisfaction with the coverage provided by the state, the ability of private insurers to develop VHI products that are affordable to a relatively low-income population and the outcome of elections due to be held in 2016.

References

Chanturidze T et al. (2009). Georgia: health system review. *Health Systems in Transition*, 11(8):1–116.

Gabrichidze S, Kechinashvili G, Baker S (2011). *Georgia Health System Strengthening Project (HSSP): mid-term evaluation*. Washington, DC, United States Agency for International Development.

Rukhadze N, Goginashvili K (2011). *Distribution of health payments and catastrophic expenditures in Georgia: analysis for 2006–2010 (annual level data)*. Tbilisi, Ministry of Labour, Health and Social Affairs.

Smith O (2013). *Georgia's Medical Insurance Program for the Poor*. UNICO Study Series No. 16. Washington, DC, World Bank.

Transparency International Georgia (2012). *The Georgian health insurance industry*. Tbilisi, Transparency International Georgia with the support of the Embassy of the Kingdom of the Netherlands.

UNICEF Georgia, University of York (2012). *The well-being of children and their families in Georgia: Georgia Welfare Monitoring Survey second stage 2011*. Tbilisi & York, UNICEF Georgia, University of York.

WHO (2016). Global Health Expenditure Database (GHED) [online database]. Geneva, WHO (http://www.who.int/health-accounts/ghed/en/, accessed 5 April 2016).

Zoidze A et al. (2012). *Health insurance for poor: Georgia's path to universal coverage?* Tbilisi, Curatio International Foundation.

13
Germany

Stefan Greß

Health system context

The health financing mix

Health care in Germany is predominantly publicly financed. In 2014, public spending accounted for 77% of total spending on health, OOP payments for 13.2% and VHI for 8.9% (WHO, 2016).

Entitlement to publicly financed health care and gaps in coverage

Health insurance coverage is mandatory for the entire population. Coverage is virtually universal and less than 1% of the population is not insured. Some groups of people can choose between publicly financed coverage provided through the statutory health insurance scheme and privately financed substitutive coverage provided by private insurers. Access to substitutive private coverage is restricted to civil servants, self-employed individuals and high-income employees (the annual earnings threshold was €50 850 in 2012). These groups may opt out of the statutory scheme, but once they do so the return options are limited. For example, employees may only return to the statutory scheme when their earnings fall below the threshold. Individuals with substitutive private coverage who are older than 55 years are prohibited from returning to the statutory scheme.

Overview of the VHI market

Market origins, aims and role

Substitutive private coverage used to provide an alternative for better-off people, namely high-income employees and the self-employed. These groups were exempt from mandatory membership of the statutory scheme and had the choice of purchasing VHI or remaining uninsured. However, when both the number of low-income, self-employed individuals and the number of uninsured persons started to grow (Greß, Walendzik & Wasem, 2006),[1] the government decided to make health coverage mandatory for the whole population (from 2009). Since 2009, substitutive private coverage is only voluntary for people aged under 55 years, who retain the option of returning to the statutory scheme if their earnings fall below the threshold.

Complementary VHI – available to the whole population – provides access mainly to luxury services not covered by the statutory scheme and cover of user charges for services only partly covered by the statutory scheme (for example, dental care). *Supplementary* VHI provides access to treatment by the chief physician in hospitals or to private rooms in hospitals.

Types of plan available

People with substitutive private coverage hold individual policies. Group policies are almost non-existent. Premiums are risk-rated and capital-funded, which means that part of the premiums paid by younger cohorts are set aside, invested in capital markets and used to fund health care in later life. Therefore, premiums are supposed to stay constant over a person's lifetime. However, this may not be the case in practice, because the calculation does not account for health care inflation or increases in life expectancy (Albrecht et al., 2010).

The range of services covered is regulated only loosely and may differ substantially between private health insurers. The same is true for the extent of user charges for privately covered services. Most policies cover inpatient care, outpatient care and medicines, but often do not cover important medical devices and mental health care. A recent study has shown that 80% of individual policies provide less coverage than the standard benefits offered by the statutory scheme (Drabinski & Gorr, 2012). A small minority of people with private coverage have a standardized basic policy; this is highly regulated by the government and must cover services comparable to those covered by the statutory scheme in return for capped premiums.

Complementary VHI mostly covers dental benefits. In contrast to substitutive private coverage, neither complementary nor supplementary VHI are capital-funded.

Why do people buy VHI

Whether individuals choose to opt out of the statutory scheme is determined by financial and non-financial incentives. The statutory scheme requires income-related contributions. In contrast, substitutive private coverage requires risk-related premiums. Premiums also rise with the age of entry, since the available time to build up savings is shorter. What is more, each family member must be insured separately, which is not the case with the statutory scheme. As a result, substitutive private coverage is financially more attractive for young, healthy and single individuals without dependants.

Most health care providers treat publicly and privately funded patients. Remuneration for GPs and outpatient specialists depends on the insurance status of patients: private health insurers pay these providers higher tariffs than statutory health insurance funds and, more importantly, do not impose volume restrictions on physicians. These differences in payments create substantial incentives for preferential treatment of individuals with substitutive private coverage in outpatient settings (Lüngen et al., 2008). Patients covered by substitutive private coverage also receive preferential treatment in hospitals (Schwierz et al., 2011). Shorter waiting times for inpatient and outpatient care provide an important non-financial incentive for individuals to opt out of the statutory scheme (Greß, 2007).

People buy supplementary VHI either to acquire the right to improved hospital amenities or to be treated by the chief physician in hospital. Complementary VHI is taken up for financial protection reasons.

Who buys VHI?

Compared to people in the statutory scheme, people with substitutive private coverage are on average healthier and

1 A growing number of the self-employed were unable to pay their substitutive private health insurance premiums and, as a result, lost their insurance benefits and had to pay for health care OOP. Many of them were unable to pay for the health care they received and physicians and hospitals were unable to recoup their expenses. In some cases, these costs were financed through social assistance (paid by the government).

richer. It is not attractive for people with high health risks to leave the statutory scheme because private health insurance premiums are risk-rated. Income differences between people in the statutory scheme and people with substitutive private coverage are somewhat moderated by the fact that the earnings threshold for opting out does not apply to self-employed individuals and civil servants (Table 13.1).

Table 13.1 *Characteristics of enrollees covered by the statutory scheme and substitutive private health insurance in Germany, 2006*

Characteristics	Statutory scheme	Substitutive private coverage
Average individual gross annual income	€22 658	€38 109
Average number of acute and chronic conditions	3.52	2.89
Poor self-assessed health status	17.9%	9.1%
Average number of hospital nights during last 12 months	2.21	2.05
Average number of physician visits during last 12 months	6.21	5.10
Share of respondents with continuous consumption of prescription medicines	47.1%	41.7%

Sources: Kriwy & Mielck (2006); Leinert (2006).

Who sells VHI?

In 2012, private health insurance was offered by 24 commercial and 19 private non-profit-making companies. Market concentration is relatively low. Since 2004, statutory health insurance funds can cooperate with private health insurers and offer complementary and supplementary VHI (to their enrollees only).

Insurer relations with providers

In general, private health insurers in Germany do not have contractual relations with health care providers due to legal restrictions. However, they are legally involved in negotiating reimbursement for inpatient services and increasingly negotiate discounts for medicines. The government determines the payment scheme for outpatient physicians, but private health insurers can pay physicians more than the official tariff.

Public policy towards VHI

The market for substitutive private coverage has undergone several important regulatory changes since 2000, both to protect the financial situation of the statutory scheme and to ensure access to private health insurance for those who rely on it (see Table 13.2). In 2000, people with substitutive coverage who were over 55 years were not allowed to return to the statutory scheme to protect the statutory scheme from adverse selection (for example, with younger people benefiting from low private health insurance premiums and returning to the statutory scheme when they became older and their premiums rose).

A highly contested reform was introduced in 2007 by a coalition government of Christian and Social Democrats – again, to protect the statutory scheme from adverse selection. Access to substitutive private coverage for high-income employees was restricted: while previously these individuals had to show that their incomes exceeded the threshold for one year to opt out of the statutory scheme, this was extended to three consecutive years. As a result, the net growth of the substitutive market dropped from 116 000 new enrollees in 2006 to 49 000 in 2008 (PKV-Verband, 2009). The new coalition government of Christian Democrats and Liberals reversed this measure in 2011 following huge political pressure from private health insurers.

The introduction of the universal mandate to take out health insurance in 2009 led to a number of new legislative acts regulating substitutive private coverage. To improve access, health insurers had to accept all admissible applicants and offer highly regulated basic policies with a standardized benefits package and premium caps. They also cannot dismiss enrollees defaulting on paying premiums (although they may restrict the level of services they provide them).

In 2010, about 21 000 individuals held basic policies (PKV-Verband, 2011). This low number is the result of adverse selection (most people who opt for these policies have high health risks) and high premiums. Although the premiums cap is set at a rather high level, private health insurers still incur a deficit that must be covered by non-basic policyholders. The same is true for costs caused by the rising number of defaulters. It is estimated that 143 000 defaulters caused a deficit of about €500 million in 2011 (Deutscher Bundestag, 2012a). To relieve financial pressure faced by insurers offering substitutive private coverage, recent legislation (2011) has allowed them to take advantage of the discounts for medicines negotiated by the statutory health insurance funds.

Table 13.2 *Reform of private health insurance in Germany, 2000–2011*

Year	Private health insurance market	Description
2000	Substitutive	Enrollees 55 years and older who have opted out are not allowed (without exception) to return to the statutory systems
2004	Complementary and supplementary	Statutory health insurance funds are allowed to sell complementary and supplementary VHI policies
2007	Substitutive	Restriction of access to private coverage for high-income employees: the income threshold must be met for three continuous years before opting out is allowed
2009	Substitutive	Universal mandate: private health insurers are required to accept all admissible applicants and have to offer highly regulated basic tariffs; defaulters cannot be dismissed
2011	Substitutive	Discounts for medicines negotiated by statutory health insurance funds are valid for private coverage also
2011	Substitutive	Access to private coverage for high-income employees is improved: individuals need to have income above the threshold for one year only

Source: Reiners & Müller (2012).

Since 2004, statutory health insurance funds can sell complementary and supplementary VHI policies in cooperation with VHI companies. They cannot sell them on their own. This reform has raised concerns that competing statutory health insurance funds may use VHI policies as an instrument to select risks (Laske-Aldershof et al., 2004). However, so far there is no strong evidence of this kind of risk selection taking place.

Debates and challenges

The existence of substitutive private coverage in Germany has been – and still is – severely challenged by political opponents. Traditionally, this challenge has been because substitutive private coverage undermines the fiscal sustainability of the statutory scheme and weakens equity of access to care by giving health care providers financial incentives for preferential treatment of people with substitutive private coverage. Substitutive private coverage undermines the fiscal sustainability of the statutory scheme in two ways. First, the statutory scheme's average revenue goes down if high-income people opt out because contributions are income-related. This effect is exacerbated by the fact that people with dependants are likely to remain in the statutory scheme. Second, the statutory scheme's average health care expenditure goes up, since people with low health risks are likely to opt out. Thus, adverse selection against the statutory scheme creates considerable fiscal pressure. Inequity in access to care is increasingly becoming a matter of public concern.

In response to these problems, several political parties (Social Democrats, Green Party and Socialists) have made proposals for a unified NHI system – similar to the reform introduced in the Netherlands in 2006. So far, these proposals have failed to gain majority support due to resistance by the Christian Democrats and the Liberal Party. Physician associations also strongly oppose the abolition of substitutive private coverage since they are afraid of the effects it would have on their income.

More recently, reports of rising expenditure and severe premium hikes of up to 40% for older people with substitutive private coverage have put pressure on the private health insurance market (Deutscher Bundestag, 2012b). Available data show that the average annual growth of health care expenditure has been more pronounced in the private health insurance market than in the statutory scheme (Table 13.3), and this translated

Table 13.3 *Comparison of health care expenditure and premiums in the statutory scheme and substitutive private coverage in Germany, 2002–2010*

Year	Statutory scheme	Substitutive VHI	
	Annual growth of health care expenditure (%)	Annual growth of health care expenditure (%)	Annual growth of premiums (%)
2002	3.3	5.7	6.2
2003	1.9	3.9	7.6
2004	–3.1	4.8	7.5
2005	2.3	4.5	3.9
2006	3.0	3.1	4.9
2007	4.1	6.1	3.7
2008	4.6	6.7	3.9
2009	6.5	4.6	3.4
2010	3.4	3.8	7.3
Average 2002–2010	**2.9**	**4.8**	**5.4**

Sources: Bundesministerium für Gesundheit (2012); Deutscher Bundestag (2012a).

into average premium growth of more than 5% per year in the 2002–2010 period, which may have been considerably higher for older people.

Rising private health insurance expenditure and premiums can be explained by the high fees they pay health care providers, the absence of contractual relations with health care providers (that is, they simply reimburse enrollees), the rising number of defaulters and low interest rates in capital markets (Deutscher Bundestag, 2012a, 2012b). Private health insurers have asked to be allowed to use more instruments to manage care and contain costs, but this would in turn lead to price cuts and volume restrictions for health care providers and, in the long run, to the disappearance of the preferential treatment given to privately financed patients. Substitutive private coverage would thus become less attractive for potential enrollees.

The future of VHI

Political support for substitutive private coverage is dwindling. Traditionally, the political left has fought it since it undermines equity and the financial sustainability of the statutory scheme. However, due to recent premium hikes in the private health insurance market, there have been growing doubts among those on the right of the political spectrum as to whether substitutive private coverage is financially viable in the end. Media reports also have increasingly questioned whether opting out of the statutory scheme is a sensible long-term option, even for young, healthy and single high-income individuals.

Private health insurers may in future obtain more instruments to manage care and contain costs. However, as a result, those with private coverage may lose their preferential treatment by health care providers and substitutive private coverage would lose its unique selling point. This mixture of political and price pressures makes the future of substitutive private coverage in Germany relatively bleak.

References

Albrecht M et al. (2010). *Die Bedeutung von Wettbewerb im Bereich der privaten Krankenversicherungen vor dem Hintergrund der erwarteten demografischen Entwicklung.* Berlin, Forschungsprojekt des Bundesministeriums für Wirtschaft und Technologie.

Bundesministerium für Gesundheit (2012). *Gesetzliche Krankenversicherung - Kennzahlen und Faustformeln.* Berlin, Bundesministerium für Gesundheit.

Deutscher Bundestag (2012a). *Nichtzahler-Tarif in der privaten Krankenversicherung. Drucksache 17/9012 vom 19. März 2012.* Berlin, Deutscher Bundestag.

Deutscher Bundestag (2012b). *Beitragssteigerungen bei privaten Krankenversicherungen. Drucksache 17/9330 vom 17. April 2012.* Berlin, Deutscher Bundestag.

Drabinski T, Gorr C-D (2012). *GKV/PKV-Systemgrenze: Bestandsaufnahme.* Kiel, Instituts für Mikrodaten-Analyse (IfMDA).

Greß S (2007). Private health insurance in Germany: consequences of a dual system. *Healthcare Policy*, 3(2):29–37.

Greß S, Walendzik A, Wasem J (2006). Hartz IV und die gesetzliche Krankenversicherung - Nichtversicherte als gesellschaftliches Problem [in German]. *Sozialer Fortschritt*, 55(8):186–192.

Kriwy P, Mielck A (2006). Versicherte der gesetzlichen Krankenversicherung und der privaten Krankenversicherung: Unterschiede in Morbidität und Gesundheitsverhalten [in German]. *Das Gesundheitswesen*, 68(5):281–288.

Laske-Aldershof T et al. (2004). Consumer mobility in social health insurance markets: a five-country comparison. *Applied Health Economics and Health Policy*, 3(4):229–241.

Leinert J (2006). Morbidität als Selektionskriterium. In: Jacobs K, Klauber J, Leinert J, eds. *Fairer Wettbewerb oder Risikoselektion? Analysen zur gesetzlichen und privaten Krankenversicherung.* Bonn, Wissenschaftliches Institut der AOK:67–76.

Lüngen M et al. (2008). Waiting times for elective treatments according to insurance status: a randomized empirical study in Germany. *International Journal for Equity in Health*, 7(1): doi: 10.1186/1475-9276-7-1.

PKV-Verband (2009). *Politischer Nackenschlag der Gesundheitsreform auch 2008 beim Netto-Neuzugang zu spüren.* Köln/Berlin, Presserklärung des Verbandes der privaten Krankenversicherung.

PKV-Verband (2011). *Zahlenbericht der Privaten Krankenversicherung 2010/2011*. Köln, Verband der privaten Krankenversicherung.

Reiners H, Müller O (2012). *Die Reformfibel. Handbuch der Gesundheitsreformen*. Berlin, KomPart-Verlag.

Schwierz C et al. (2011). Discrimination in waiting times by insurance type and financial soundness of German acute care hospitals. *European Journal of Health Economics*, 12(5):405–416.

WHO (2016). Global Health Expenditure Database (GHED) [online database]. Geneva, WHO (http://www.who.int/health-accounts/ghed/en/, accessed 5 April 2016).

14
Greece

Charalampos Economou

Health system context

The health financing mix

In 2014, public spending accounted for 61.7% of total spending on health and came from general taxes and earmarked payroll taxes. OOP payments and VHI accounted for 34.9% and 3.4% of total spending on health, respectively (WHO, 2016).

Entitlement to publicly financed health care and gaps in coverage

Health is enshrined in the Greek Constitution as a social right. There are two main principles of entitlement. One is citizenship in the case of outpatient services provided by the NHS (*Ethniko Systima Ygeias* (ESY)). The other is occupational status and payment of payroll taxes in the case of services provided or financed by social insurance funds, including services provided in urban polyclinics owned by social insurance funds, inpatient care provided by ESY hospitals and services provided by private providers contracted by social insurance funds. The poor are also entitled to services and free access to ESY health centres and hospitals. Undocumented migrants are entitled only to access hospital emergency services for the treatment of life-threatening conditions and may remain there only until their health has stabilized. They also have free access to primary care offered in a small number of local authority settings and to services provided by nongovernmental organizations.

The establishment of the ESY in 1983 aimed to achieve comprehensive and universal coverage of the population based on the principle of equity. Until recently, there were significant differences among social insurance funds regarding the scope and quality of coverage and freedom of choice; this means that this objective has been only partially met. Health care reform measures introduced by the government after 2010 aimed to confront this problem by merging all the major social insurance funds (IKA, OGA, OAEE, OPAD) into a single health insurance fund (National Organization for Health Care Provision, EOPYY). However, the adopted measures also included an increase in user charges for outpatient visits, diagnostic services in public hospitals and health centres, and medicines.

Overview of the VHI market

Market origins, aims and role

VHI mainly plays a *supplementary* role, with commercial insurers providing cover for faster access, better quality of services and increased choice. VHI is largely sold in combination with life insurance policies or private pension schemes. A major milestone took place in 1998, when two privately managed health care schemes with their own health care facilities were established. In addition, large companies started to offer group VHI contracts to their employees as employment perks.

Types of plan available

Supplementary VHI can be classified as follows (Siskou et al., 2009):

- *plans covering expenses in private hospitals*: accommodation, food, laboratory tests, medicines, surgical expenses, physicians' fees, dedicated nursing
- *plans covering expenses for private outpatient care*: reimbursement for expenses including physicians' fees, medicines and diagnostic tests; and
- *managed care programmes*: providing an integrated package of outpatient and inpatient services.

VHI plans do not cover plastic surgery, alternative medicine, routine ophthalmological services, and pre-existing conditions and chronic illnesses such as diabetes. Insurers use risk-rating in setting their premiums (risk factors include age, profession and individual medical record). People who wish to purchase VHI must provide information about their own and their family's medical history and undergo medical examinations and tests.

Why do people buy VHI?

According to the results of a survey conducted in 2003 on behalf of the Hellenic Association of Insurers (n=1100, aged 25–45 years, living in urban areas), VHI plans were purchased to:

- obtain access to better quality services (54% of those with VHI plans);
- avoid trouble and discomfort in relation to the way services are provided (49%);
- obtain faster access to services and jump waiting lists for publicly financed treatment (45%);
- supplement other forms of coverage (43%);
- because they did not trust social insurance (31%);
- because they were not covered by other schemes (8%); and
- to cover childbirth expenses (8%) (ICAP, 2003).

Who buys VHI?

During the 1980s, only 2% of the population was covered by VHI. This percentage had risen to 10% by 2005 and to about 11% in 2012. Most subscribers are middle to high earners and are about 45–60 years old. They are mainly employers (purchasing VHI cover for their employees), professionals, civil servants, white-collar workers and managers working for large private companies and banks and living in urban areas (Siskou et al., 2009). According to the 2003 survey, 53% of those with VHI plans were males, 43% had tertiary education and 68% belonged to the middle and upper classes.

Who sells VHI?

The overwhelming majority of insurers are non-specialist private commercial entities also engaged in other insurance activity, mainly life insurance. Most of them (87.5%) are Greek joint-stock insurers; the others are branch offices of foreign companies. The number of insurers operating in the life insurance and VHI market has fallen over time due to mergers and buyouts. Measured in premium revenue, the five biggest companies had 71% of the market share in 2010 (Hellenic Association of Insurers, 2011).

Insurer relations with providers

Private insurers can contract selectively with providers. They negotiate prices and pay providers on a FFS basis. Physicians in managed care schemes may also be paid on a salary basis. Capitation is applied mainly to outpatient diagnostic centres. However, in recent years, there is a growing trend among private insurers to engage in active purchasing and not simply to reimburse providers or subscribers, to control costs. In this context, either insurers develop their own health services or they make use of PPNs and apply financial incentives to encourage subscribers to use those providers.

Until 2010, insurers had been purchasing services from private hospitals and clinics; the law forbade the use of private beds in public hospitals. The situation changed in 2011, when new legislation allowed private insurers to use up to 10% of public hospital beds with the aim of giving public hospitals an additional source of income.

Public policy towards VHI

Table 14.1 summarizes the relevant legislation pertaining to the VHI market in Greece. The main changes in public policy in the last 20 years include the lowering of tax incentives for people to take up VHI in 1997, the abolition of these tax incentives in 2013 and the move to allow private insurers to use beds in public hospitals in 2011.

Debates and challenges

Some experts believe that the expansion of the VHI market will lower the public sector's contribution to health care financing and further increase private spending. Others see the role of VHI as purely supplementary and thus not affecting the public–private mix. Politicians have not generally supported a stronger role for VHI, although the 2011 reform allowing private insurers to use 10% of public hospital beds may indicate a change in direction.

In fully covering new technologies (in contrast to social insurance funds), VHI may have supported the development of the private diagnostic services and hospital market. While this has been beneficial in assuring faster access to new technologies, it may also have induced overuse of services and increased health care costs.

Table 14.1 *Development and regulation of the VHI market in Greece, 1970–2013*

Year	Legislation
General legislation	
1970	Legislative Decree 400/1970: Establishment and functioning of private insurance undertakings
2011	Ministerial Decision Y4a/oik.93320: NHS hospitals are allowed to conclude contracts with private insurance companies
Regulation of technical reserves of insurers	
2001	Ministerial Decisions K3-4382/7-6-2001 and K3-9124/30-11-2001
Regulation of the mediation process in private insurance contracts	
1985	Law 1569/1985
2006	Presidential Decree 190/2006
2007	Ministerial Decision K3-8010/8-8-2007
2011	Decision Number 2647/7-11/2011 of the Bank of Greece Board of Directors
Underwriting and duration of private insurance contracts	
1997	Law 2496/1997: Tax incentives for purchasing VHI are lowered
2013	Law 4110/2013: Tax incentives for purchasing VHI are abolished
Supervision of private insurance	
2004	Law 3229/2004
2010	Law 3867/2010: Supervision of insurers is transferred to the Bank of Greece
Adaptation of the Greek legal framework to EU Directives	
1985	Presidential Decree 118/1985 adopted Directives 73/239/EEC, 73/240/EEC, 76/580/EEC, 79/267/EEC
1996	Presidential Decree 252/1996 adopted Directives 88/357/EEC, 90/618/EEC, 90/619/EEC, 92/49/EEC, 92/96/EEC
2005	Presidential Decree 23/2005 adopts Directive 2002/83/EC
2009	Law 3769/2009: The principle of equal treatment between men and women in the access to and supply of goods and services is implemented

Source: Author.

VHI offers people an alternative to OOP payments and is thought to have helped improve transparency by formalizing informal payments and lowering waiting times (Economou, 2010). In recent years, it may also have allowed some costs to be shifted from social insurance funds to private health insurers, especially where people have double coverage. Social insurance funds contract private hospitals to provide their subscribers with faster access to elective surgery, but due to delays in payment from EOPYY and growing scrutiny of private hospital expenditure by EOPYY – leading to legal actions – private hospitals and their patients prefer to pay through VHI.

The effects of the 2011 change are hard to evaluate since there are no studies on the topic and the health sector is in a situation of continuous change due to the financial and economic crisis. On the one hand, it seems unlikely that patients with VHI would opt to be treated in public hospitals, given the problems the latter face because of austerity measures. On the other hand, recent cuts in hospital budgets may motivate hospital managers to attract VHI subscribers, for example, by offering better quality of accommodation if they pay through VHI. This may result in a two-tier system within the public delivery system.

There is much discussion in Greece about the optimal level and content of VHI regulation, and the cost–effectiveness of such policies. Data on the pros and cons of VHI are still being gathered and it is thus difficult to provide definitive policy conclusions. For example, there are no scientific studies to document whether VHI provides a stimulus for better quality or higher efficiency. The crisis and policy responses to the crisis – increased user charges and other OOP payments, cuts to public hospital budgets and high long-term unemployment leading to the loss of entitlement to social insurance fund coverage – have negatively affected access to health care and, at the same time, exacerbated the fact that only the better off can afford VHI. In these circumstances, mechanisms may be needed to ensure broader access to VHI coverage and to ensure VHI does not undermine the social character of the health system.

The future of VHI

VHI coverage remains relatively low in Greece due to economic, social and cultural factors – downward pressure on household incomes, high unemployment, full coverage provided by the social insurance system, people's preference to pay a doctor or hospital directly when the need arises – and factors concerning the VHI market itself, such as low organizational capacity, cream-skimming and the absence of insurance products meeting consumer requirements – for example, increased market concentration does not seem to have led to efficiency gains being passed on to consumers in the form of lower premiums (Siskou et al., 2009).

A significant determinant of future VHI development is the evolution of the publicly financed health system and the effects of the reforms introduced since 2010. Many of the measures implemented (for example, increased user charges) limit social insurance coverage and raise serious questions about the accessibility of publicly financed health services (Economou, 2012). These measures can be seen as a stimulus for the growth of VHI. However, austerity measures have reduced disposable incomes and the ability of citizens to take up VHI. VHI market growth may therefore depend on the willingness and capacity of private insurers to introduce plans that cover the needs of consumers at reasonable cost.

References

Economou C (2010). Greece: health system review. *Health Systems in Transition*, 12(7):1–180.

Economou C (2012). The performance of the Greek healthcare system and the economic adjustment programme: "economic crisis" versus "system-specific deficits" driven reform. *Social Theory*, 2:33–70.

Hellenic Association of Insurers (various years). *The Greek insurance market in figures*. Athens, Hellenic Association of Insurers.

ICAP (2003). *Results of a survey about life and health private insurance*. Athens, ICAP.

Siskou O et al. (2009). Private expenditure and the role of private health insurance in Greece: status quo and future trends. *European Journal of Health Economics*, 10(4):467–474.

WHO (2016). Global Health Expenditure Database (GHED) [online database]. Geneva, WHO (http://www.who.int/health-accounts/ghed/en/, accessed 5 April 2016).

15
Hungary

Szabolcs Szigeti, Ferenc Lindeisz and Péter Gaál

Health system context

The health financing mix

In 2014, public spending accounted for 66% of total spending on health, with OOP payments accounting for most of the remainder (WHO, 2016). A substantial share of private spending on health can be attributed to informal payments, a deeply rooted characteristic of the health system, although the magnitude of informal payments is unclear, with estimates ranging from 0.06 to 0.6% of GDP (Gaál et al., 2011). The VHI share of private spending on health increased from 0.6% in 2000 to 7.6% in 2014 (WHO, 2016). However, these data should be interpreted with caution, because National Health Accounts data for Hungary do not clearly distinguish between VHI and voluntary medical savings accounts (VMSAs) managed by voluntary mutual health funds (WHO, 2016). According to our own estimates, between 2007 and 2012, around 94–97% of VHI expenditure could be attributed to VMSAs (Hungarian Financial Supervisory Authority, 2014; MABISZ, 2014) – that is, VHI accounted for only around 0.2–0.5% of private health expenditure and around 0.1–0.2% of total spending on health.

Entitlement to publicly financed health care and gaps in coverage

Participation in the statutory scheme is compulsory for all citizens living in Hungary; opting out is not allowed. Entitlement of employees to benefits is based on having paid contributions, but regulations ensure that almost all non-paying social groups are entitled to health services (excluding cash benefits); necessary care cannot be denied to patients with unpaid contributions. As a result, population coverage is virtually universal (although the coverage status of approximately 4% of the population was unclear in 2009) (Gaál et al., 2011). The benefits package is comprehensive but not exhaustive. Both a positive and a negative list are in place. Coinsurance and copayments are required for medicines, medical aids and prostheses, balneotherapy, dental prostheses, treatment in sanatoria, long-term chronic care and some hotel services in hospitals. Copayments are also required for non-emergency specialist services obtained without a referral, visiting a provider other than the one referred to and when patients desire more services than those prescribed by their physician (Gaál et al., 2011).

Overview of the VHI market

Market origins, aims and role

VHI was virtually non-existent until 1993,[1] when the Act on Voluntary Mutual Health Funds created the legal framework for complementary VHI to operate on a non-profit-making basis, according to the model of the French mutual associations. Initially, the larger part of VHI premiums went to individual accounts and could be used by the account holder; only a smaller portion of the premium was a real health insurance premium, paid into a common fund or risk pool. Consequently, VHI was mainly a VMSA scheme. The risk-pooling element of the system was abolished in 2003 and since then the VHI system has worked as a pure VMSA, with no VHI element (Gaál et al., 2011). The stated aim of the abolition of risk pooling was to encourage people's own responsibility for financing their health care. The services offered by voluntary mutual insurance funds range from home care to medicines, medical aids and recreational activities. In 2013, 79% of expenditure on services was spent on reimbursing medicines and medical aids and 18% on supplementing services covered by the statutory health insurance system, managed by the National Health Insurance Fund Administration of Hungary (NHIFA) (Hungarian Financial Supervisory Authority, 2014).

Commercial VHI is very limited, but *supplementary* plans seem to be developing. The reason for VHI not having taken root may lie in the near universal coverage of the statutory scheme or the higher quality services that can be bought less expensively in return for informal payments, but this is a matter of debate (Gaál et al., 2011). In addition, while VMSAs have been encouraged by tax incentives since the mid-1990s, until 2012 there were no such incentives for VHI.

Types of plan available

Commercial VHI is very limited and mainly offers cash benefits in case of sickness. There have been recent attempts to extend the market by offering in-kind benefits in the form of above-standard hotel services (a *supplementary* role for VHI), but the outcome of these efforts has not yet been assessed.

Why do people buy VHI?

People buy supplementary VHI to have access to better amenities and faster access to care. The main motivation for joining the mutual funds (VMSAs) is to benefit from tax advantages to pay for user charges.

Who buys VHI?

No public information is available on the socioeconomic characteristics of those who purchase VHI or whether VHI take-up is more common for individuals or groups. Only a few employers use the tax exemption (available since 2012) to purchase VHI for their employees.

Who sells VHI?

In 2011, 11 of the 32 commercial insurers offered sickness insurance, but these were mainly income replacement cash-benefit policies for certain illnesses and not real VHI (MABISZ, 2014). In 2012, 33 958 sickness insurance contracts were sold, down from 55 204 in 2001. In the same year, only five companies offered real VHI, but it is not known how many policies they sold.

With regard to VMSAs, at the end of 2012, there were 31 voluntary mutual health funds in Hungary (Hungarian Financial Supervisory Authority, 2012), covering over 1 million residents in 2013 (close to 10% of the population) compared to only around 71 000 in 2000. The VMSA market is highly concentrated. The four largest funds (owned by large financial and private profit-making institutions) hold 62% of membership and 54% of total financial assets.

1 The exception was the voluntary supplementary employee insurance scheme of the Hungarian State Railway, which has operated since 1930 and whose members pay 0.5% of their salary.

Insurer relations with providers

Providers are paid on a FFS basis.

Public policy towards VHI

Since 1995, the government has subsidized participation in voluntary mutual health funds through tax incentives (currently equal to 20% of the premium amount up to HUF 150 000/€480 per year), which has had a significant impact on extending both the membership and revenue of these funds (Hungarian Financial Supervisory Authority, 2014). The tax incentive was lowered from 30 to 20% in 2011. Employers who pay contributions on behalf of their employees benefit from a tax exemption of up to 30% of the monthly minimum wage. Contributions paid by employers constitute the main revenue source of the voluntary mutual health funds (78% of their total revenue in 2012) (Hungarian Financial Supervisory Authority, 2014).

At the beginning of 2012, following negotiations with commercial insurers on how to channel more private resources to the health system (likely resulting from lobbying by commercial insurers), the government decided to exempt from tax all health insurance premiums (including for policies purchased from private insurers) paid by employers for their employees. Although this was meant to increase spending through VHI, data from the Hungarian Financial Supervisory Authority show that the revenues and expenditures of insurers were lower in 2012 than in 2010 (Hungarian Financial Supervisory Authority, 2014).

Debates and challenges

Starting in 2006, one of the highest priorities of the government was to introduce managed competition in the statutory scheme by replacing the single payer, the NHIFA, with a number of mandatory health insurers under partial private ownership. The stated aims of this measure were to reduce inequities in the use of health care services, to improve efficiency and to ensure financial sustainability and transparency. This was the third and the most elaborate attempt since the early 1990s to introduce a system of multiple, competing health insurers.

In December 2007, the National Assembly approved a bill introducing the new system, but the President sent it back to the National Assembly for reconsideration shortly after. In February 2008, the National Assembly decided to disregard presidential concerns and passed the bill in the face of widespread public protest. In March, the main opposition parties initiated a referendum on user charges for physician visits and hospital stays and on tuition fees in state-funded higher education. By an overwhelming majority (over 80%), voters approved a reversal of both measures. In the meantime, the opposition parties had signalled their intention to hold a referendum on the managed competition law in September. Expecting that this would have the same outcome as the referendum held in March, the National Assembly repealed the act in May.

Commercial insurers have repeatedly tried to extend the VHI market and hospitals also have shown an interest in expanding VHI. In 2014, one of the main public hospitals began to introduce options for patients to be treated privately in return for OOP payments, in an attempt to reduce waiting lists (WebORVOS, 2014). The prices charged for these private services are twice as high as reimbursement rates paid by the NHIFA, which could boost demand for VHI if middle-class people find waiting times and the financial uncertainties of informal payments in the public system increasingly unacceptable. Waiting times have become an issue since the introduction of volume caps for the quantity of services reimbursed by the NHIFA in 2007. These caps have also led to some spare capacity in public hospitals (Gaál et al., 2011).

The future of VHI

Over the past 20 years, despite sharp increases in GDP and OOP payments, VHI's share of total spending on health has remained negligible. Recent government attempts to increase spending through VHI by introducing tax exemptions for plans purchased by employers have not had a significant impact on the VHI market. A common assumption is that the weak development of the VHI market partly relates to the fact that patients use informal payments to obtain greater choice of physician and faster access to quality care by public providers – an option that may feel cheaper to households than purchasing VHI. As a result, VHI seems likely to continue to play a marginal role in health financing in Hungary, with higher take-up largely dependent on demand from richer households.

References

Gaál P et al. (2011). Hungary: health system review. *Health Systems in Transition*, 13(5):1–266.

Hungarian Financial Supervisory Authority (2012). *Annual Report*. Budapest, Hungarian Financial Supervisory Authority (http://alk.mnb.hu/en/left_menu/pszafen_publication/pszafen_reports, accessed 1 June 2014).

Hungarian Financial Supervisory Authority (2014). Time series on the insurance sector and on the mutual funds. Budapest, Hungarian Financial Supervisory Authority (http://felugyelet.mnb.hu/bal_menu/jelentesek_statisztikak/statisztikak/pszaf_idosorok/idosorok, accessed 1 June 2014).

MABISZ (2014). Hungarian insurers' yearbooks. Budapest, Magyar Biztosítók Szövetsége (MABISZ) [Association of Hungarian Insurers]. (http://www.mabisz.hu/en/market-reports.html, accessed 22 November 2015).

Weborvospro WebORVOS (2014). *Gyorsító sávot nyitott azUzsoki a fizető betegeknek [The Uzsoki hospital opened acceleration lane for patients who pay for services]* (http://www.weborvospro.hu/cikkek/lapszemle/gyorsito savotnyitottazuzsokiafizetobetegeknek.html, accessed 22 November 2015).

WHO (2016). Global Health Expenditure Database (GHED) [online database]. Geneva, WHO (http://www.who.int/health-accounts/ghed/en/, accessed 5 April 2016).

16
Iceland

Sigurbjörg Sigurgeirsdóttir

Health system context

The health financing mix

In 2014, public spending accounted for 81% of total spending on health, down from 84.0% in 1995 (WHO, 2016). Private spending comes almost entirely from OOP payments (17.5% of total spending on health). Financing from private health insurance is so small that it is not considered as a separate source of health care financing.

Entitlement to publicly financed health care and gaps in coverage

The publicly financed health system offers universal coverage linked to residence. By law, all residents should have access to the best health care available regardless of age, gender, race or ability to pay. Eligibility and coverage are regulated in the Health Insurance Act of 1957. Everyone who has been legally residing in Iceland for six months is automatically covered, regardless of nationality, unless intergovernmental treaties state otherwise. Public health coverage in the first six months of stay is regulated by international treaties. If no such agreements are in place, the individual must pay health care costs incurred during this period in full. However, exemptions can be issued by the Minister of Health in case of emergency on a case-by-case basis; in such cases, Icelandic Health Insurance (IHI) – which is publicly funded by the state budget – will pay for necessary care. People who have been insured, employed, or held residence in another Nordic country or other European Economic Area (EEA) member state prior to acquiring legal residency in Iceland can count the time spent in those countries towards the fulfilment of their six months' qualification period, as long as they supply proper documentation.

Children and adolescents under the age of 18 are covered by IHI as dependants of their parents. It is not possible to opt out of the publicly financed system. With the exception of inpatient care, all other IHI-covered health services are subject to user charges.

The six-month exclusion described earlier is the key coverage gap in the publicly financed system and is the main reason for purchasing VHI. Once the waiting period is over and IHI coverage applies, VHI cover is no longer needed.

Overview of the VHI market

Market origins, aims and role

VHI plays a *substitutive* role as a person's only source of coverage during the temporary six-month period of exclusion from the IHI. Although OOP expenditure is substantial, this has not caused complementary VHI for user charges to develop. The reason for this may be the small size of the VHI market and its low attractiveness to private insurers.

Types of plan available

Substitutive VHI plans reimburse the health care costs of goods and services covered by the IHI. Treatment of pre-existing conditions is typically not covered.

Why do people buy VHI?

People buy VHI to obtain health care cover in the first six months of residence in the country. For those individuals who plan to apply for residential permits in Iceland, buying VHI cover is an important requirement in that process.

Who buys VHI?

People purchase substitutive VHI plans in the first six months of their residence in Iceland (when they are temporarily excluded from statutory cover).

Who sells VHI?

There are four commercial insurers selling substitutive VHI plans. The Financial Supervisory Authority regulates all these companies.

Insurer relations with providers

There is no integration between insurers and providers. Insurers reimburse services based on FFS payment, with the fee being set by the providers or the IHI. Both private and public providers can treat the insured. Medical doctors can work both in private and public sectors but no private beds exist in public hospitals in Iceland.

Public policy towards VHI

No particular legislation applies to private health insurance.

Debates and challenges

VHI has not been subject to public debate or discussion.

References

WHO (2016). Global Health Expenditure Database (GHED) [online database]. Geneva, WHO (http://www.who.int/health-accounts/ghed/en/, accessed 5 April 2016).

17
Ireland

Brian Turner

Health system context

The health financing mix

In 2014, public spending accounted for 66.1% of total spending on health and mainly came from general tax revenues. OOP payments and VHI accounted for 17.7 and 14% of total spending on health, respectively, meaning Ireland currently has one of the three largest markets for VHI in Europe (WHO, 2016).

Entitlement to publicly financed health care and gaps in coverage

There are two categories of eligibility for publicly financed health care (Table 17.1):

- People in Category I (nearly 1.8 million people or 39% of the population in 2015) are entitled to free public hospital care, primary care and other community care and personal social services (HSE, 2015). They are in possession of a full medical card. Medical cards are means-tested, although the income threshold for a medical card is higher for those aged 70 and older.
- People in Category II are entitled to public hospital care with charges per night and for outpatient services. Patients are required to pay in full for GP services, where fees are unregulated and tend to be approximately €50 per visit (Bourke & Roper, 2012). However, there is some high-cost protection from the state for prescription medicines for outpatients in Category II. (Medicines prescribed to inpatients are covered under hospital costs.) For claimants

Table 17.1 *Entitlement to publicly financed health benefits in Ireland, 2015*

Service	Category I	Category II	
	Medical Card	GP Visit Card	No GP Visit Card
Population covered in 2011 (%)	37	3	60
GP	Free	Free	Full fee (exemptions apply, for example, for neonates up to six weeks old)
Prescription medicines	€2.50 per item up to a maximum of €25 per month per family	DPS: Full cost (monthly maximum €144 per family) LTI/HTD: Free for specific illnesses/medicines	
Acute hospital inpatient	Free public care	€75 per night (annual maximum €750)	
Acute hospital outpatient (A&E/emergency department)	Free public care	Free with referral from GP; €100 without referral	
Other services	Vary by service and entitlement category		

Source: http://www.citizensinformation.ie/en/.

Notes: Other services include services for older people, mental illness, disability, child protection and other community, personal and social care services, as well as dental, ophthalmic and aural services. DPS: Drugs Payment Scheme; LTI: Long-Term Illness Scheme; HTD: High Tech Drugs Scheme.

under the Drugs Payment Scheme (DPS; less than 16% of the population), the state covered less than 65% of the total cost of medicines over the period 2003–2007 (PCRS, 2007). Some people in Category II are eligible for a GP Visit Card (introduced in 2005), which entitles them to free GP visits but not the other benefits of a medical card. The income threshold for the GP Visit Card is higher than for the full medical card. At the end of 2014, almost 160 000 people held GP Visit Cards (HSE, 2015). In 2015, universal eligibility for GP Visit Cards was introduced for the under-6s and those aged 70 and older who do not qualify for a medical card, as the first step in the government's plan to make GP care free at the point of use for the entire population (although it has acknowledged that this will only be achieved in a second term of office).

Nearly 60% of the population lacks publicly financed coverage of primary care services and must pay user charges for publicly financed inpatient and outpatient care in public hospitals.

Overview of the VHI market

Market origins, aims and role

The VHI Act of 1957 aimed to provide substitutive cover for the top 15% of earners who, at that time, were not entitled to free access to care in public hospitals. However, those who already had access entitlements could also take it out, so it played a supplementary role for these people. Since then, access to public hospital care has been extended to the whole population and VHI no longer plays a *substitutive* role. It plays a mainly *supplementary* role, providing faster access to elective treatment in hospitals, and a smaller *complementary* role, covering ancillary services (for example, GP visits, physiotherapy).

Types of plan available

VHI is mainly in the form of hospital plans providing access to semi-private or private rooms in public and private hospitals (depending on the level of cover chosen). Most hospital plans provide limited cover for ancillary services, which must otherwise be paid for OOP by those without medical cards. In recent years, insurers have introduced hospital plans with significant ancillary cover and stand-alone ancillary plans.

Why do people buy VHI?

The market has seen significant growth since 1957 and in 2015 covers almost 46% of the population (HIA, 2015). Although this represents a decline from over 50% at the peak of the market in 2008, the level of VHI take-up is very high in comparison to other OECD countries (Colombo & Tapay, 2004). Survey data suggest that people who buy VHI do so to obtain a better level of health care service and to jump waiting lists for treatment (Figure 17.1).

Who buys VHI?

Table 17.2 shows how VHI take-up is concentrated in higher socioeconomic groups. More recent survey evidence shows that A, B and C1 consumers, who account for 41% of the population, account for 58% of VHI holders (HIA, 2014a). About 41% of the population has VHI and no medical card, 30% has a medical card but no VHI, 23% has neither VHI nor medical card and 6% has both (CSO, 2011). Take-up rates are highest

Figure 17.1 *Motivation for buying VHI in Ireland (% agreeing), 2003–2010*

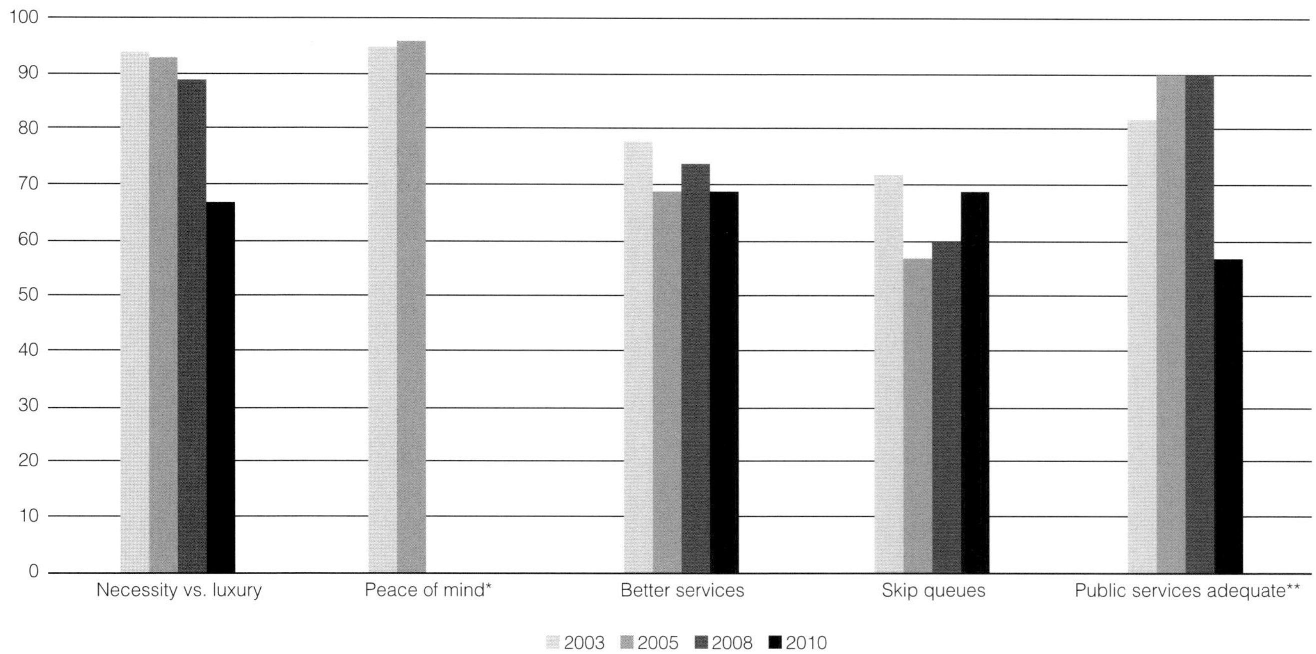

Source: HIA (2003, 2005, 2008, 2010).
Notes: *Not asked in 2008 and 2010; **Percentage disagreeing.

Table 17.2 *VHI take-up in Ireland by social class, 2003–2008*

Social class	2003 (%)	2005 (%)	2008 (%)
Upper middle and middle class (A)	70	85	89
Lower middle class (B)		75	65
Skilled working class (C1)	31	46	42
Other working class, casual workers and those dependent on welfare		18	18
Farming	39	55	49
Overall	47	52	49

Sources: HIA (2003, 2005, 2008).

in the 40–80 age groups (HIA, 2014b) and research suggests Vhi Healthcare has a larger proportion of older members than its competitors (HIA, 2014c).

Table 17.3 *Overview of VHI insurers in Ireland, 2015*

Insurer (year of market entry)	Market share (%)*	Regulated by	Profit orientation
Vhi Healthcare (1957)	53	HIA, Central Bank	Non-profit-making
Laya Healthcare (1997; BUPA Ireland until 2007, QUINN Healthcare from 2007–2012)	23	HIA, Central Bank**	For-profit (BUPA Ireland was non-profit-making)
Aviva Health (2004; VIVAS Health until 2008)	15	HIA, Central Bank	For-profit
GloHealth (2012)	5	HIA, Central Bank	For-profit
Restricted membership schemes	4	HIA	Non-profit-making

Sources: *HIA (2014c).
Note: **BUPA Ireland was regulated by the Financial Services Authority (the insurance regulator in the United Kingdom).

Who sells VHI?

Between 1957 and 1997, Vhi Healthcare was effectively the only voluntary health insurer in the Irish market (alongside a number of small schemes with restricted membership, for example, covering police officers). Following the introduction of the EU's Third Non-Life Insurance Directive in 1992, the VHI market was opened up to competition in 1994. In 2015, there are four insurers in the open part of the market (Table 17.3).

Survey data suggest rates of switching from one insurer to another have increased over time from 6% in 2003 to 10% in 2005 and 2007, 16% in 2010 and 23% in 2012, although this dipped to 20% in 2014 (HIA, 2003, 2005, 2008, 2010, 2012, 2014a). Cost savings were the main reason given for switching, while the main reason for not switching was satisfaction with the current insurer.

Insurer relations with providers

Private insurers are not integrated with providers. People with VHI can be treated in private hospitals and as private patients in private, semi-private or public beds in public hospitals. Hospital specialists are paid a salary for treating publicly financed patients and on a FFS basis for treating the privately insured. Public hospitals traditionally received payments from insurers for private patients using private beds (which accounted for 20% of beds in public hospitals). In recent years, the charges for these private beds have increased significantly, with a view to charging the full economic cost. More recently, in December 2011, the Minister for Health announced a decision to begin charging insurers for the use of public beds by private patients. Approximately half of the private patients treated in public hospitals are treated in public or non-designated beds (Comptroller and Auditor General, 2009), for which insurers are not charged. After being delayed on a number of occasions, charges for private patients in any beds in public hospitals came into effect from 1 January 2014.

Public policy towards VHI

Private insurers must operate on the principles of community rating, open enrolment and lifetime cover, with risk equalization in place to support community rating. Risk equalization has been highly contested (see Table 17.4), so an interim set of measures to try to equalize some of the costs of older consumers was in place from 2009 to 2012 and a full risk equalization

Table 17.4 *Development and regulation of the VHI market in Ireland, 1957–2015*

Year	Policy
1957	Health Insurance Act: VHI Board (now Vhi Healthcare) is established as a statutory body
1992	European Third Non-Life Insurance Directive: EU member states are required to open their non-life insurance markets to competition
1994	Health Insurance Act: three pillars of the Irish VHI market are enshrined into legislation (community rating, open enrolment, lifetime cover)
1995	Tax relief on VHI premiums is reduced from the marginal rate of tax to the standard rate (20%) to make it less regressive
1996	Minimum benefits are introduced; a risk equalization scheme is to operate between insurers
1999	Risk equalization scheme is revoked Publication of the White Paper on VHI; one of its commitments is to increase the private bed charge in public hospitals over a phased period to reflect the full economic cost
2001	Health Insurance (Amendment) Act: a new risk equalization scheme is to be developed; an independent statutory body, the HIA, is introduced to regulate VHI in Ireland; provisions are made for regulations governing the introduction of lifetime community rating (proposed in the White Paper)
2002	National Treatment Purchase Fund (NTPF) is established to allow public patients waiting longer than three months for public hospital treatment to be treated free of charge (at the state's expense) in a private hospital in Ireland or the United Kingdom
2003	Risk Equalization Scheme is introduced; the EC rules against a complaint from BUPA Ireland that the scheme constituted illegal state aid and the challenge is brought to the European Court of First Instance
2006	Minister for Health and Children decides to commence equalization payments in January; a stay on payments under the Risk Equalization Scheme is put in place subject to the outcome of the legal challenge; BUPA Ireland challenges the scheme in the Irish courts but its case is dismissed in November 2006
2007	BUPA Ireland withdraws from the market; its business is taken over by QUINN Healthcare
2008	BUPA Ireland's challenge to the EC decision is dismissed by the European Court of First Instance BUPA Ireland's challenge to the High Court decision on risk equalization is upheld in the Supreme Court Interim measures introduced for three years, while work is carried out on a new risk equalization scheme* VHI (Amendment) Act: Vhi Healthcare is to be regulated by the Financial Regulator from the end of 2008 (and to meet solvency requirements laid down in the EU regulation) but deadline is extended on a number of occasions**
2009	Health Insurance (Miscellaneous Provisions) Act: the HIA is granted greater powers of enforcement; definition of community rating in the 1994 Act is amended to reflect the issues highlighted in the Supreme Court judgement Automatic entitlement to a full medical card (available in 2001–2008) for those aged >70 removed (they are now subject to a means test)
2011	ECJ rules against Vhi Healthcare's exemption status (with regard to the solvency requirements)
2013	Risk equalization scheme commences
2014	Insurers are charged for the use of all beds in public hospitals
2015	Lifetime community rating introduced on 1 May. Insurers permitted to reduce premiums for young adults aged up to 26 Vhi Healthcare authorized by the Central Bank in July Universal eligibility for GP Visit Cards for under-6s and over-70s is rolled out

Source: Turner & Smith (in press).

Notes: *The interim measures comprise two elements: a community rating levy on health insurers for each person they insure and increased tax relief for older people with VHI, on a sliding scale. **The main reason for the delay was the fact that Vhi Healthcare will require a capital injection to bring its solvency reserves up to the level required for authorization by the Financial Regulator/Central Bank.

scheme commenced on 1 January 2013. VHI plans must also include a minimum level of benefits. VHI has always been subsidized through tax relief, although in 2013 the amount of premium subject to tax relief was capped at €1000 per adult and €500 per child aged under 18. The current rate is equal to 20% of the cost of the premium up to the cap.

Debates and challenges

Although VHI has, in the past, accounted for a moderate share of total spending on health (around 8% prior to the crisis), it commands a high profile in media and policy discussions and substantial leverage in the health system. Key issues include the status of Vhi Healthcare in relation to its competitors (recently resolved), an incentive structure that distorts public resources in favour of the privately insured and the role of VHI in facilitating two-tier access to health care.

Vhi Healthcare's competitors claimed that its exemption from the regulations of the Insurance Acts gave it unfair advantages because it was not required to hold a minimum level of reserves to guarantee solvency and did not need to establish subsidiaries to engage in other business activities. Changing the regulatory status of Vhi Healthcare to bring it in line with its competitors was initially proposed in 1999 (Department of Health and Children, 1999), and again in 2008, but has only recently been fully implemented. In 2011, the ECJ found the exemption to be unlawful.

Direct and indirect public subsidies for VHI and the incentive structures in place serve to distort resource allocation in favour of people with VHI. In addition to tax relief on VHI premiums, the government indirectly subsidizes VHI-financed health care by training the health professionals who treat VHI patients and by failing to charge insurers the full economic cost of using private and public beds in public hospitals, although as noted earlier, this is being addressed. In the past, the government has noted that public subsidies are justified "on the basis that those who opt for voluntary cover effectively forgo a statutory entitlement while continuing to contribute to the funding of the public health service through taxation" (Department of Health and Children, 1999:24). It has also been argued that VHI reduces demand for publicly financed care. However, the evidence does not support this claim. Public hospitals, specialist doctors and private insurers all face strong financial incentives to treat privately insured people in public hospitals. Consequently, a significant proportion of VHI-financed care takes place in public hospitals. Recent figures suggest that in a 12-month period 60% of adult inpatients with VHI were admitted to public hospitals (CSO, 2011).

Another source of criticism is the preferential treatment given to the privately insured. Some evidence suggests that waiting times are longer for those without VHI and there are concerns about private patients being treated by specialists, while public patients are treated by more junior doctors (Tussing & Wren, 2006; Wren, 2003). A common waiting list for public and private patients has been called for, but not implemented (O'Morain, 2007). In 2002, the NTPF was established to provide faster access to care to public patients, mainly by purchasing treatment in private hospitals or even abroad. The NTPF was subsumed into a Special Delivery Unit in 2011. The revised 2008 consultant contract contains measures to restrict the number of private patients treated within the public hospital system and requires specialists to work in teams to deliver specialist-provided (rather than specialist-led) services to patients (McDaid et al., 2009). However, breaches in the contract are not being penalized.

The future of VHI

As the market for VHI is possibly close to saturation and VHI premiums are likely to increase further in nominal and real terms, private insurers may diversify into other insurance and non-insurance offerings (for example, travel and dental insurance). The Programme for Government issued by the coalition government elected in 2011 (Department of the Taoiseach, 2011) outlined a plan to introduce, by 2016, a system of universal health insurance – mandatory coverage of the whole population provided by competing private insurers. Under these proposals, VHI will no longer be able to offer faster access to hospital care, but it will still be able to provide better amenities in hospital. A primary objective is to tackle unequal access to hospital care. There is considerable uncertainty around the development of universal health insurance. Initially, it was to be rolled out as the final element of the government's health reforms in 2016, but then the timescale was pushed back to 2019. When the current Minister for Health was appointed in 2014, he indicated that even this timescale might be ambitious. If universal health insurance is implemented, it is likely to have a significant impact on the role and regulation of VHI.

References

Bourke J, Roper S (2012). In with the new: the determinants of prescribing innovation by Irish general practitioners. *European Journal of Health Economics*, 13(4):393–407.

Colombo F, Tapay N (2004). *Private health insurance in OECD countries*. Paris, Organisation for Economic Co-operation and Development.

Comptroller and Auditor General (2009). *Accounts of the public services 2008: Comptroller and Auditor General annual report*. Dublin, Office of the Comptroller and Auditor General.

CSO (2011). *Health status and health service utilisation: quarterly national household survey: health*. Quarter 3 2011. Dublin, Central Statistics Office.

Department of Health and Children (1999). *White paper: private health insurance*. Dublin, Government Stationery Office.

Department of the Taoiseach (2011). *Programme for Government 2011–2016*. Dublin, Department of the Taoiseach (http://www.taoiseach.gov.ie/eng/Work_Of_The_Department/Programme_for_Government/Programme_for_Government_2011-2016.pdf, accessed 31 August 2011).

HIA (2003). *The private health insurance market in Ireland*. Report prepared by Amárach Consulting. Dublin, Health Insurance Authority (HIA).

HIA (2005). *The private health insurance market in Ireland: a market review*. Report prepared by Insight Statistical Consulting. Dublin, HIA.

HIA (2008). *The private health insurance market in Ireland: a market review*. Report prepared by Insight Statistical Consulting. Dublin, HIA.

HIA (2010). *The private health insurance market in Ireland*. Report prepared by Red C Research & Marketing Limited. Dublin, HIA.

HIA (2012). *Report on the health insurance market*. Report prepared by Millward Brown Lansdowne to the Health Insurance Authority. Dublin, HIA.

HIA (2014a). *Report on the health insurance market*. By Millward Brown Landsdowne to The Health Insurance Authority. Dublin, HIA.

HIA (2014b). *Newsletter*, May 2014 edition. Dublin, HIA (http://www.hia.ie/sites/default/files/HIA_May_Newsletter_2014_Final.pdf, accessed 22 November 2015).

HIA (2014c). *Market Statistics: Website Statistics 2014*. Dublin, HIA (http://www.hia.ie/publication/market-statistics, accessed 22 November 2015).

HIA (2015). *Newsletter*, June 2015 edition. Dublin, HIA (http://www.hia.ie/sites/default/files/HIA_June_Newsletter_2015.pdf, accessed 22 November 2015).

HSE (2015). *Annual report and financial statements 2014*. Naas, Health Service Executive.

McDaid D et al. (2009). Ireland: health system review. *Health Systems in Transition*, 11(4):1–268.

O'Morain P (2007). *The health of the nation: the Irish healthcare system 1957–2007*. Dublin, Gill & Macmillan Ltd.

PCRS (2007). *Finance shared services: primary care reimbursement service: statistical analysis of claims and payments 2007*. Dublin, Health Service Executive.

Turner B, Smith S (in press). Uncovering the complex role of private health insurance in Ireland. In: Thomson S, Mossialos E, eds. *Private health insurance and medical savings accounts: history, politics, performance*. Cambridge, Cambridge University Press.

Tussing D. Wren M-A (2006). *How Ireland cares: the case for health care reform*. Dublin, New Island.

WHO (2016). Global Health Expenditure Database (GHED) [online database]. Geneva, WHO (http://www.who.int/health-accounts/ghed/en/, accessed 5 April 2016).

Wren M-A (2003). *Unhealthy state: anatomy of a sick society*. Dublin, New Island.

18
Italy

Francesca Ferré

Health system context

The health financing mix

In 2014, public spending accounted for 75.6% of total spending on health, mainly from general tax revenues, while OOP payments and VHI accounted for 21.2 and 0.9%, respectively (WHO, 2016). These shares have been relatively stable in the last 15 years (Armeni & Ferré, 2012).

Entitlement to publicly financed health care and gaps in coverage

Coverage by the National Health Service (known as the *Servizio Sanitario Nazionale* (SSN)) is compulsory for all residents and opting out is not allowed. Patients are free to choose between public and private providers for many health care services, since it is possible for the public sector to outsource the delivery of health services to accredited private providers. Accredited private hospital beds account for 28% of the total number of beds, but there are great differences in the geographical distribution of private beds among Italy's 20 regions, with Lombardy and Lazio having a larger share of private beds (Ministry of Health, 2009). The minimum benefits package of services and goods guaranteed by the SSN involves user charges, especially for medicines and outpatient visits.

Overview of the VHI market

Market origins, aims and role

The role of VHI is mainly *supplementary*, covering faster access and enhancing consumer choice of provider. This is particularly the case for people wishing to use the services of specialists who engage in part-time private practice (inpatient and outpatient) within public hospitals (*intramoenia* services) (Cavazza & De Pietro, 2011). VHI also plays a *complementary* role covering: (1) SSN user charges, for example, for medicines, laboratory and diagnostic tests, specialist visits, hospital prostheses and rehabilitation; and (2) services excluded from the SSN, such as dental care, home care for older people (but not residential LTC), cosmetic treatment, thermal care and alternative medicine. VHI has generally been slow to develop, perhaps due to the lack of strong fiscal incentives to encourage VHI take-up among individuals and companies (see further on) and high insurance premiums, which makes VHI unaffordable, especially in the poorer southern areas of the country.

Types of plan available

VHI plans may provide full coverage of all health expenditure, regardless of the nature of provider (public, accredited private or non-accredited private providers). However, there are always limits with regard to excluded benefits (for example, the number of laboratory tests covered) and eligibility (for example, serious pre-existing and often expensive conditions, such as drug and alcohol addiction, AIDS and severe mental health problems are not covered). Most policies restrict access to people over 65–75 years old. Limits are also often applied to cancer patients if treatment does not start within the first two years after diagnosis.

Why do people buy VHI?

Survey data suggest that people buy individual supplementary cover to jump waiting lists for treatment (Thomson & Mossialos, 2009) and, in some cases, to obtain better quality of care through access to centres of excellence listed in the coverage plan (or to any other provider in return for a user charge of 5–25% of the cost known as *scoperto fuori rete*). The availability of, and waiting times for, public and accredited health services vary across regions and areas of care. For example, the average waiting time for some diagnostic tests (such as osseous computerized mineralography, mammography, and MRI, PET and CT scans) and specialist consultations (for example, urology, ophthalmology and cardiology consultations) is over 7.5 months (Fattore, Mariotti & Rebba, 2013). Also, people subscribe to VHI plans to obtain a daily allowance in case of post-surgery or other recovery needs; such schemes are particularly appealing to the self-employed. Moreover, it is becoming common for one-income families to buy VHI to insure against the risk of permanent invalidity due to illness. Finally, companies purchase VHI plans for their employees as employment perks.

Who buys VHI?

Estimates suggest that around 6 million people are covered by some form of VHI. This proportion appears to have remained constant over the last 3–4 years (Giannoni, 2009). In 2010, around 5.5% of the population had individual VHI cover (1.33 million families), which constitutes a 0.5 percentage point increase compared to 2008, while around 2.5 million people had group cover.

Individual VHI take-up is concentrated in higher socioeconomic groups (16.3% of the families in the highest income quintiles versus 1.4% in the lowest quintiles) and among middle-aged groups compared to younger and older age groups. There is a geographical variation in the diffusion of VHI: families in the north and centre are more inclined to buy VHI (7.6% and 7.2%, respectively) compared to those living in the south (1.3%). Education is another determinant of VHI take-up, with people with higher education being more likely to be insured (Bank of Italy, 2012). The diffusion of group VHI increased slightly between 2008 and 2010.[1] The individual VHI market is still dominated by self-employed subscribers (Figure 18.1).

Figure 18.1 *Individual VHI take-up in Italy by employment type, 2008 and 2010*

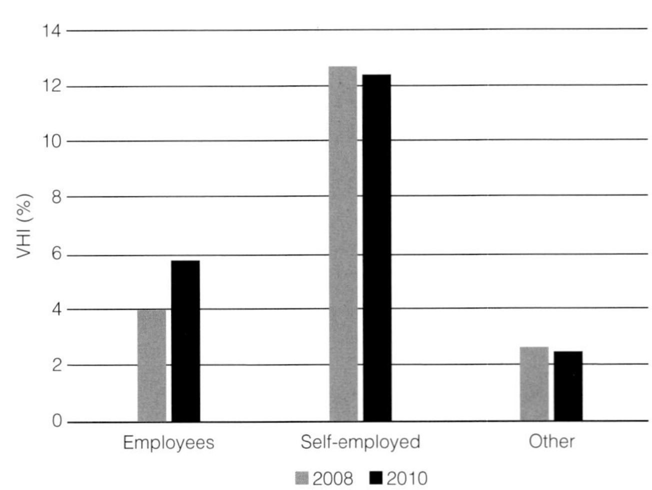

Sources: Bank of Italy (2012); ANIA (2012).

Note: No information for group VHI is available.

1 It is noteworthy that while the number of employees decreased by 257 000 between 2008 and 2010, the number of group VHI plans increased by 148 000 in the same period. On the other hand, the number of the self-employed increased by 93 000 between 2008 and 2010 but the number of VHI policyholders among the self-employed remained stable (at 487 000 individuals).

Who sells VHI?

VHI plans are sold by for-profit and non-profit-making insurers (see Table 18.1). There is no information on the number of policies sold by each type of VHI provider but non-profit-making insurers cover the majority of the insured.

Insurer relations with providers

Private insurers are not vertically integrated with health care providers. People with VHI can usually seek treatment in public hospitals, accredited private hospitals and non-accredited private hospitals. Some commercial insurers allow their clients to choose only among selected providers. Commercial insurers also tend to encourage people to use public services to reduce their costs – many policies offer no-claim bonuses when public facilities are used (since they can be used free of charge for patients and insurers) and daily cash benefits for inpatient stays in public hospitals (Giannoni, 2009).

Hospital specialists are paid a salary for treating publicly financed patients and typically on a FFS basis for treating privately insured patients. Benefits are provided in kind if the insurer has a contract with the provider. If not, the patient pays and is later reimbursed by the insurer.

Public policy towards VHI

The development and regulation of the VHI market in Italy are summarized in Table 18.2. VHI was introduced and promoted to manage the growth of private spending on health, without undermining the solidarity and universality of the SSN. VHI is subsidized through tax incentives; 19% of medical expenses can be deducted from an individual's taxable income, even if part or all of these expenses were covered by VHI (there is a deductible of €129). In addition, premiums for non-supplementary VHI (*doc* plans that mainly focus on complementary cover) may be deducted from taxable income. Since 2003, tax-deductible income has been capped at €3615 per year. Employer-paid VHI premiums are taxed at a reduced social contribution rate, requiring the employer to pay 10% of salary to the Italian Social Security Institute instead of ordinary social security contributions.

The Private Insurance Supervisory Authority (*Istituto per la vigilanza sulle assicurazioni private*) is the primary body, along with the Ministry of Health, responsible for regulating and monitoring the VHI market. Commercial insurers are also regulated by the Code for Private Insurance of 2005.

Private health insurers enjoy significant control over their activities, including total discretion in the selection of providers and in the design of benefits packages (Cavazza & De Pietro, 2011). The only constraints they face are the requirements to offer open enrolment and to allocate at least 20% of premium revenue to dental and social care (LTC) for people who need assistance with activities of daily living to benefit from tax incentives.

Table 18.1 *Types of VHI providers in Italy, 2010*

Type of VHI provider (profit status)	Types of plans	Details	Number of providers
Fondi aziendali (non-profit-making)	Group	Employer-specific insurance funds provided by companies such as FIAT (FASIV) and ENEL/ENI (FISDE); can be managed internally by the companies themselves or by commercial insurers on their behalf; people over 75 years old are usually not eligible for such schemes, but the plans may cover retired people provided that they had been enrolled for a certain amount of time before retiring; the biggest funds use group rating; others usually use community rating	n/a
Fondi di categoria (non-profit-making)	Group	Insurance funds managed by organizations of various categories of professional workers, for example, public employees; they cover retired people provided that they had been enrolled for a certain amount of time before retiring; the biggest funds use group rating; others usually use community rating	n/a
Società di mutuo soccorso (non-profit-making)	Group and individual	Insurance funds organized in the form of mutual aid societies; they are open to the whole population; age limits for enrolment may be fixed at around 65–75 years old; retired people remain covered and pay lower premiums; the biggest funds use group rating; others usually use community rating	3
Commercial insurers (for-profit)	Group and individual	Non-life health insurers; the largest eight account for 50% of the commercial health insurance market (ANIA, 2012); individual risk-rating is applied in setting premiums	65

Sources: Author; ISTAT (2012) for the number of providers.

Note: n/a = not available.

Table 18.2 *Development and regulation of the VHI market in Italy, 1886–2012*

Year	Policy
1886	Mutual aid societies (*Società di mutuo soccorso*) open on a voluntary basis to artisans and workers
1978	The SSN is established
1992	The VHI market is formally opened, with VHI intended to play a *substitutive* role (there was no commercial VHI before 1992)
1993	Quick shift towards Integrated Health Funds (IHFs) takes place, providing complementary and supplementary VHI
1999	The SSN minimum benefits package is defined and health services provided by IHFs are identified; services available through IHFs can be provided by public and accredited private hospitals only; selection of patients is still not allowed (open enrolment)
2000	Regulation and tax treatment of individual and group VHI premiums is revised; tax relief is assured for contributions to IHFs and other insurers
2005	The new Code for Private Insurance is adopted
2008	A Ministry of Health Decree states that IHFs will have to cover LTC and dental services not fully covered by the SSN to qualify for fiscal benefits The National Financial Law for 2008 requires that IHFs are solvent, adequately capitalized and offer competitive premiums (they should be lower than commercial premiums)
2009	A government *Green Paper on Welfare for people who are not self-sufficient* discusses the idea that IHFs should cover LTC; a *White Paper on Welfare* clearly supports the development of IHFs
2010	New legislation requires all IHFs to be listed in the national register of IHFs and to allocate at least 20% of total premium revenue (that is, from the whole IHF market) to dental care and social care (mainly LTC) for people requiring assistance with daily living to gain fiscal benefits
2011	The government publishes a report on the state of the welfare programme proposed in the 2009 Green Paper, supporting the need for IHFs to take part in collective contracting at national and company levels
2012	The government supports the development of IHFs as a strong second pillar of the health system to secure the financial sustainability of the SSN and to promote integration between health and social care

Sources: Adapted from Giannoni (2001); Cavazza & De Pietro (2011).

Debates and challenges

Although VHI accounts for a very small share of total health spending, it has recently attracted high interest in the media and policy discussions. The government has called for further development of the IHFs as a strong second pillar of the health system to secure the SSN's financial sustainability and to promote integration between health and social care – a position influenced by the financial and economic crisis. In addition, because access to dental and LTC is not uniform across the country, the role, organization and regulation of IHFs and VHI in general have found their way into the spotlight (ISTAT, 2012).

Since 2009, the central government has explicitly favoured the development of the IHFs (see Table 18.2). However, this has been criticized on a number of grounds. First, there is evidence that most types of VHI significantly increase income-related horizontal inequity in access to specialist services and VHI could exacerbate the economic and social disparities between the north and the south of the country, especially since devolution of power and fiscal federalism is still on the government's agenda. This may lead to increased variability in the public–private mix across regions and greater differences in VHI take-up, with VHI coverage increasing in the northern regions (Giannoni, 2009). There is a risk that, without taking into account existing inequities across regions, increasing VHI coverage could further weaken the capacity of the SSN to guarantee uniform access to services across the country (Giannoni & Masseria, 2007; Rebba, 2010), with patients with VHI being given preferential treatment. Some evidence already suggests that waiting times are longer for those without VHI cover. Second, there are also concerns about the gradual decrease in public investment in health, which may further affect access to care to patients without VHI. Third, the low level of regulation and monitoring of all types of private health insurers means there is considerable variation in the scope and depth of VHI coverage and in the level of premiums paid.

Regions and public health care organizations also favour an increased role for supplementary and complementary VHI since it constitutes an additional source of financing, helps assure more uniform coverage for patients seeking care, provides additional services and can allow a more efficient management of patients, as activities can be shifted to private providers.

The future of VHI

Although the government has tried to promote the development of the IHFs, the VHI market has not significantly grown over time. Unless the government continues to promote an increased role for VHI, it seems unlikely that VHI take-up will increase significantly.

References

ANIA (2012). *L'assicurazione italiana 2011–2012 [The Italian insurance 2011–2012]*. Rome, Associazione Nazionale fra le Imprese Assicuratrici [Italian National Association of Insurers] (http://www.ania.it/export/sites/default/it/pubblicazioni/rapporti-annuali/Assicurazione-italiana-Appendice-statistica/Assicurazione-Italiana-2011-2012.pdf, accessed 22 November 2015).

Armeni P, Ferré F (2012). La spesa sanitaria: composizione ed evoluzione [Health expenditure: composition and evolution]. In: Cantù E, ed. *Rapporto OASI 2012. L'aziendalizzazione della sanità in Italia [OASI Report 2012: The managerialism of health in Italy]*. Milan, EGEA:109–166.

Bank of Italy (2012). *I bilanci delle famiglie italiane nell'anno 2010 [The financial statements of Italian families]*. Rome, Bank of Italy (https://www.bancaditalia.it/pubblicazioni/indagine-famiglie/bil-fam2010/suppl_06_12new.pdf accessed 22 November 2015).

Cavazza M, De Pietro C (2011). *Sviluppo e prospettive dei fondi integrativi del Servizio Sanitario Nazionale [Development and prospects of the matching funds of the National Health Service]*. In: Cantù E, ed. *Rapporto OASI 2011. L'aziendalizzazione della sanità in Italia [OASI Report 2011: The managerialism of health in Italy]*. Milan, EGEA:173–200.

Fattore G, Mariotti G, Rebba V (2013). Italy. In: Siciliani L, Borowitz M, Moran V, eds. *Waiting time policies in the health sector. What works?* OECD Health Policy Studies. Paris, Organisation for Economic Co-operation and Development.

Giannoni M (2001). Fondi sanitari integrativi: situazione attuale e prospettive [Supplementary health funds: current situation and prospects]. *Tendenze Nuove*, 1.

Giannoni M (2009). Italy. In: Thomson S, Mossialos E, eds. *Private health insurance in the European Union*. Final report prepared for the European Commission, Directorate General for Employment, Social Affairs and Equal Opportunities. London and Brussels, LSE Health and Social Care, London School of Economics and Political Science and European Commission:226–255.

Giannoni M, Masseria C (2007). Assicurazioni sanitarie volontarie in Italia: problemi di accesso e prime stime di indicatori di equità orizzontale [Voluntary health insurance in Italy: problems of access and first estimates of indicators of horizontal equity]. In: *Forme di copertura dei costi delle prestazioni complementari a quelle erogate dal SSN in un contesto di federalismo [Coverage forms of costs for additional health benefitsnot provided by the NHS in a context of federalism]*. Report for the Italian Ministry of Health (Direzione Generale della Ricerca sanitaria e della Vigilanza sugli Enti).

ISTAT (2012). *Italia in cifre [Italy in figures]*. Rome, Istituto Nazionale di Statistica (http://www.istat.it/it/files/2011/06/Italia-in-cifre-03-ago-2012-Italia-in-cifre-edizione-2012.pdf, accessed 2 December 2015).

Ministry of Health (2009). *Attività gestionali ed economiche delle ASL e Aziende Ospedalieri. Annuario Statistico del Servizio Sanitario Nazionale 2009 [Management and economic activities of the local health authority and hospital enterprises. Statistical yearbook of the National Health Service 2009]*. Rome, Ministry of Health (http://www.salute.gov.it/portale/documentazione/p6_2_2_1.jsp?lingua=italiano&id=1677, accessed 2 December 2015).

Rebba V (2010). Le assicurazioni integrative [Supplementary insurance]. In: Gori C, ed. *Il sistema di protezione e cura delle persone non autosufficienti. Prospettive, risorse e gradualità degli interventi [The system of protection and care of dependent persons. Perspectives, resources and interventions]*. Project promoted by the Ministry of Labour and Social Policy and IRS. Rome and Milan, Ministry of Labour and Social Policy and IRS.

Thomson S, Mossialos E (2009). *Private health insurance in the European Union*. Final report prepared for the European Commission, Directorate General for Employment, Social Affairs and Equal Opportunities. London and Brussels, LSE Health and Social Care, London School of Economics and Political Science and European Commission.

WHO (2016). Global Health Expenditure Database (GHED) [online database]. Geneva, WHO (http://www.who.int/health-accounts/ghed/en/, accessed 5 April 2016).

19
Latvia

Girts Brigis

Health system context

The health financing mix

In 2014, public spending accounted for 63.2% of total spending on health, with OOP payments and VHI accounting for 35.1 and 1.6%, respectively (WHO, 2016). In 2014, public spending on health accounted for only 3.7% of GDP, one of the lowest levels among EU countries (WHO, 2016). The private share of total spending on health has increased since the onset of the financial and economic crisis.

Entitlement to publicly financed health care and gaps in coverage

The NHS[1] is a state-run organization under the Ministry of Health that contracts with private and public health care providers (Tragakes et al., 2008). By law (Law on Medical Treatment of 2006, paras. 16 and 17), the NHS covers the whole population (Latvian citizens and non-citizens, EU and EEA nationals residing in Latvia and non-EU and non-EEA nationals with permanent residence in Latvia) (Mitenbergs et al., 2012). Although the publicly financed benefits package is broad, patients are exposed to substantial user charges and other OOP payments.

Overview of the VHI market

Market origins, aims and role

The VHI market emerged as part of the general private insurance market after independence was established in

1 Previously known as the State Compulsory Health Insurance Agency.

1991 and was politically supported as an expression of a free market economy. In the first decade of its existence, the VHI market was negligible and VHI mainly played a *supplementary* role, providing access to better amenities during hospital stays. Over time, direct OOP payments started to rise, user charges were introduced and waiting times for NHS services increased. In this context, in spite of insurers' complaints about the low profitability of the VHI business,[1] the VHI market has grown, playing both supplementary and *complementary* roles (covering user charges and services excluded from NHS cover).

Types of plan available

All insurers offer a wide variety of VHI plans. Terms are often negotiated, usually by employers for their employees, since most VHI is sold on a group basis. VHI can offer cover of user charges, a fixed sum for any inpatient and outpatient service, non-NHS services and faster access to services in the private and public sectors. The existence of a wide range of plans causes confusion among service providers about what is covered and what is not. VHI plans are usually sold as independent products (not linked to other insurance products).

Why do people buy VHI?

The main factor stimulating demand for VHI is limited access to publicly financed health services due to the low level of public financing. People purchase VHI to gain faster access to care (NHS waiting times are currently very long), to cover user charges or to obtain access to non-NHS services. The main factor limiting market growth is the wealth of the population and its capacity to purchase VHI.

Who buys VHI?

According to the European Health Interview Study, 23% of the female and 24.2% of the male adult population in Latvia reported having some kind of VHI policy in 2008 (Central Statistical Bureau, 2010). Most of those with VHI cover were economically active people of working age with higher education and were covered by their employers. Only 19.2% of those with VHI cover paid for it out of their own pocket (that is, they were covered by a collective plan but this cover was not paid for by the employer).

1 According to the author's own calculations based on Financial and Capital Market Commission data (2012), on average claims in the VHI sector (health, excluding accidents) accounted for 95.4% of revenue in 2011. This ratio has increased since 2008, most likely due to the economic crisis. However, it is important to note that reporting requirements for life and non-life insurance companies differ and it is therefore difficult to make separate estimations for VHI business.

Demand for VHI has fallen dramatically since 2008 because of the economic crisis. For example, due to consolidation of the state budget, governmental and municipal institutions and organizations were forbidden to purchase VHI for their employees for several years.

Who sells VHI?

VHI is sold exclusively by commercial, mainly international, insurers. None of them is specialized in VHI; all offer a range of life or non-life insurance products. According to the Latvian Financial and Capital Market Commission, there were 6 insurers in 2015 (Financial and Capital Market Commission, 2015), but the Association of Insurers of Latvia gives a higher number (15). The explanation for this difference may be that some companies are actually not active. Market concentration is high, with the three largest companies covering 65% of the market.

In 2010, only one insurer offered individual VHI plans. These were mainly low-cost plans covering user charges. In 2010, the owner of this company – the municipality of Riga city – decided to close it as it was practically bankrupt. Since then, several insurers have started to offer individual VHI policies, but this type of cover is not popular because plans are very limited, premiums are high and few individuals can afford to purchase them, especially in the current economic environment.

Insurer relations with providers

The relationship between insurers and service providers (including the quality of provided services) is regulated by individual contracts. There is no vertical integration between insurers and providers as insurers are not specialized and providers cannot fulfil the capital requirements necessary for vertical integration. Selective contracting is permitted, but not practised widely. In theory, insurers can influence the costs of services, but such negotiations are complicated in practice.

Before the economic crisis, service providers were usually reimbursed by insurers, without the involvement of patients. As the economic situation worsened and providers started experiencing problems with non-payment and delayed payments, they have started to charge patients the full price and insurers now reimburse patients rather than providers.

Prices of services are negotiated between insurers and providers. Services covered by the NHS have relatively low prices (NHS contracts often dictate prices below cost), but services purchased on an OOP basis, especially those reimbursed by VHI, are usually very expensive. This may, to some extent, be influenced by tax evasion, which increases ability to pay and motivates providers to charge higher prices. All providers can work in the public and private sectors at the same time.

Public policy towards VHI

As the availability of public funding for the health system has traditionally been limited, public policy towards VHI has always been highly supportive, with VHI seen as an additional source of funding. Despite some negative effects VHI may have in terms of access to care (see following section), there is no VHI-specific regulation. The only institution that supervises the VHI market is the Financial and Capital Market Commission, which supervises all financial institutions in the country.

Debates and challenges

Several characteristics of the health system influence the relationship between the public and private sectors, in both financing and service provision. NHS prices are determined more by the size of the health budget than by actual costs; because the prices paid by privately financed patients are higher, providers have an incentive to prioritize privately financed patients and an increasing number of specialists refuse to sign contracts with the NHS. Since most VHI policyholders are covered by group policies purchased by their employer, they are more likely to be young (working age) and healthy, but – as *preferred* patients – they may benefit from better access than those who have greater need for treatment.

Although many specialists and hospitals would be ready to increase the volume of NHS-financed services provided, current budgetary restrictions do not allow it. As the economy returns to growth, demand for VHI may increase – for example, restrictions on government purchasing of VHI for employees have been lifted.

Since 2010, there has been debate about the government's plans to change the basis for entitlement to NHS benefits from residence to payment of a new earmarked payroll tax (Mitenbergs, Brigis & Quentin, 2014). The reason for this is to exclude from NHS coverage those who avoid or do not pay tax, including the substantial numbers of Latvians living abroad (Ministry of Health, 2012). The Bank of Latvia and other institutions have proposed that this new mandatory insurance scheme be administered by competing private insurers, similar to the changes introduced in the Netherlands in 2006. However, current plans leave the administration of the new scheme to the NHS.

Private insurers feel that one of the main shortcomings of the current system is the unclear definition of NHS benefits. The key document describing the organization and financing of the NHS, the Regulations of the Cabinet of Ministers No. 1046 (Ministry of Health, 2012), essentially defines a negative list of services that usually changes several times a year. Insurers would prefer a stable, positive list of services to better plan their products. They also call for an improvement in information exchange with the NHS to avoid double payment (by VHI and the NHS) for the same services.

The future of VHI

Although the economic situation is improving, public spending on health is expected to grow slowly and stay below the optimal level for a considerable period. This would bode well for the VHI market if households could afford to pay for VHI.

References

Central Statistical Bureau (2010). *Iedzīvotāju veselības apsekojuma rezultāti Latvijā [Health survey results in Latvia]*. Riga, Central Statistical Bureau.

Financial and Capital Market Commission (2015) [website]. Licenses Issued to Insurance Companies. (http://www.fktk.lv/en/market/insurance/licences-issued-to-insurance-c.html, accessed 22 November 2015).

Ministry of Health (2012). *Veselības obligātās apdrošināšanas koncepcijas projekts [Project of mandatory health insurance concept]*. Riga, Ministry of Health (http://www.lvportals.lv/wwwraksti/LVPORTALS/KONC_VES_APDROS_GALA_2012.PDF, accessed 2 December 2015).

Mitenbergs U et al. (2012). Latvia: health system review. *Health Systems in Transition*, 14(8):1–191.

Mitenbergs U, Brigis G, Quentin W (2014). Healthcare financing reform in Latvia: switching from social health insurance to NHS and back? *Health Policy*, 118(2): 147-152.

Tragakes E et al. (2008). Latvia: health system review. *Health Systems in Transition*, 10(2):1–253.

WHO (2016). Global Health Expenditure Database (GHED) [online database]. Geneva, WHO (http://www.who.int/health-accounts/ghed/en/, accessed 5 April 2016).

20
Lithuania

Gintaras Kacevicius

Health system context

The health financing mix

In 2014, public spending accounted for 67.9% of total spending on health, with OOP payments and VHI accounting for 31.3 and <1%, respectively (WHO, 2016).

Entitlement to publicly financed health care and gaps in coverage

All permanent residents, including foreign citizens, and temporary residents legally working in the country are entitled to publicly financed health coverage. All economically active persons (42% of the population) pay contributions and the government pays contributions on behalf of 19 categories of economically inactive people (58%). In 2011, 91% of those entitled to publicly financed coverage were actually covered. The remaining 9% of the population (for example, people who did not declare that they had left the country, those in the shadow economy, homeless people) had access to free emergency care only.

The publicly financed benefits package is broad and services are usually free of charge. The key exceptions are medicines (up to 50% coinsurance), rehabilitation for chronic diseases (50% coinsurance) and health services if treatments above the normal standard are chosen (patients pay the difference in price). Most private providers are contracted by the NHIF and usually charge additional fees than public providers. Both public and private providers also provide services excluded from publicly financed coverage; these are usually paid for by patients on an OOP basis. Due to scope and depth of publicly financed health coverage, there has not been much scope for the development of VHI.

Overview of the VHI market

Market origins, aims and role

After independence in 1990, the National Health Concept adopted by parliament in 1991 established the framework for the future development of the health system. It foresaw the development of compulsory health insurance and VHI, given the scarcity of public resources, and both types of cover were established in 1996 through the Health Insurance Law (No. I-1343). Today, VHI mainly plays a *supplementary* role, providing faster access to services that are provided mostly by private providers. It also plays a minor *complementary* role, covering some services excluded from statutory coverage.

Types of plan available

VHI plans provide access to services provided mainly by private providers but also by public providers (GP consultations, specialist outpatient care, rehabilitation, dental care, medicines, glasses, diagnostics, prevention, inpatient care).

Why do people buy VHI?

The VHI market has not developed much since 1996 and in 2009 covered under 1% of the population (Murauskiene et al., 2013). According to survey data (Buivydas et al., 2010), the main reasons why people buy VHI are: (1) for an additional financial guarantee for cover in case of a serious disease; and (2) higher quality and faster access to services.

Who buys VHI?

VHI plans are mainly purchased on a group basis by multinational or large national companies (for example, banks, foreign-owned companies) for their employees as an employment perk (supported by tax policy, see further on). Therefore, VHI covers mainly middle- to high-income people living in major cities. There are very few individual purchasers of VHI.

Who sells VHI?

In 2011, there were seven insurers in the market (Table 20.1). All of them were commercial companies. Until the end of 2011, they were supervised by the Insurance Supervision Commission (ISC). Since 2012, when the ISC was abolished, this function has been performed by the Central Bank of Lithuania. Market concentration is relatively high, with two insurers accounting for almost 60% of the market.

Table 20.1 *Market shares of VHI companies (%), at the end of 2011*

Companies	Market shares (%)
SEB Gyvybės draudimas	31
ERGO Life Insurance SE	27
Compensa Life Vienna Insurance Group SE	13
If P&C Insurance	11
PZU	9
BTA Baltic Insurance Company JSC	6
Gjensidige Baltic	4

Source: ISC (2011).

Note: Market shares add up to 101% due to rounding.

Insurer relations with providers

Private insurers are not integrated with providers. People with VHI can be treated by private providers or as private patients in public hospitals. Both private and public providers are paid on a FFS basis for treating privately insured patients. Reimbursement of cases incurring extraordinarily expensive treatment has to be agreed with insurers in advance.

Public policy towards VHI

From the beginning of its existence VHI has been seen as an additional source of health care financing. The idea of VHI expansion has also been strongly supported by private providers as a means of entering and expanding their share of the health care market. For example, private providers expect VHI to provide them with extra revenue. For private providers contracted by the NHIF, VHI is expected to cover (fully or partially) the OOP payments paid by patients. For non-contracted private providers, VHI may increase the financial accessibility of their services to consumers with limited purchasing power. From the perspective of the population, the development of VHI promises better access to (and probably also better quality of) specialized care.

For these reasons, since 1996 almost all governments have included the development of the VHI market in their political programmes. Since 2007, VHI has been subsidized through tax relief. The government in power between 2006 and 2008 expounded a concept based on the idea of family MSAs instead of VHI. The coalition government that followed (in office from 2008 to 2012) ordered a comprehensive feasibility study on the VHI market in 2010. The study identified conditions likely to promote the development of the market, including: low administrative costs (capping administrative costs at 4–7%); making the purchase of VHI compulsory for a substantial part (up to 50%) of the population; financial support from the government (tax relief); low premiums; low barriers to market entry for insurers; and the availability of both group and individual policies. The study proposed the combination of two alternative models: commercial insurance and MSAs (Buivydas et al., 2010).

Debates and challenges

Due to its very low population coverage, the impact of VHI on health system performance is limited. However, VHI receives substantial attention among health professionals in policy discussions as well as in the media. The main advocates of VHI are health professionals working in the private sector and those working both in the public sector and in private practice. Non-contracted private providers actively seek to contract with private insurers to increase their revenues, citing positive benefits such as greater choice for patients and competition among providers. Greater VHI take-up would probably increase the availability of privately provided services.

Political support for VHI is influenced by support from health care providers and is also based on a set of beliefs regarding the advantages of VHI (Figure 20.1). However, analysis of European VHI experiences, conducted as part of the 2010 feasibility study, revealed that the majority of expectations regarding the benefits of supplementary VHI are only partially met or not met at all; for example, there is only partial evidence that supplementary VHI will increase accessibility and decrease waiting times (Buivydas et al., 2010:20).

The study also surveyed public opinion regarding VHI (Figure 20.1). The survey showed that while health professionals are optimistic about the potential benefits of VHI development, the general public is less positive. VHI development was supported by 25% of respondents and by 50% of respondents on condition that it would not affect those with no VHI coverage. The majority of

Figure 20.1 *Potential benefits of VHI cover in Lithuania, 2010*

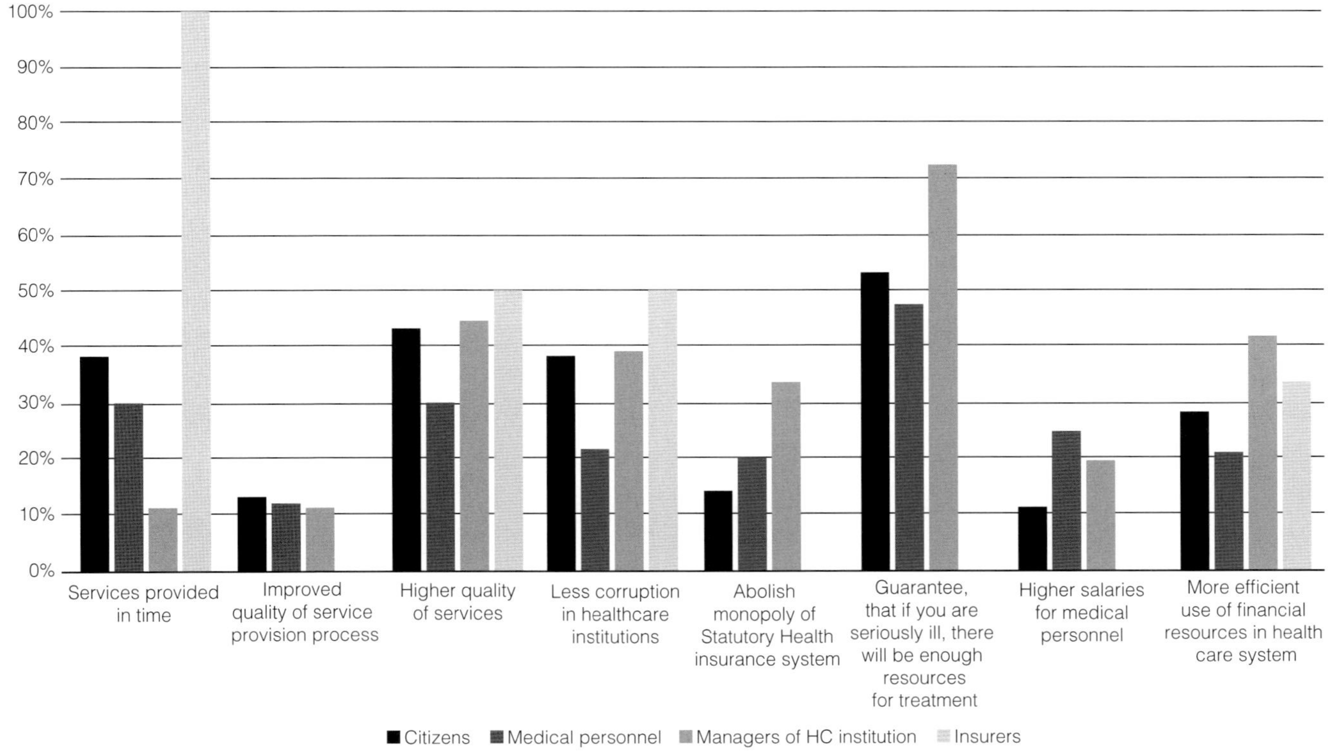

Source: Health Economics Centre (2011).

respondents (59%) agreed that VHI should cover a large share of the population.

However, an equal share of respondents (59%) would refuse to pay more for health care than they pay presently and would expect VHI premiums to be paid by employers or the government. This position can be explained by the fact that since 2009 contributions for publicly financed health coverage, which previously had been collected as part of income tax, have instead been collected as a separate earmarked tax – this has made some people more aware of the costs of health care. More importantly, the survey took place during a period of deep economic decline and the general attitude towards any additional payments (for example, VHI premiums and user charges) was understandably negative. Mainly due to negative public opinion, the government has stopped further initiatives to develop the VHI market.

Overall, the limited development of VHI can be attributed to the low purchasing power of the population, the wide range of services that are publicly financed and the absence of significant user charges. People prefer to pay OOP payments directly to health care providers when the need arises rather than pay VHI premiums on a regular basis. In terms of VHI supply, insurers do not spend a high proportion of premium income on claims (69% in 2011), administrative costs are correspondingly high and reimbursement is often substantially lower than the premiums paid.

The future of VHI

A number of health system developments may support the development of the VHI market in the future. First, fiscal consolidation aimed at meeting the Maastricht Treaty criteria means public spending on health has been frozen at below the pre-crisis level. This makes VHI an obvious option for generating additional health system revenue. Second, pressure to define the publicly financed benefits package more explicitly and to strengthen the NHIF's regulatory powers led to amendments being put to the parliamentary health committee. However, the amendments were not adopted and are no longer on the political agenda. A more recent proposal is to prohibit health care providers from charging publicly covered patients any additional payments. Third, the various analyses of VHI conducted in the last few years have generated more evidence on its advantages and disadvantages.

The left-wing coalition government in power since the end of 2012 has included VHI in its programme, proposing greater integration between compulsory and voluntary health insurance, although it has taken a more cautious approach than the previous government. However, there are few reasons to believe that the population's attitude towards the introduction of semi-obligatory premiums to purchase private health insurance will change. As a result, it is unlikely that VHI will expand significantly in the next few years.

References

Buivydas R et al. (2010). *Papildomo savanoriškojo sveikatos draudimo analizė [Supplementary voluntary health insurance analysis]*. Vilnius, Health Economics Centre.

Health Economics Centre (2011). New developments in Lithuanian health care system. Presentation by Buivydas R, Cerniauskas G. March 2011, Vilnius, Health Economics Centre.

ISC (2011). *Draudimas Lietuvoje metinė ataskaita 2010 [Insurance in Lithuania, annual report 2010]*. DPK, Vilnius. (https://www.lb.lt/2010_metu_veiklos_apzvalga, accessed 8 November 2015).

Murauskiene L et al. (2013). Lithuania: health system review. *Health Systems in Transition*, 15(2):1–150.

WHO (2016). Global Health Expenditure Database (GHED) [online database]. Geneva, WHO (http://www.who.int/health-accounts/ghed/en/, accessed 5 April 2016).

21 Malta

Natasha Azzopardi-Muscat

Health system context

The health financing mix

In 2014, public spending on health accounted for 69.2% of total spending on health, with OOP payments and VHI accounting for 28.9 and 1.7%, respectively (WHO, 2016).

Entitlement to publicly financed health care and gaps in coverage

Publicly financed health coverage provides a comprehensive range of preventive, diagnostic, curative and rehabilitative health services to residents covered by the social security system. It also provides all necessary care to special population groups such as undocumented migrants or foreign workers with work permits. Although health services are free at the point of use, there may be long waiting times for accessing certain specialist outpatient appointments, diagnostic tests such as MRI scans and procedures such as cataract surgery and joint replacement.

Private financing plays a significant role in primary care (which is mainly provided by private providers) and ambulatory specialist care. OOP payments remain the main means of paying for outpatient medicines[1] (inpatient medicines are available free of charge) and paying private GPs; they are also still widely used for private ambulatory specialist consultations. However, consultations, day care and inpatient treatment in the

1 Medicines for around 70 chronic conditions are available free of charge; also those whose incomes fall below a certain threshold are entitled to free medicines on a limited positive list.

private sector are now mostly covered by private health insurance.

Overview of the VHI market

Market origins, aims and role

Traditionally, privately provided care has been paid for on an OOP basis. VHI take-up started to increase since the mid-1990s and in 2010 21.2% of the population was covered by VHI (Malta Insurance Association, 2012). VHI mainly plays a *supplementary* role, providing faster access to treatment and superior room amenities, and in general does not cover services that are not available in the public sector. However, some VHI policies may cover treatment abroad that is not always available in Malta and, more recently, some VHI plans have begun to cover dental treatment, for which publicly financed coverage is limited (that is, a *complementary* role).

VHI's share of total spending on health has doubled in the past 15 years due to a combination of increasing competition among private insurers, with new providers entering the market, the increasing costs of private care and a general increase in socioeconomic conditions, including stable employment.

Types of plan available

VHI plans vary tremendously in the scope of their coverage and in eligibility criteria. Most insurers do not accept new applicants over 65 years old; however, existing policies can normally be renewed infinitely. Most plans do not cover chronic and pre-existing conditions. Also usually excluded are routine check-ups, screening, cosmetic surgery, normal childbirth, palliative treatment, certain dental care services, experimental treatment and treatment for chronic conditions. Premiums are normally community rated. However, certain insurance plans link premiums to age or risk factors. Some insurers may ask applicants, particularly older people, to provide the results of a medical examination. Premiums for group policies for groups above a certain size are experience rated. Premiums for smaller groups are community rated. Group policies also benefit from group discounts.

Why do people buy VHI?

VHI plans provide a wider choice of health care providers than the publicly financed system and cash benefits for patients treated in public facilities. They are popular among people who wish to avoid waiting lists, obtain appointments at more convenient times and have superior accommodation in hospitals (single rooms).

Who buys VHI?

Approximately 70% of insured persons were covered by group policies in 2010 (Malta Insurance Association, 2012). These policies are purchased by companies for their employees and may also cover employees' dependants. The remaining 30% of those with VHI are individuals with middle to high incomes, mostly families rather than single people. The share of group policies in monetary terms is substantially lower than their share in the number of covered people as groups normally benefit from premium discounts and companies normally purchase schemes with limited benefits. Around 52% of people with VHI plans have very limited cover, mostly for outpatient care and limited inpatient treatment (Malta Insurance Association, 2012). The scope of coverage under the basic and standard VHI schemes is much narrower than the scope of publicly financed coverage.

According to the European Health Interview Survey conducted in 2008 (Department of Health Information and Research, 2010), one-fifth of the surveyed population in Malta claimed to have VHI cover. Individuals with higher incomes and with higher education were more likely to be covered. The degree of competition between insurers has increased; however, policies with extensive coverage are still only affordable for those with the highest incomes.

Who sells VHI?

There are currently eight VHI insurers in Malta: one provident association (BUPA Insurance Limited) and seven commercial insurers. Provident associations were the first to enter the VHI market and commercial insurers came in at a later stage. A gradual increase in the number of market players has been observed over time.

Insurer relations with providers

Insurers negotiate terms on an individual basis with hospitals/clinics. There is no integration between insurers and health care providers and usually all providers are contracted. Fees paid to private doctors are not negotiated and insurers pay what they deem is fair and reasonable – that is, patients may need to pay the difference in price if they choose a more expensive provider than what is specified in their insurance policy. Market-wide negotiations with private doctors took place in the early 2000s but were stopped after the Office for Fair Trading deemed them to represent price fixing. Benefits are received in kind or, less commonly, via a cash benefit (after the event) or retrospective reimbursement of eligible bills. Private hospitals are largely financed by VHI. Some insurers negotiate block payments for certain procedures in place of per diem and FFS payment.

Public policy towards VHI

The VHI market is regulated by the Ministry of Finance through the Malta Financial Services Authority (MFSA), in the same way as other insurance businesses. There is no VHI-specific regulation. In 2007, the MFSA issued an insurance rule *Information for Policyholders* determining what kind of information an insurer has to communicate to potential policyholders before a contract is concluded or to policyholders during the term of their contract and the manner in which that information is to be provided. Over the years, the Consumer Complaints Manager of the MFSA has received a number of complaints against private health insurers, usually related to increases in premiums and to the fact that VHI policies become unaffordable for older age groups (MFSA, 2012). Price increases are more common in the VHI market than in other types of insurance, mainly due to medical inflation and increased use of private care, but they have slowed down in the past couple of years, possibly due to increasing competition.

Debates and challenges

The opening of private hospitals in recent years and the increasing provision of private specialist and secondary/ tertiary care have increased demand for VHI, but the market remains small in terms of its share of total spending on health. Barriers to VHI market growth include the absence of user charges for publicly financed health care, the high cost of VHI plans and the affordability of OOP payments for primary and ambulatory care.

VHI makes the management of the publicly financed system more difficult because of the role conflict doctors working in both public and private sectors may be experiencing; demand for private services depends on the length of waiting lists in the public sector and the level of remuneration per consultation or procedure is much higher in the private sector than in the public sector. Another problem in the VHI market is the high cost of care; insurers have often complained about the lack of regulation of prices in the private sector. The small number of private specialists in certain medical specialities hinders price competition and insurers complain that some procedures and consultations in the private sector are more expensive than in richer European countries.

Debates about the role of VHI sometimes appear in the press. In 2008, the Malta Insurance Association issued a position paper making the case for giving VHI a larger role. The Minister for Social Policy at the time had mentioned the need to examine more closely the role of VHI, not excluding the possibility that it could be linked to publicly financed coverage, but no clear policy proposal was formulated and no policy changes have been introduced since then (Debono, 2008).

The future of VHI

The dual system of public and private coverage has existed for a long time and appears to be acceptable to the population as long as the public system delivers well. The outlook for VHI is unlikely to change given broad political consensus around publicly financed health care that is free at the point of use.

References

Debono J (2008). Dalli still thinks insurance companies should pay for hospital costs. *Malta Today*, 26 March 2008 (http://www.maltatoday.com.mt/2008/03/26/n1.html, accessed 22 November 2015).

Department of Health Information and Research (2010). *European health interview survey 2008*. Valletta, Ministry for Health, the Elderly and Community Care (https://health.gov.mt/en/dhir/Pages/Surveys/eurohealthintervsurvey2008.aspx, accessed 2 December 2015).

Malta Insurance Association (2012) [website]. Malta Insurance Association (http://maltainsurance.org/, accessed 22 November 2012).

MFSA (2012) [website]. Malta Financial Services Authority (http://www.mfsa.com.mt/pages/default.aspx, accessed 22 November 2015).

WHO (2016). Global Health Expenditure Database (GHED) [online database]. Geneva, WHO (http://www.who.int/health-accounts/ghed/en/, accessed 5 April 2016).

22
Netherlands

Hans Maarse

Health system context

The health financing mix

In 2014, public spending on health and LTC accounted for 87% of total spending on health, while OOP payments and VHI accounted for 5.2 and 5.9%, respectively (WHO, 2016). The Netherlands does not include the compulsory deductibles paid by all adults using health services as OOP spending. As the deductible amounts to €375 per adult per year (in 2015), OOP payments are underestimated in national health accounts data for the Netherlands (OECD & European Union, 2014). Public spending on health and LTC rose from 4.6% of GDP in 2000 to 9.5% of GDP in 2014 (WHO, 2016) due to the incorporation of the former private health insurance arrangements into a single universal and mandatory health insurance scheme.

Entitlement to publicly financed health care and gaps in coverage

The 2006 HIA (*Zorgverzekeringswet*) put an end to the traditional division between publicly financed health coverage operated by sickness funds, covering about 63% of the population, and a complex mix of substitutive private and other health insurance arrangements covering the remaining 37%. The new law integrated both forms of coverage into a single scheme covering all legal residents (including foreigners working in the Netherlands). It also made health insurance universally compulsory. Although the HIA scheme is based on private law and operated by competing private insurers, the many state regulations on access and consumer choice make it essentially public (Maarse, Jeurissen & Ruwaard, 2015).

The HIA benefits package is relatively comprehensive and user charges are uncommon. Instead, all adults must pay a mandatory annual deductible (€375 in 2015) when using health services. GP visits, maternity care and children are exempt from the deductible. People can choose to pay a higher deductible (up to €500 more – that is, €875 in total) in exchange for paying a lower contribution to the HIA scheme.

Overview of the VHI market

Market origins, aims and role

The 2006 health insurance law implied a significant reduction in demand for private health insurance. VHI lost its traditional substitutive role (Van de Ven & Schut, 2008) and now only plays a *complementary* role, covering services not covered by the HIA scheme. Some VHI plans also cover the mandatory deductible. Before 2006, both sickness funds and private insurers offered complementary plans on a voluntary basis.

Between 2008 and 2012 revenues from VHI premium income rose from €3.9 billion to €4.7 billion. However, since 2012 revenues have been steadily declining, reaching €4.3 billion in 2014 (Vektis, 2015a). VHI profits have also declined significantly, from €436 million in 2012 to €154 million in 2014 (Vektis, 2015a). Nevertheless, VHI has remained an important marketing instrument for insurers in the HIA scheme.

Types of plan available

Complementary VHI plans vary widely and may cover dental care for adults, physiotherapy, glasses, orthodontic care, alternative medicine, contraceptives, preventive programmes including physical exercise programmes, dietary services, hearing aids, skin treatments, sterilization and user charges for hospice care. Plans may be standard (basic), silver or gold (most comprehensive). Insurers also offer special plans for dental care and plans covering other services. More recently, insurers have started to target plans at specific population groups, offering plans for young people (vaccinations for travelling abroad, dental care and condoms), families (orthodontic care and some forms of maternity care) and people aged 50 and older (hearing aids, for example).

In 2014, dental care accounted for 43.3% of total VHI expenditure, physiotherapy and other supplementary care for 27.2%, medical devices for 8.4%, alternative medicine for 4.9% and assistance abroad for 1.8% (Vektis, 2015b).

Insurers are free to reject applications, introduce age limits or apply exclusion waivers. In the first years after the implementation of the HIA scheme, they voluntarily abstained from exclusion waivers in VHI or applied them in only specific cases. However, this practice has changed. The Dutch Health Care Authority found that, in 2012, 42% of VHI plans (n=544) had entry requirements (NZa, 2012).

Why do people buy VHI?

Dutch people tend to be risk averse and the share of the population purchasing complementary plans is very high: 84% of people covered by the HIA scheme in 2015 (about 74% of people with an individual HIA plan and about 90% of people with a group HIA plan in 2015). However, VHI population coverage has steadily decreased from a peak of 93% of HIA insured in 2006 (Vektis, 2015b). One reason for this negative trend is that complementary VHI is considered expensive. Another reason is that people prefer to pay directly for health services not covered by the HIA scheme rather than buying VHI, partly because they feel that VHI plans cover many services they will never use.

VHI premiums have increased significantly since 2006. The average premium rose from €222 in 2006 to €314 in 2013 (Vektis, 2015b). Note that these figures are averages and that there is a huge variation in premiums given the wide variety in types of plans.

Who buys VHI?

Most people purchase VHI, but there are no quantitative data available on the characteristics of people who do not buy VHI.

Who sells VHI?

All health insurers offer complementary VHI plans. There are no data on concentration in the VHI market. However, assuming a strong correlation between the HIA market share and VHI market share, the market share of the four largest insurance concerns (each of which operates several insurance brands) can be estimated at about 90%. Administrative costs in the VHI market were calculated at 13.4% of total premium income in 2014. This is significantly higher than the administrative costs in the HIA scheme (3.5% in 2014) (Vektis, 2015a).

The HIA scheme bans insurers from requiring HIA enrollees to purchase complementary VHI from the same company or to terminate a VHI policy if an enrollee moves to another company for HIA cover. However, only 0.2% of the HIA insured are covered by two insurers (one for HIA and another for VHI) (Nza, 2012).

Insurer relations with providers

Selective contracting is permitted in the complementary VHI market. Glasses are a good example: purchasing glasses from non-preferred providers is discouraged by lower reimbursement rates. Vertical integration barely exists. Insurers usually reimburse their customers for using services covered in their plan. They may reimburse the full cost, a percentage of the cost or a fixed amount.

Public policy towards VHI

Regulation of complementary VHI is limited to standard market regulation applied to all insurance business, such as solvency and reporting requirements, anti-cartel regulation and patient safety regulation. The main regulatory body is the Dutch Bank, which supervises solvency requirements.

Debates and challenges

There is not much debate on VHI as its role in health care financing remains relatively small.

The future of VHI

The expansion of the complementary VHI market is highly dependent on developments in the HIA market, in particular with regard to the scope of HIA coverage. For example, the decision to delist (exclude) most dental care for adults from publicly financed health coverage in 2004 and later in 2011, and to limit entitlement of publicly financed physiotherapy, created new demand for complementary VHI. However, delisting is very unpopular: in mid-2013, a plan by the government to reduce HIA scheme coverage by €1.3 billion was dropped. Instead, the government signed an agreement with the national associations of provider organizations for GPs to take over some hospital tasks to save costs and be more careful in referring patients to hospital, prescribing medicines and applying medical tests. The role of complementary VHI may also increase in response to the substantial revision of publicly financed LTC that is being implemented (Maarse H, Emeritus Professor, unpublished research memo, 2013).

References

Maarse H, Jeurissen P, Ruwaard D (2015). Results of the market-oriented reform in the Netherlands: a review. *Health Economics, Policy and Law*. doi:10.1017/S1744133115000353.

OECD (2014). *Health at a glance: Europe 2014*. Paris, OECD Publishing (http://ec.europa.eu/health/reports/docs/health_glance_2014_en.pdf, accessed 22 November 2015).

NZa (2012). *Marktscan zorgverzekeringsmarkt [Market scan health insurance market]*. Utrecht, NZa [Dutch Healthcare Authority] (http://www.nza.nl/104107/105773/475605/Marktscan_Zorgverzekeringsmarkt.pdf, accessed 2 December 2015).

Van de Ven W, Schut F (2008). Universal mandatory health insurance in the Netherlands: a model for the United States? *Health Affairs (Millwood)*, 27(3):771–781.

Vektis (2015a). *Jaarcijfers 2015. Zorgfinanciering en zorgverzekeraars [Annual results 2015. Health care financing and health insurers]*. Zeist, Vektis (http://www.vektis.nl/images/Jaarcijfers_2015.pdf, accessed 2 December 2015).

Vektis (2015b). Zorgthermometer 2015 [Care thermometer 2015]. Zeist, Vektis (http://www.vektis.nl, accessed 22 November 2015).

WHO (2016). Global Health Expenditure Database (GHED) [online database]. Geneva, WHO (http://www.who.int/health-accounts/ghed/en/, accessed 5 April 2016).

23
Norway

Jan Roth Johnsen

Health system context

The health financing mix

Health care in Norway is financed from direct taxes (mainly proportional income tax), indirect taxes, national social insurance contributions and private expenditure (OOP payments and VHI). The public–private financing mix has been very stable since the 1980s, with public spending accounting for 85.5% of total spending on health in 2014 and OOP payments for 13.6 (there is no data on VHI) (WHO, 2016).

Entitlement to publicly financed health care and gaps in coverage

The health system is built on the principle of assuring equal access to health care services to all inhabitants, regardless of their social status, place of residence and income. These rights are regulated by law and are also embedded in the culture of the Norwegian welfare state. All residents are entitled to publicly financed health services. The scope of coverage is broad, excluding only non-medical eye care, adult dental care and complementary and alternative medicine. User charges are applied to all except inpatient care and are usually moderate. General dental care for adults is one area where private participation in costs is very high. Nursing and LTC also incur very high user charges. Exemptions from and caps on user charges apply to certain diseases and population groups. Waiting times for elective care are long and constitute an important barrier to accessing care (Ringard et al., 2013).

Overview of the VHI market

Market origins, aims and role

VHI plays mainly a *supplementary* role, providing faster access to ambulatory and inpatient elective care treatment, often in private clinics.

Types of plan available

VHI plans usually cover ambulatory care and elective inpatient care in private hospitals. Emergency care is excluded.

Why do people buy VHI?

The VHI market has seen significant growth in the last decade, with population coverage increasing from around 34 000 people in 2003 to around 300 000 in 2011 (Figure 23.1). Premium income rose by 27% between 2009 and 2010 and by over 50% between 2010 and 2011 (Finansnæringens hovedorganisasjon, 2012). People buy VHI to obtain a better level of health care services (private care is perceived to be of better quality and the public system is thought to provide only necessary care) and to jump waiting lists for publicly financed treatment.

Figure 23.1 *Number of people with VHI in Norway, 2003–2011*

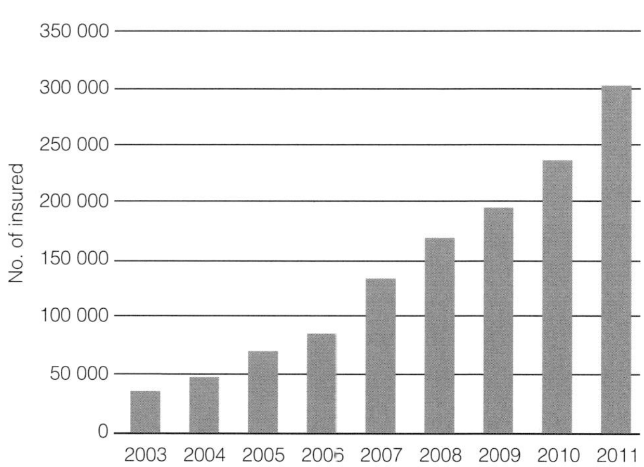

Source: Finansnæringens hovedorganisasjon (2012).

Who buys VHI?

Group contracts dominate. In 2011, there were 10 times more group contracts than individual contracts (210 944 compared to 23 065). Group contracts are mainly purchased by companies as employment perks for their employees.

A national survey conducted in 2004 by one insurer (Synovate MMI) among people aged between 30 and 55 years old (the age group with the highest VHI take-up) showed that VHI take-up is higher among smokers, people with higher incomes (but tails off in the upper income segment; also confirmed in 2007 for group policies; Pedersen, 2007) and white-collar workers in leading positions (Table 23.1). In general, blue-collar workers are more likely to possess VHI than white-collar workers. One possible explanation for this is that blue-collar workers are more likely to work for small employers where the economic consequences of accidents and sickness absence cannot be easily diversified away. People with higher education are less likely to possess individual

Table 23.1 *Distribution of health insurance in Norway by socioeconomic categories (%), 2004*

	Employer provided	Privately bought	No health insurance
Age			
30–34	10.3	3.3	86.3
35–39	8.4	6.2	85.4
40–44	6.0	6.0	87.9
45–49	5.1	2.3	92.6
50–54	5.5	2.3	92.2
Gender			
Male	8.0	4.0	88.0
Female	5.8	3.6	90.5
Occupation			
Blue-collar	9.4	4.0	86.6
Leading position white-collar	10.3	4.2	85.4
White-collar	5.8	3.0	91.2
Self-employed	2.4	5.9	91.7
Other	4.9	3.7	91.4
Income (Norway krone)			
Up to 300 000	4.4	4.0	91.6
300 000–600 000	8.6	3.8	87.6
Over 600 000	6.6	4.4	89.0
Education			
Old primary school (8 years)	0.0	0.0	100.0
New primary school (10 years)	7.6	2.9	89.5
High school	8.6	4.0	87.4
Bachelor's/Master's degree	6.1	4.0	89.9
Smoking habit			
Daily	9.6	4.6	85.8
Sporadically	6.9	4.1	89.0
Not at all	6.0	3.6	90.4

Source: Aarbu (2007).

Note: These data may also include cover for critical illness and child illness.

VHI. On the other hand, for group policies, VHI take-up is more likely among people with more education (Pedersen, 2007). The likelihood of having VHI is the highest among people between 35 and 45 years old.

Who sells VHI?

All insurers offering VHI, except for Vertikal Helse,[1] are commercial companies offering a broad range of other types of insurance products. Market concentration is higher in the individual VHI market, with one insurance company accounting for over 50% of the market. In the group market, the company with the highest market share has just under 27% of the market. Overall, there were seven insurers in the VHI market in 2011. One was exclusively active in the individual VHI market and one in the group market, with the remaining five companies offering both individual and group insurance products (Table 23.2).

Insurer relations with providers

Private insurers are not integrated with providers but sign agreements with selected private providers. People with VHI can be treated in private hospitals and clinics only because public hospitals do not provide services for private insurers.

1 Vertikal Helse provides assistance in case of illness by helping to identify the fastest and best treatment available (in practice, hospital choice), but does not cover medical care.

Public policy towards VHI

Although population coverage of VHI plans has increased significantly over the past 10 years, VHI continues to play a marginal role in health financing. During the 1990s, the market for VHI was nearly non-existent but since 2000 some growth has been observed. In 2001, the conservative right-of-centre government provided financial incentives (a tax reduction) to companies that purchased VHI cover for their employees. Introduced in 2003, the tax subsidy increased the number of VHI subscriptions. However, the withdrawal of this tax subsidy by the left-of-centre government in 2006 did not bring about a reversal of this trend.

Waiting times have been the subject of public debate for several years, especially in relation to their effect on the labour market (employees being on waiting lists and not able to work) and costs for the National Insurance Scheme and companies (sick leave benefits). Schemes aimed at helping employees avoid waiting times were supported by a Royal Commission (*Sandman-utvalget*) in

Table 23.2 *Overview of VHI providers in Norway, 2009–2011*

	Number of insured			Market share (%)		
Individual contracts	2009	2010	2011	2009	2010	2011
Codan Forsikring/Vertikal Helse	–	–	6639	0.00	0.00	28.78
Försäkrings AB Skandia, filial Norge	719	–	–	4.55	0.00	0.00
Gjensidige Forsikring ASA	1391	1707	2006	8.80	10.86	8.70
SpareBank 1 Skadeforsikring	–	894	874	0.00	5.69	3.79
Storebrand Helseforsikring AS	12 699	12 024	12 083	80.36	76.47	52.39
Terra Forsikring	45	36	34	0.28	0.23	0.15
Tryg Forsikring	949	1062	1429	6.01	6.75	6.20
Total	**15 803**	**15 723**	**23 065**	**100.00**	**100.00**	**100.00**
Group contracts						
Codan Forsikring/Vertikal Helse	–	–	32 904	0.00	0.00	15.60
Försäkrings AB Skandia, filial Norge	17 765	–	–	17.79	0.00	0.00
Gjensidige Forsikring ASA	16 199	27 506	37 094	16.22	21.83	17.58
If Skadeforsikring NUF	19 161	25 264	56 016	19.19	20.05	26.55
SpareBank 1 Skadeforsikring	–	16 502	21 287	0.00	13.09	10.09
Storebrand Helseforsikring AS	32 345	32 082	37 894	32.39	25.46	17.96
Tryg Forsikring	14 378	24 665	25 749	14.40	19.57	12.21
Total	**99 848**	**126 019**	**210 944**	**100.00**	**100.00**	**100.00**
Grand total	**115 651**	**141 742**	**234 009**			

Source: Finansnæringens hovedorganisasjon (2012).

Note: All data as of 31 December (of all years included in the table).

2000 on the grounds that faster access to health care for workers would increase national income, leaving room for more spending on hospital services in the future (NOU: 2000 No 27; Ministry of Labour and Social Affairs, 2000). This argument was opposed by a previous Royal Commission (NOU: 1997 No 18; Ministry of Health and Care Services, 1997), which considered it unethical for social background (employment status) to have an influence on access to health services. In 1999, the National Insurance Administration set up a scheme that offered faster access to health care for employees. In the peak year (2003) around 10 000 patients were treated under this arrangement. The scheme was abandoned by the government in 2005, but in 2007 a new scheme was set up to provide special needs-based ambulatory care facilities for ordinary treatments for employees through public and private providers. The scheme should not, under any circumstances, influence access to care for ordinary patients, but should be based on available capacities. So far around 8000 people have been referred in this scheme.

Debates and challenges

Long waiting times for publicly financed health care (or the perception of long waiting times, partly fuelled by the insurance industry) and public subsidies for group VHI through tax relief have been central to the growth of VHI over the last few years. Growing demand for health services adds to the pressure on the publicly financed system. This, combined with the increasing purchasing power of the middle class (Norwegians being among the richest people in the world) creates room for private options.

The future of VHI

The market for VHI has been growing since 2003 despite high levels of public spending on health and the existence of a public scheme assuring faster access to health care for employees. The reasons for this are increasing real incomes and negative perceptions regarding the public health care system. Nevertheless, VHI take-up is still small. The most recent extension of patient choice of hospital to all public and private hospitals in Norway (currently under implementation) could lead to an increase in the number of private health care providers and contribute to a reduction in waiting times, which have been key to VHI growth. This may reduce interest in VHI, but it is too early to tell.

References

Aarbu K (2007). *Do smokers pay too little – or do insurers pay too little attention?* Bergen, Rokkansenteret.

Finansnæringens hovedorganisasjon (2012). *Statistics. Non-life insurance.* Oslo, The Norwegian Financial Services Association.

Ministry of Health and Care Services (1997). *Prioritering på ny - Gjennomgang av retningslinjer for prioriteringer innen norsk helsetjeneste [Prioritizing again - Review of the guidelines for priorities within the Norwegian health care].* NOU [Norwegian Official Report] 1997: No. 18. Oslo, Government Administration Services.

Ministry of Labour and Social Affairs (2000). *Sykefravær og uførepensjonering – Et inkluderende arbeidsliv [Sickness and disability pensions - an inclusive workplace].* NOU [Norwegian Official Report] 2000: No. 27. Oslo, Government Administration Services.

Pedersen I (2007). *Private helseforsikringer – status og betydning for utvikling i sosial helseskilnader [Private health insurance - status and importance to the development of social health inequalities].* Bergen, Program for Helseøkonomi i Bergen.

Ringard Å et al. (2013). Norway: health system review. *Health Systems in Transition*, 15(8):1–162.

WHO (2016). Global Health Expenditure Database (GHED) [online database]. Geneva, WHO (http://www.who.int/health-accounts/ghed/en/, accessed 5 April 2016).

24
Poland

Alicja Sobczak

Health system context

The health financing mix

Health expenditure in Poland has grown rapidly in the past decade, but its composition has remained fairly stable, with public sources accounting for 71% of total spending on health in 2014 (WHO, 2016). Private expenditure mainly comprised OOP payments (23.5% of total health expenditure, while VHI accounted for 4% of total health expenditure). Other private sources, such as private companies (for example, expenditure on occupational health services) and foundations, accounted for the remaining share of total spending on health.

Entitlement to publicly financed health care and gaps in coverage

Publicly financed health coverage is almost universal, with 97.6% of the population covered in 2009 (Sagan et al., 2011). Membership of the National Health Fund (NHF) is mandatory for everyone. NHF benefits are broad, with user charges for prescribed outpatient medicines, orthopaedic and auxiliary products, spa treatment, inpatient long-term nursing treatment and some over-standard medical procedures, including some innovative procedures. Waiting lists are applied to outpatient specialist consultations and treatment procedures, elective inpatient care, rehabilitation and chosen diagnostic procedures (ultrasonography, CT, MRI). Waiting times may vary significantly (up to many months) depending on the area of care, region and provider.

Overview of the VHI market

Market origins, aims and role

VHI's key role is *supplementary*. There is also a niche market for *complementary* cover of user charges and for goods and services excluded from NHF coverage (for example, non-refunded medicines, some dental services, over-standard procedures and treatment courses).

There are two main categories of VHI product in Poland – medical packages/subscriptions and health insurance policies. The most common VHI products are health care packages or subscriptions offered mainly by commercial insurers but also by some public health care providers.[1] Although subscriptions are not legally recognized as insurance products and do not operate under the 2003 Insurance Activity Act, they guarantee their beneficiaries access to health services in the event of health problems. While subscriptions are rooted in employers' legal obligation to provide employees with occupational health services, they often also cover other medical services for employees and their families.

Recently, banks have started to offer relatively cheap VHI packages and policies covering varying ranges of health care services. These products are offered in cooperation with insurance or subscription companies.

Subscriptions predate and dominate the VHI market. They were initiated in the 1990s, while health insurance policies have only seen growth since the middle of the 2000s. Respective market sizes are difficult to assess in financial terms as subscription companies have no obligation to report their financial results while other VHI products are counted as part of accident and health insurance products and not reported separately. When looking at population coverage, subscriptions dominate, accounting for approximately 72% of the entire VHI market.

According to the Polish Insurance Chamber (PIU, undated), more than 2.5 million people (approximately 6.6% of the population) had VHI cover in 2010: 2 million had subscriptions and about 0.5 million had other VHI policies. Social Diagnosis surveys showed that about 20% of the population was willing to pay for VHI cover if it was not too expensive (up to €20 per month) (Czapiński & Panek, 2005, 2007, 2009). Another survey of a representative sample of 999 people found that 19% of respondents had VHI cover (subscription or other VHI) (CBOS, 2012). At the end of 2014, approximately 1.2 million people had health insurance policies, compared to 850 000 in 2013 (an increase of 41%), with the number of individual policies rising from approximately 35 500 in 2013 to 197 000 in the first quarter of 2015 (that is, a growth of 455%; PIU, 2015). The number of subscription holders was estimated at approximately 3 million people in 2014 (out of which approximately 2.5 million received it as an employment perk) (Skibińska, 2015). Subscriptions continue to dominate the VHI market.

Types of plan available

Subscriptions mainly provide faster access to and better quality of outpatient services. Basic subscription packages (for groups and individuals) usually cover services related to the provision of occupational health services, such as ambulatory specialist consultations and procedures, and diagnostic procedures. In recent years the leading subscription companies have also included inpatient treatment (in their own or cooperating hospitals), rehabilitation, medical transport, nursing care, dental care, higher hospitalization standards and auxiliary products. Packages range from basic to VIP.

Health insurance policies offered by insurance companies are sold as separate policies or as supplements to other insurance policies, especially life insurance. They provide benefits in kind or cash benefits. Plans may cover primary and specialist ambulatory care, dental care and elective hospital procedures, rehabilitation, home visits and vaccinations on an in-kind basis. User charges may be applied. Plans that provide cash benefits (for example, a lump sum payment for a hospital day or a refund for the cost of medicines) usually cover hospital stays, surgery and serious illnesses (Ubezpieczenia Online.pl, 2010). Bank VHI policies may cover medical consultations, transport, nursing care, delivery of medicines and medical auxiliary products. The cheapest packages cover only a narrow range of assistance-like services, such as medical information and access to help centres, and transport to a health care provider in case of emergency.

Why do people buy VHI?

Survey data suggest that faster access to health care (avoiding long waiting times for treatment) and better quality of care are the main reasons for buying VHI

1 Independent public health care institutions providing occupational health services that are not covered by the NHF but are contracted and paid for by employers. Public health care providers are not allowed to charge additionally for NHF services, so occupational services became the basis for developing subscriptions/health packages.

(CBOS, 2012). The latest Social Diagnosis survey indicates that people are mainly interested in policies covering standard outpatient services (Czapiński & Panek, 2005, 2007, 2009).

Who buys VHI?

According to recent estimates by the Polish Insurance Chamber, approximately 90% of the insured are covered by group policies as VHI is mainly purchased by employers for their employees (PIU, undated). In recent years (2014, 2015), the share of group policies has decreased by a few percentage points due to the rapid growth in the number of individual policies. Employers remain the key purchasers of subscriptions, which are offered as employment perks, but their share is decreasing (over 90% of all subscriptions in 2010; PIU, undated) and approximately 84% in 2014; see figures on the number of VHI policy and subscription holders cited earlier). As a result, VHI take-up (subscriptions and other VHI products) is concentrated in the working population under 65 years old, especially those with higher education, working in large and medium-sized companies, and living in big cities. The highest VHI take-up is observed among the self-employed working outside the agriculture sector (37% of this group). VHI take-up is also particularly high among skilled workers with higher incomes (managers, skilled working class and middle technical staff) (CBOS, 2009).

Who sells VHI?

Subscriptions are sold by private companies. Three companies (Medicover, ENEL-MED and LUX MED Group) are market leaders and together with several others (Centrum Medyczne Damiana, POLMED, Swissmed Centrum Zdrowia, Falck) cover almost the entire country, while smaller companies cater to regional or local populations. More recently, the larger subscription firms either have become subcontractors for insurers or have registered part of their activity as insurance business (under the Insurance Activity Act).

Health insurance policies are sold by a mix of around 20 commercial (among them PZU, AXA, Allianz, SIGNAL IDUNA Group, ING Życie, Generali, INTER Polska, UNIQUA, InterRisk, TU Zdrowie insurers). Due to tough competition, the need for investment and development and low profitability of some new VHI products, only around 10 of them count as significant players in the health insurance policies market.

Insurer relations with providers

Subscription companies provide health care services via networks of their own health facilities and/or subcontracted private and public providers. Depending on the type of subscription, choice of provider may be very broad (for example, across the whole country) or very limited. Insurers and banks sign contracts with private and public health care providers or, more recently, with subscription firms. Patient choice of provider depends on policy terms. Providers are paid on a FFS basis (for outpatient consultations and tests) or via a diagnosis-related group (DRG)-like mechanism for hospital treatment. Tariffs are determined during contract negotiations.

Public policy towards VHI

Commercial insurers and banks are supervised by the Polish Financial Supervision Authority. Firms offering subscriptions are not part of the financial sector and not subject to supervision (which may be considered to constitute unfair competition).

VHI products do not benefit from tax subsidies. Employer expenditure on subscriptions or other VHI products for employees (but not for their family members) are treated as current operational costs. Employees must include the value of their subscription or VHI policy as part of their income in their personal income tax declaration.

Debates and challenges

VHI has been subject to extensive debate since 1989. In 2011, the Ministry of Health under the coalition government led by the Civic Platform proposed a bill on Additional Health Insurance. This was met with criticism from almost all sides, and was under consideration until the parliamentary, elections in October 2015, after which the opposition party (Law and Justice) assumed power (Chłoń-Domińczak et al., 2008; Sagan et al., 2011). The proposal strengthened the role of insurers with regard to subscription companies and, as a result, the latter would be likely to be relegated to the role of subcontractors for insurers (a shift already visible in recent years). It provided a legal definition of VHI, distinguishing between supplementary and complementary cover. It defined price, coverage and other requirements intended to secure access to good-quality services and introduces tax subsidies for VHI. Finally, it allowed public providers to charge patients extra for services already contracted by the NHF, allowed occupational health services to be included in insurance policies and allowed employers to finance VHI from their social funds. The idea of introducing tax subsidies was rejected by the Ministry of Finance.

The insurance sector has gone further and proposed allowing private insurers to compete with the NHF to offer publicly financed benefits (in a proposal developed by the Polish Insurance Chamber) (Chłoń-Domińczak et al., 2008). For people opting for a private insurer, the NHF would pay the private insurers a sex- and age-adjusted capitation fee and private insurers could also charge additional premiums. This proposal also had many opponents.

The debate over VHI's role and arrangements continues. Advocates argue that VHI reduces demand for publicly financed care, supplies health care providers with additional funding and substantially reduces corruption in health care. Opponents stress that equity and access may worsen if the role of VHI is strengthened.

The future of VHI

Despite the economic slowdown, the market for VHI continues to grow. According to recent estimates, expenditure on VHI (subscriptions and other VHI products) grew faster than other types of private health expenditure between 2010 and 2012 (Skonieczna, 2012). Market competition is growing as new players enter the market, resulting in diversification of products and mergers. The subscription market is assessed as mature and it is growing more slowly than before (less than 10% per year). The health insurance policies market is seen as a developing market, with high levels of competition and high growth rates.

Legislative proposals put forward before the October 2015 parliamentary election were in favour of strengthening the role of the private sector, including private insurers, in the health sector. At the same time, the importance of ensuring access to good-quality care was stressed. No major legislative changes took place before the parliamentary election in October 2015. VHI providers expected that in the future increases in wages and private consumption (assuming growing GDP) would stimulate further market development and predicted high growth in the private health care market as a whole in 2015–2020 (PMR, 2015).

References

CBOS (2009). *Characteristics of private health care users based on: Opinie o opiece zdrowotnej. Komunikat z badań [Opinions on health care. The research report].* Warsaw, Centrum Badania Opinii Społecznej [Public Opinion Research Center].

CBOS (2012). *Polacy o państwowej i prywatnej opiece zdrowotnej [Poles on public and private health care].* Warsaw, Centrum Badania Opinii Społecznej [Public Opinion Research Center].

Chłoń-Domińczak A et al. (2008). *Budowanie system prywatnych ubezpieczeń zdrowotnych w Polsce. Propozycje rozwiązań [Constructing a system of private health insurance in Poland. Proposed solutions].* Raport Polskiej Izby Ubezpieczeń [Report of the Polish Insurance Chamber]. Warsaw, Instytut Badań Strukturalnych [Institute for Structural Research].

CSO (2012). *Health and health care in 2010.* Warsaw, Central Statistical Office.

Czapiński J, Panek T, eds. (2005, 2007, 2009). *Diagnoza społeczna. Raport [Social diagnosis. Report].* Warsaw, Council for Social Monitoring.

PIU (undated). *Rola prywatnych ubezpieczeń zdrowotnych w systemie ochrony zdrowia. Jak wpływają na dostęp do świadczeń, innowacji i leków – kluczowe tezy i rekomendacje [The role of private health insurance in healthcare system. How they influence access to services, innovations and medicines – key theses and recommendations].* Warsaw, PIU [Polish Insurance Association] (http://piu.org.pl/public/upload/ibrowser/110908_PIU_Infarma_Sequence_opracowanie_dodatkowe_ubezpieczenia.pdf, accessed 22 November 2015).

PIU (2015). *Rynek ubezpieczeń zdrowotnych po I kw. 2015 r [The market of health insurance after the first quarter of 2015]* (http://piu.org.pl/analizy/project/1903/pagination/1, accessed 22 November 2015).

PMR (2015). *Rynek prywatnej opieki zdrowotnej w Polsce 2015. Prognozy rozwoju na lata 2015-2020 [The market of private health care in Poland 2015. Development prognosis for the years 2015–2020]* (http://www.pmrpublications.com/product/Rynek-prywatnej-opieki-zdrowotnej-w-Polsce-2015, accessed 22 November 2015).

Sagan A et al. (2011). Poland: health system review. *Health Systems in Transition*, 13(8):1–193.

Skibińska R (2015). *Abonamenty wygrywają z polisami [Subscriptions win against insurance policies]* (http://www.obserwatorfinansowy.pl/tematyka/rynki-finansowe/abonamenty-wygrywaja-z-polisami/, accessed 2 December 2015).

Skonieczna A (2012). *5% increase in private healthcare market in Poland between 2012 and 2014.* Based on: *Private healthcare market in Poland 2012. Development forecast 2012–2014.* PMR Report. Cracow, PMR Publications.

Ubezpieczenia Online.pl (2010). *Prywatne ubezpieczenia zdrowotne. Polska 2010, Raporty ubezpieczeniowe [Private health insurance. Poland 2010].* Wrocław, Ubezpieczenia Online.pl (http://www.zdrowotne.ubezpieczenie.com.pl/raport_rynek_prywatnych_ubezpieczen_zdrowotnych_2010/81,9916.html, accessed 2 December 2015).

WHO (2016). Global Health Expenditure Database (GHED) [online database]. Geneva, WHO (http://www.who.int/health-accounts/ghed/en/, accessed 5 April 2016).

25
Portugal

Mónica Duarte Oliveira and
Sofia Nogueira da Silva

Health system context

The health financing mix

In 2014, public spending accounted for 64.8% of total spending on health, with OOP payments and VHI accounting for 26.8 and 5.1%, respectively (WHO, 2016). The private share of total spending on health has risen from 32% in 2000 to around 35% in 2014 (WHO, 2016).

Entitlement to publicly financed health care and gaps in coverage

A NHS system was introduced in 1979. Today, the NHS coexists with several public and private occupation-based schemes known as *subsystems*, most of which provide compulsory coverage. Subsystems predated the introduction of the NHS and also coexist with a VHI market, which has grown in recent decades.

As specified in the Portuguese Constitution (Assembleia da República, 1992), the NHS covers the whole population with a comprehensive range of benefits; in theory, no services are explicitly excluded from NHS coverage. Nonetheless, there are gaps in provision due to geographical imbalances and in practice the NHS does not cover dental care. User charges (copayments) are in place for most NHS services. Until recently, with the exception of copayments for medicines, user charges were very low, accounting for only 1% of NHS expenditure (Barros & de Almeida Simões, 2007). Reforms in 2012 increased the level of user charges and the range of benefits to which they are applied (see further on).

Overview of the VHI market

Market origins, aims and role

The VHI market has developed since the 1980s and covers approximately 17% of the population (Barros, Machado & de Almeida Simões, 2011) (Table 25.1). Less than 2% of the population is covered by both VHI and one or more subsystems (INSA & INE, 2007). The role of VHI is *supplementary* (providing faster access to elective hospital treatment and ambulatory consultations and choice of provider) and, only rarely, *complementary* (covering services excluded from the NHS) (Companhia Portuguesa de Seguros de Saúde, 2005; Martins, 2006).

Table 25.1 *Key figures in the Portuguese VHI market, 2010 and 2013*

	2010	2013
Total number of insured individuals	2.15 million (around 20% of the population)	1.8 million (around 17% of the population)
Average monthly premium paid by an insured individual	€248.34	€281.87
Share of VHI policies that are group policies	64%	62%
Share of VHI policies that are reimbursement plans	15%	26%
Total premium income	€535 million	€507 million
Share of premium income spent on claims	74.8%	70.1%
Share of claims value covered by the insurer	70.4%	67.6%

Sources: Associação Portuguesa de Seguradores (2010, 2014).

A handful of VHI plans cover user charges for medicines. Insurers have never shown a real interest in assuming a substitutive role towards the NHS.

Types of plan available

Basic VHI policies covering inpatient care, ambulatory care and/or external consultations dominate the market (Associação Portuguesa de Seguradores, 2010). VHI plans do not usually cover NHS user charges; only a few expensive plans cover copayments for medicines (Oliveira & Silva, unpublished report, 2008). Most plans offer limited coverage, multiple exclusions apply (for pre-existing, chronic and psychiatric diseases) and few products cover individuals aged over 70 and at high risks. There are also benefits ceilings, user charges (balance billing, coinsurance and copayments), moratorium underwriting periods and pre-authorizations for the use of some services (Thomson & Mossialos, 2009). VHI premiums are based on risk, measured mainly by age and, to a lesser extent, by health status.

Why do people buy VHI?

People buy VHI because of generous tax incentives for high-income individuals and companies, due to the social status it confers (Barros, Machado & de Almeida Simões, 2011) and due to access problems in the NHS – for example, having VHI coverage allows a person to jump waiting lists and choose providers.

Although there is little evidence on the criteria people use to choose VHI products, price, reputation of the insurer and quality of services seem to be important variables (Autoridade da Concorrência, 2004). It is very difficult for consumers to compare the prices and policy conditions of different VHI products. The Portuguese Association for Consumer Protection (*Associação Portuguesa para a Defesa de Consumidores*, DECO) produces brief reports on VHI products and provides information to the public on VHI products, coverage limits and the key factors to take into account when choosing a VHI policy.

Who buys VHI?

In 2010, 64% of VHI policies were group policies purchased by employers and the remainder were individual contracts (Associação Portuguesa de Seguradores, 2010; Instituto de Seguros de Portugal, 2011). Group policies often cover employees' dependants. Around half of all VHI policies are established through banking channels (Autoridade da Concorrência, 2004), The average VHI client is aged between 20 and 54, lives in an urban area, has a medium to high income and works in a medium-sized or large company (Nunes, 2006).

Who sells VHI?

Over time the VHI market has become more concentrated, reflecting trends also observed in the banking and insurance sectors (Oliveira & Silva, unpublished report, 2008). In 2011, there were 19 commercial (non-specialist) insurers in the VHI market, all Portuguese (Instituto de Seguros de Portugal, 2012). In 2010, the three largest insurers had a market share of 56% (Instituto de Seguros de Portugal, 2011). An earlier study supported the hypothesis that there was a low level of competition in the non-life insurance market, suggesting low price competition, market barriers to entry and economies of scope for the largest companies (Autoridade da Concorrência, 2004). In 2011, the VHI market registered a total premium income of €508 million (excluding reinsurance) (Instituto de Seguros de Portugal, 2012), and most insurers registered profits (Instituto de Seguros de Portugal, 2011).

Insurer relations with providers

Insurers usually negotiate contracts with private hospitals and pay for private ambulatory care on a FFS basis. Several insurers use PPNs to minimize costs and increase efficiency, even though there is no evidence that this has been achieved. These networks do not generally require exclusivity and providers commonly belong to more than one network (that is, with more than one insurer) and may also hold contracts with the NHS, as well as provide private services to the general public on an OOP payment basis. Providers must apply and conform to the insurer's rules to enter its network (Barros, Machado & de Almeida Simões, 2011). Typically, plans with PPNs involve user charges in the form of copayments, while coinsurance and balance billing are applied to plans that offer reimbursement. Some of the larger insurers have their own providers, giving them better control over costs and quality. In theory, the prices of services are negotiated between providers and insurers. However, since many providers depend on insurers to survive, their negotiating power is rather low.

Public policy towards VHI

There is no VHI-specific legislation; general insurance legislation is applied to VHI, which is regulated by the following bodies: the Portuguese Insurance Institute (*Instituto de Seguros de Portugal*); DECO; the Portuguese Competition Authority (*Autoridade da Concorrência*); and the Health Regulatory Agency (*Entidade Reguladora da Saúde*), an independent public body whose responsibilities include protecting the rights of health care users (including access to health care and freedom of choice), assuring compliance with the legislation and transparency in the economic relations between providers, purchasers and users, and promoting fair competition.

Tax incentives for companies and individuals have promoted the growth of the VHI market. Since 1988, tax reforms have made most private health care expenditure, including user charges for NHS services, OOP payments in the private sector and VHI premiums, deductible from personal taxable income – a policy that has had a substantial impact on VHI and private spending on health. The value of the tax subsidy associated with VHI premiums was estimated at €32 million in 2007 (Direcção-Geral do Orçamento, 2007).

Tax incentives for private spending on health are high by international standards (Comissão para a Sustentabilidade do Financiamento do Serviço Nacional de Saúde, 2007). In 2012, in the context of reforms intended to address the public deficit and increase tax revenue, the tax deduction for VHI premiums was reduced from 30 to 10% and the maximum amount of tax benefit was lowered. It is still too early to estimate the impact of this change on the VHI market.

Stronger tax incentives for group VHI policies mean that group VHI benefits are relatively generous (Barros, Machado & de Almeida Simões, 2011). However, relatively few businesses provide VHI for their employees.

Since the 1990s, the possibility of opting out of the NHS has been widely discussed in Portugal. As an experiment, between 1998 and 2007 some employees of Portugal Telecom, for whom a private health subsystem is in place, were allowed to opt out of the NHS. A small number of employees chose to do so. Because the NHS is funded through general taxation, this implied a transfer of a capitation fee by the NHS to the private subsystem, which then became responsible for paying the full price for NHS services whenever the beneficiary decided to use them. However, the negotiation of this capitation fee proved to be extremely difficult and generated regular complaints by the subsystem, which argued that the amount was far too low. The subsystem eventually abandoned this model in 2007. Since then, opting out of the NHS has been allowed by law but no opting out has taken place.

Debates and challenges

VHI has not generally attracted much public attention as it plays a marginal role in health financing. Direct and indirect incentives have favoured the development of the VHI market and increases in private spending, but there has been no serious discussion about the interaction between public and private coverage and spending.

Access to VHI depends on the ability to pay, and demand for such products has mainly come from higher-income groups (Nunes, 2006). The existence of a considerable share of the population enjoying double coverage through VHI as well as the NHS suggests that inequalities in access exist. Coverage by either VHI or subsystems is associated with higher use of services – especially ambulatory care – and better self-reported health status (Barros, Machado & de Almeida Simões, 2011). Evidence highlights that VHI exacerbates inequalities in use by enabling easier access to health care (Moreira & Barros, 2010) and also exacerbates socioeconomic inequity – not only is VHI mainly bought by middle- and high-income groups, these groups also benefit disproportionately from tax relief on private spending on health. In fact, until 2011, tax relief had been provided at the marginal rate of taxation and 30% of non-reimbursed expenses was tax deductible. Since 2011, tax relief has been limited to 10% of non-reimbursed expenses (up to a ceiling) to address the inequities described here.

Many aspects of the VHI market would benefit from greater scrutiny by regulators. For instance, more attention should be paid to the conditions of annual contract renewal, since insurers do not always announce changes in prices or coverage in advance. In addition, there are some products in the market that, despite being similar to health insurance (for example, insurance products associated with credit cards and dental health plans or products similar to those offered in some subsystems), are not covered by the jurisdiction of the Portuguese Insurance Institute (*Instituto de Seguros de Portugal*). Furthermore, in order to promote a transparent market and to protect consumers, prices, policy conditions and other relevant aspects of the VHI market should be monitored (this is not currently the case).

The future of VHI

Ongoing coverage reductions in public and private subsystems[1] aimed at promoting their financial sustainability may stimulate greater demand for VHI. The increasing expansion of private health care provision, on which VHI largely depends, is also likely to contribute to growth in the VHI market. For instance, the size of PPNs may increase, leading to more choice for VHI policyholders, and as many providers belong to large financial groups, these have an interest in extending their VHI activities. It is also possible that new insurers (for example, foreign companies) will enter the market and contribute to the reshaping of the VHI market. At the same time, the economic situation inevitably constrains the growth of the VHI market in the short term.

1 Such as ADSE (Direção-Geral de Protecção Social aos Funcionários e Agentes da Administração Pública), the largest public subsystem that covers civil servants, and PT ACS (Portugal Telecom – Associação de Cuidados de Saúde), one of the largest private subsystems, which emerged when the Portuguese public telecommunications company was privatized.

References

Assembleia da República (1992). *Constituição da República Portuguesa [Constitution of the Portuguese Republic]*. Lisbon, Assembleia da República.

Associação Portuguesa de Seguradores (2010). *Estatística do Seguro de Saúde 2009/2010 [Health Insurance Statistics 2009/2010]*. Lisbon, Associação Portuguesa de Seguradores.

Associação Portuguesa de Seguradores (2014). *Estatística do Seguro de Saúde 2013/2014 [Health Insurance Statistics 2013/2014]*. Lisbon, Associação Portuguesa de Seguradores.

Autoridade da Concorrência (2004). *Decisão da Autoridade da Concorrência sobre a venda do sector segurador do BCP à Caixa Seguros, Processo nº28/2004 [Decision of the Competition Authority about the sale of the BCP insurance sector to Caixa Seguros, Process No. 28/2004]*. Lisbon, Autoridade da Concorrência.

Barros P, de Almeida Simões J (2007). Portugal: health system review. *Health Systems in Transition*, 9(5):1–140.

Barros P, Machado S, de Almeida Simões J (2011). Portugal: health system review. *Health Systems in Transition*, 13(4):1–156.

Comissão para a Sustentabilidade do Financiamento do Serviço Nacional de Saúde (2007). *Relatório da "Comissão para a Sustentabilidade do Financiamento do Serviço Nacional de Saúde". Despacho conjunto nº 296/2006 dos Ministérios das Finanças e da Administração Pública e da Saúde [Report of the "Commission for Sustainability of the National Health Service". Joint order No. 296/2006 of the Ministries of Finance, Public Administration and Health]*. Lisbon, Ministry of Health.

Companhia Portuguesa de Seguros de Saúde (2005). *Relatório do Conselho de Administração, Exercício de 2004 [Report of the Board of Directors, 2004]*. Lisbon, Médis.

Direcção-Geral do Orçamento (2007). *Conta Geral do Estado Direcção Geral do Orçamento.[General State Account – Directorate General for Budget].* Lisbon, Direcção-Geral do Orçamento.

INSA, INE (2007). *Inquérito Nacional de Saúde 2005/2006 [National Health Survey 2005/2006].* Lisbon, National Institute of Health Dr Ricardo Jorge and National Statistics Institute.

Instituto de Seguros de Portugal (2011). *Relatório do sector segurador e fundos de pensões 2010 [Report of the insurance sector and oension funds 2010].* Lisbon, Instituto de Seguros de Portugal.

Instituto de Seguros de Portugal (2012). *Estatísticas de Seguros 2011 [Statistics of insurance 2011].* Lisbon, Instituto de Seguros de Portugal.

Martins R (2006). *SNS e seguradoras de saúde – a coabitação real. [SNS and health insurers – the real actual cohabitation].* Lisbon, Especial Seguros – Associação Portuguesa de Seguradores.

Moreira S, Barros P (2010). Double health insurance coverage and health care utilisation: evidence from quantile regression. *Health Economics*, 19(9):1075–1092.

Nunes D (2006). Seguros de saúde: Ter ou não ter? [Health insurance: to have or not to have?]. *Prémio*, III:9–13.

Thomson S, Mossialos E (2009). *Private health insurance in the European Union.* Final report prepared for the European Commission, Directorate General for Employment, Social Affairs and Equal Opportunities. London and Brussels, LSE Health and Social Care, London School of Economics and Political Science and European Commission.

WHO (2016). Global Health Expenditure Database (GHED) [online database]. Geneva, WHO (http://www.who.int/health-accounts/ghed/en/, accessed 5 April 2016).

26
Romania

Victor Olsavszky

Health system context

The health financing mix

In 2014, public spending accounted for 80.8% of total spending on health, with OOP payments and VHI accounting for 18.9% and 0.1% respectively (WHO, 2016). Informal payments appear to be a significant feature of the health system and are estimated to account for over 40% of total OOP spending (Belli, 2003; World Bank, 2011).

Entitlement to publicly financed health care and gaps in coverage

Publicly financed health coverage is mandatory and covers the whole population. The publicly financed benefits package offered by the National Health Insurance Fund is considered to be comprehensive. Dental care is the main area of care not publicly covered (Vlădescu, Scîntee & Olsavszky, 2008). User charges are mainly applied to prescription medicines and inpatient care, with some exemption for vulnerable groups, pregnant women and children.

Almost all ambulatory care is provided by private providers who can be freely contracted by any patient or third-party payer. The few private hospitals in operation tend to have better infrastructure and are perceived to be more patient-friendly. Differences in quality of care across public and private providers have not been assessed but are unlikely to be significant since the same doctors work in both sectors, although up-to-date medical technologies may be more prevalent in private hospitals.

Overview of the VHI market

Market origins, aims and role

According to Law 95/2006 (see Table 26.1), VHI can play a *complementary* and a *supplementary* role. However, the VHI market mainly plays a supplementary role. In the late 1990s, subscriptions (contracts for health services with providers) were popular among many employers, especially among international companies, who offered them as employment perks. This market grew alongside the development of private provision offering better quality compared to public provision. Subscriptions were organized by private providers, who offered treatment through their own facilities or through contracted providers, including state-owned or state-financed providers. Following the passing of the 2006 law, the subscription system continued to play a role, but its take-up has remained at the 2004 level because coverage of publicly financed health services grew once the NHIF was allowed to contract both public and private providers.

Types of plan available

VHI plans mainly offer access to superior accommodation in hospital, choice of provider and private care (supplementary cover). Premiums and policy conditions are not regulated and are linked to health status.

Why do people buy VHI?

Possible reasons for buying VHI include access to more patient-friendly and (perceived) better-quality services, cover of extra charges in private hospitals, and a means of avoiding informal payments in public hospitals. Some people obtain VHI cover as an employment benefit.

Who buys VHI?

A typical person purchasing VHI cover would be under 45–50 years old, better educated, with a higher income, in paid employment (typically working for a multinational or large national corporation) or self-employed, and living in an urban area. VHI can be purchased individually, or by employers as a health benefit for their employees. There are no available data on the share of the population with VHI or on the share of individual versus employer-based VHI cover (Vlădescu, Scîntee & Olsavszky, 2008).

Since 2006 (Law 95/2006), to be eligible for VHI, applicants must first pay their contributions to the statutory health insurance scheme for the basic package of services (Vlădescu, Scîntee & Olsavszky, 2008). Payment of these contributions can be easily verified by using a person's NHI card (introduced in 2015) to check an online database.

Who sells VHI?

VHI is offered by 12 commercial insurers. The NHIF can in theory also offer VHI but its actual role in the VHI market is marginal. VHI forms a very small part of the overall insurance market, but its share has grown in recent years (Insurance Supervisory Commission, 2010).

Insurer relations with providers

Insurers contract selected providers and pay them on a FFS basis. Integration of insurers and providers is rare.

Public policy towards VHI

The Ministry of Health and the Insurance Supervisory Commission regulate the activity of commercial VHI companies (Vlădescu, Scîntee & Olsavszky, 2008). The Commission publishes annual reports on the activity and evolution of the insurance market. These reports are the only source of information about the VHI market. Development and regulation of the VHI market is described in Table 26.1. The 2006 law provides the legislative framework for VHI but does not cover the following areas: occupational health, work-related accidents and health care subscriptions (subscriptions are not regulated).

Debates and challenges

Although the VHI market is very small, one of the challenges it raises is the potential to skew the distribution of NHIF resources in favour of the mainly higher-income people with VHI. This is because anybody can freely access any NHIF-contracted provider: if VHI policyholders obtain treatment from an NHIF-contracted provider, the insurer has no incentive to reimburse the costs of that treatment and will only pay for improved ancillary services (for example, better accommodation, meals) or for services not covered by the NHIF.

Policy debate has mainly focused on ways of expanding the VHI market. National conferences on VHI that took place between 2007 and 2009[1] identified the comprehensive

1 The conferences were organized by Media XPRIMM, a press, public relations and events group that specializes in insurance (http://www.xprimm.ro).

Table 26.1 *Development and regulation of the VHI market in Romania, 1995–2015*

Year	Policy	Key measures/effects on VHI
1995	Law 136/1995 on insurance and reinsurance	Sets the legal framework
2000	Law 32/2000 on insurance activities and supervision of insurance plans	Sets the legal framework and regulates relations between the insured and insurers
2004	Private Health Insurance Law (No. 212)	The implementation procedures for this law were never elaborated; it was replaced by Chapter 10 of Law 95/2006
2006	Chapter 10 of Law 95/2006 on Health Care Reform entitled *Voluntary health insurance*	Defines VHI; people must pay their statutory health insurance contribution (for the NHIF benefits package) to be able to apply for VHI cover
2007	Methodological norms of 22 February 2007 on VHI	Regulate the relationship between the insurer and the insured
2006	Law 343/2006 to modify and add to Law 571/2003 regarding the fiscal code	Introduces a tax deduction of €200 per year for all insurance plans purchased (not only for VHI)
2015	Law 571/2003 on the fiscal code and Government Decision 20/14.01.2015 on methodological norms	Introduces a separate tax deduction of €250 per year for VHI. Tax deduction for other insurance plans is now €400 per year

Source: Author.

nature of publicly financed health coverage, including the relatively limited extent of user charges, as a major barrier to VHI market development. However, it is interesting to note two things. First, publicly financed access to dental care is very limited and no VHI plans cover dental care as yet. Second, user charges do apply to medicines, but again, no insurer is willing to offer a VHI plan that covers user charges for medicines due to the lack of control over prescriptions and the possibility of fraud. In 2013, the Ministry of Health put forward new proposals for the publicly financed benefits package with the aim of reducing the scope of these benefits and introducing more user charges to limit public spending and expand the VHI market. At the time of writing, the proposal was under public discussion.

In 2012, the Ministry of Health submitted a more radical health care reform proposal for public debate (perhaps motivated by imminent elections). Its proposed new law would introduce competition for NHIF benefits, allowing private insurers to take over regional branches of the NHIF (and offer both NHIF benefits and VHI) and allowing people to choose their insurer. The NHIF would provide supervision, norms (policy) and risk equalization. However, following mass protests over austerity measures introduced in 2010, the government was forced to resign in 2012 and this proposal failed.

The future of VHI

Public debate on VHI continues. Various stakeholders would like to see the VHI market expanded based on the widespread conviction among health care providers and some opinion leaders that VHI will improve the financing of the health system. However, there is less agreement on how this should happen. After discussion about the new health care law was dropped, the only option for stimulating the VHI market seems to be the Ministry of Health's 2013 initiative to reduce the scope and depth of publicly financed health coverage. So far, this possibility has not generated discussion around implications for equitable access, equity in financing or financial protection for households, but these questions may surface in public debate.

References

Belli P (2003). *Formal and informal household spending on health: a multi-country study in central and eastern Europe.* Cambridge, MA, Harvard School of Public Health.

Insurance Supervisory Commission (2010). *Annual Reports on the Romanian insurance market and the insurance supervision.* Bucharest, Insurance Supervisory Commission (http://www.csa-isc.ro/publicatii/rapoarte-anuale/rapoarte-anuale, accessed 2 December 2015).

Vlădescu C, Scîntee G, Olsavszky V (2008). Romania: health system review. *Health Systems in Transition,* 10(3):1–172.

WHO (2016). Global Health Expenditure Database (GHED) [online database]. Geneva, WHO (http://www.who.int/health-accounts/ghed/en/, accessed 5 April 2016).

World Bank (2011). *Romania Functional Review: health sector.* Final report. Washington, DC, World Bank (http://www-wds.worldbank.org/external/default/WDSContentServer/WDSP/IB/2012/12/10/000425962_20121210160554/Rendered/PDF/NonAsciiFileName0.pdf, accessed 22 November 2013).

27 Russian Federation

Elena Potapchik

Health system context

The health financing mix

In 2014, public spending accounted for 52.2% of total spending on health, OOP payments for 45.8% and VHI for 1.7% (WHO, 2016).

Entitlement to publicly financed health care and gaps in coverage

Russian citizens have a constitutional right (Article 41 of the Constitution) to access medical care provided in state and municipal medical facilities free of charge. In accordance with the Federal Law on Mandatory Health Insurance (2010), publicly financed health coverage is available to all Russian citizens, foreign citizens permanently or temporarily living in the Russian Federation and people who have the right to medical care in accordance with the federal law on refugees.

The scope of the publicly financed benefits package excludes outpatient medicines (except for certain population groups), dental care (except for children and some privileged groups), cosmetic surgery, medical prostheses including dentures (except for privileged groups) and rehabilitation in institutions other than those approved by the Ministry of Health. User charges are not applied to services in the publicly financed benefits package.

Overview of the VHI market

Market origins, aims and role

VHI appeared in 1991. Originally, it was assumed that VHI would cover services excluded from the publicly financed benefits package. However, VHI plays mainly a *supplementary* role (providing access to better facilities and offering better conditions) and a minor *complementary* role, covering dental care.

Types of plan available

Several VHI plans are available. The majority of plans cover outpatient care, while a minority of plans cover inpatient care – about 10% of all policies (2009 data) (Expert RA, 2011). There are no VHI plans for outpatient medicines, even though outpatient medicines are generally not publicly covered (only some population groups receive them free of charge or at a discount).

Why do people buy VHI?

Employers purchase VHI for employees as an employment perk to attract better staff, reduce the number of working days lost because of sick leave and lower staff turnover. In 2009, an increase in the employee medical expenses ceiling (including purchasing VHI policies), from 3 to 6% of gross wages, created incentives for purchasing VHI among small and medium-sized businesses. Tax relief (through a tax deduction) is also available for people who have paid up to Russian ruble (RUB) 120 000 per year for health care, including VHI premiums.

Who buys VHI?

The VHI market is dominated by corporate plans and take-up is heavily concentrated in the Moscow area. About 95% of insurance premiums are paid by employers. The individual VHI market is very small and accounts for about 5% of premium income (2010 data) (Expert RA, 2012). VHI policies are mainly purchased by large businesses. At the same time, in 2010, only 40% of all business entities had VHI.[1]

Who sells VHI?

According to data from the Expert RA rating agency, in 2010 there were about 350 insurers with a licence to sell VHI, some of which are only allowed to sell mandatory health insurance or VHI (keeping both lines of business separate). All insurers are private and VHI is carried out on a profit-making basis. The market is not very concentrated – the top five insurers had 45% of the market. Table 27.1 presents an overview of the top five insurers selling VHI.

Insurers can be grouped according to their strategy to attract customers: (1) subsidiaries of financial services holding companies (examples include SOGAS, which has the highest market share among VHI providers, JASO and Energogarant), who provide cover for employees of affiliated companies; (2) insurers providing mandatory and voluntary cover (examples are Rosno and ZAO MAKS), who are already well known to people and have relations with health care providers under the mandatory system; and (3) general insurers (examples include Ingosstrakh, Rosgosstrakh and UralSib) (Expert RA, undated a).

Insurer relations with providers

The relations between insurers and providers are regulated by contracts, with prices subject to negotiation and benefits provided in kind. Because privately provided services are underdeveloped (around 2% of hospitals and 20% of outpatient facilities), VHI-covered services are mainly provided by public facilities belonging to

1 Data from a special sociological survey of enterprise directors carried out by the Higher School of Economics in 2010 as part of the project *Monitoring of economic developments in health sector* (http://www.hse.ru).

Table 27.1 *Overview of the five largest insurers selling VHI in Russia, 2011*

Insurer	Premium income (RUB, in millions)	Market share (%)	Claims as a share of premium income (%)	Change in premiums 2010–2011 (%)
SOGAS	17 797	18.3	94.5	12.1
Alyans	7194	7.4	76.3	4.2
JASO	6754	7.1	85.2	9.9
Ingosstrakh	6124	6.3	79.3	16.6
Rosgosstrakh	5771	5.9	55.2	68.8

Source: Expert RA (2012).

the Ministry of Health provider network or a parallel network of facilities belonging to other ministries (for example, the Ministry of Finance or the Ministry of Defence) (Popovich et al., 2011). Some insurers have established their own facility networks.

Public policy towards VHI

There is no special regulation of the VHI market. From 1991 to 2011, VHI was regulated by the Health Insurance Law as well as the Civil Code and the Federal Law on the Organization of Insurance in the Russian Federation. Guidelines applicable to all types of insurance are issued by the Federal Service of Financial Market. In 2010, a new Federal Law on Mandatory Health Insurance was adopted but it did not mention VHI. VHI is encouraged through tax incentives aimed at employers and individuals.

Debates and challenges

The recent global economic crisis has affected the VHI market. In 2009, the market stagnated in terms of premium income because businesses reduced their staff numbers and health budgets. In 2010, the VHI market started growing again (Figure 27.1), largely due to premium inflation rather than new subscribers (Expert RA, 2012).

Figure 27.1 *Trends in VHI premium income in the Russian Federation, 2007–2012*

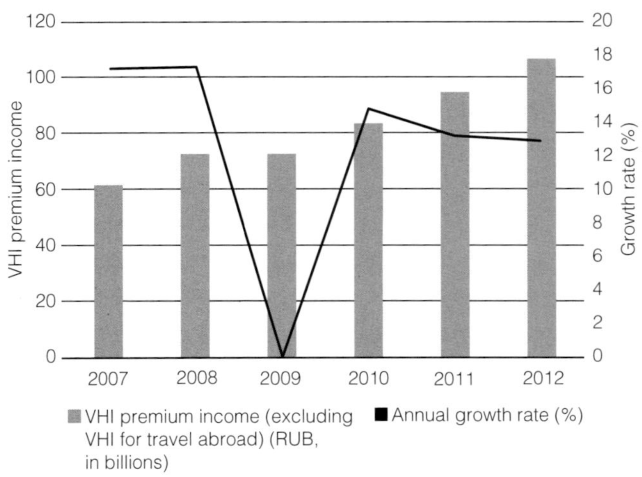

Source: Expert RA (2012).

VHI coverage is very unequally distributed across the country. Moscow and the Moscow region account for 85% of total VHI premium income (Federal State Statistics Service, 2011). There is no VHI in 45% of regions and no VHI or VHI is very minor (premium income less than RUB 10 million) in 55% of regions. As almost all corporate clients in Moscow and the Moscow region are already insured, the scope for further development of the VHI market lies mainly in other regions.

The VHI market could also be expanded by extending coverage to small and medium-sized enterprises. The increase in corporate tax relief introduced in 2009 did not affect small and medium-sized enterprises during the economic crisis but had a positive influence on their VHI take-up later on. At the same time, the rise in the employer payroll contribution for mandatory health coverage from 3.1 to 5.1% in 2011 might have offset the effect of the increase in corporate tax relief.

Low levels of individual VHI coverage may be explained by the limited purchasing power of the majority of the population, the general lack of an insurance culture, the high cost of VHI policies, the fact that insurers do not favour individual policies (Expert RA, 2012) and the fact that most facilities are owned by the State or municipalities and there is little scope for private provision.

Important stakeholders and the main players in the VHI market argue that the following two measures would contribute to VHI market growth: first, there should be a clear separation between mandatory health insurance and VHI; second, special legislation should be developed to regulate the VHI market – for example, insurers would like to be able to offer cover of user charges for mandatory benefits. However, the Ministry of Health and the Federal Mandatory Health Insurance Fund are opposed to this idea as mixing public and private financing in this way may be difficult for people to understand and may undermine transparency (Expert RA, undated b).

The future of VHI

It seems that the VHI market is close to saturation and will not grow unless insurers can develop new products that are cheaper and more tailored to individual demand and a strategy of marketing VHI in regions beyond Moscow. One of the versions of the *Concept for the Development of Healthcare to 2020* published on the Ministry of Health's website (https://www.

rosminzdrav.ru/) stated that, in the absence of exacting regulation, private sources of financing (OOP payments and VHI) reduced access and lowered the quality of publicly financed health care. Insurers interpreted this as an unwillingness on the part of the state to support the development of VHI. The government is currently paying much more attention to mandatory health insurance than to VHI development and is focused on implementing the newly adopted Law on Mandatory Health Insurance that came into force in 2011.

References

Expert RA (2011). *2009 data from Expert RA's Bulletin VHI market and rating of medical providers*. 10 March 2011. Moscow, Expert RA.

Expert RA (2012). *2011 data from Expert RA's Bulletin Health insurance*. 14 March 2012. Moscow, Expert RA.

Expert RA (undated a). *The current state of VHI in Russia*. Moscow, Expert RA (http://www.raexpert.ru, accessed January 2011).

Expert RA (undated b). *Health insurance: VHI and MHI synergy*. Moscow, Expert RA (http://www.raexpert.ru, accessed January 2011).

Federal State Statistics Service (2011). *Insurance service market in 2010*. Bulletin No. 7 (178) 2011. Moscow, Federal State Statistics Service.

Popovich L et al. (2011). Russian Federation: health system review. *Health Systems in Transition*, 13(7):1–190.

WHO (2016). Global Health Expenditure Database (GHED) [online database]. Geneva, WHO (http://www.who.int/health-accounts/ghed/en/, accessed 5 April 2016).

28
Slovakia

Peter Pazitny and Peter Balik

Health system context

The health financing mix

In 2014, public spending accounted for 72.5% of total spending on health, while OOP payments accounted for 22.5% (VHI does not appear in the national health accounts data) (WHO, 2016).

Entitlement to publicly financed health care and gaps in coverage

The health system provides universal coverage for a broad range of benefits. User charges were introduced in 2003 and abolished several times. Currently, they are only applied to emergency care visits (€1.99 per visit), outpatient prescriptions and spa treatments. Publicly financed health coverage is offered by three autonomous, competing health insurers: the state-owned General Health Insurance Company (*Všeobecná zdravotná poisťovňa*, VšZP) (3.5 million insured), Dôvera (1.4 million) and Union Health Insurance Company (0.4 million). These insurers compete by providing additional benefits for different age groups (for example, eye care, vitamins, vaccinations, stays in spas and health resorts, use of sports facilities). Waiting times for elective procedures and patient complaints about the public system may indicate scope for the development of a VHI market.

Overview of the VHI market

Market origins, aims and role

VHI emerged in Slovakia in 2004 during the 2002–2006 reform period when competition among purchasers was introduced. It became part of the Health Insurers Act 581/2004 and was encouraged by the government. However, the VHI market is not well developed for two main reasons. First, the definition of the publicly financed benefits package is vague and user charges are limited. Second, the types of benefits for which patients pay OOP (medicines, prepaid programmes of private providers) are not attractive for insurers. When patients have to pay OOP, they choose a specific health care provider, with whom they have experience, rather than a VHI plan, which might not guarantee free choice of provider.

VHI mainly plays a *supplementary* role, covering, among other things, easier access to outpatient care or a higher standard of hospital room. (The popularity of these rooms is increasing, although their number is still low.) Fees for high-standard rooms range from €5 to €50 per night. People do not feel it is necessary to purchase VHI plans covering such benefits.

Types of plan available

VHI plans mainly cover preventive care, higher-standard inpatient amenities and easier access to outpatient treatment. Coverage may include: preventive check-ups; simplified booking of doctors' appointments through call centres; daily cash benefits during hospitalization; higher-standard room in hospitals; eye and dental care; and rehabilitation. Although eye care, dental care and rehabilitation are included in the publicly financed benefits package, VHI plans assure a higher standard, easier access to treatments and shorter waiting times.

Why do people buy VHI?

Interest in purchasing VHI plans is very limited. In 2011, only 51 000 VHI polices were sold (see Table 28.1) among a population of over 5 million people. The existence of long waiting times makes the underdevelopment of VHI particularly interesting, as jumping waiting lists is one of the main driving forces for purchasing VHI cover in other countries. However, outpatient care is readily accessible in the private sector and inpatient care in the public system can be accessed through informal payments.

Table 28.1 *Number and value of VHI policies in Slovakia, 2008–2011*

	2008	2009	2010	2011
Number of VHI policies	46 282	51 136	51 027	50 837
Total premium income (€ thousands)	1682	1812	2060	2326
Average annual premium per contract (€ per year)	36.3	35.4	40.4	45.7

Source: National Bank of Slovakia (2012).

Who buys VHI?

Information on who buys VHI is scarce. According to anecdotal evidence, VHI is usually purchased by employers for their employees as an employment perk.

Who sells VHI?

VHI is offered by three commercial insurers which are independent from the three health insurers providing publicly financed health coverage: Union (owned by Achmea, a multinational insurance company that also operates in the publicly financed health insurance market), Wüstenrot and UNIQA (also multinational companies).

In 2005, an exclusive VHI contract was negotiated between the state-owned VšZP and the commercial insurer Union, enabling those insured in VšZP to purchase VHI plans from Union at a 10% discount. A similar partnership agreement was later negotiated between Union and the Union Health Insurance Company (two separate companies; the agreement was for a 50% discount) after the latter entered the health insurance market. The exclusive contract with VšZP has ended.

In 2006, only Union offered VHI cover. Other subsequent entrants to the market (Generali, UNIQA) focused on specific VHI products, such as daily cash benefits for hospital stays. Today, the VHI market remains highly concentrated.

Insurer relations with providers

Insurers are not vertically integrated with health care providers. People with VHI cover can be treated in public and private health care facilities. Providers are paid on a FFS basis and fees are negotiated. VHI policyholders make payments directly to providers and are reimbursed afterwards. No user charges are required; however, an upper ceiling on benefits may be applicable for specific treatments and insurance products.

Public policy towards VHI

The VHI market is regulated by the National Bank of Slovakia and the Healthcare Surveillance Authority. The key piece of legislation in the VHI market is the Health Insurers Act 580/2004, which came into force on 1 January 2005 and made a distinction between publicly financed health coverage and VHI.

Debates and challenges

VHI plays a marginal role and does not command much interest in the debate about health care reform, even though this debate tends to focus on financing challenges. The main reasons for this are the limited scope for developing VHI due to the comprehensive scope and vague definition of the publicly financed benefits package, the low level of user charges and the deep-rooted perception among the population that health care should be free of charge.

Before the 2012 parliamentary elections, several political parties advocated reducing the scope of the publicly financed benefits package and launching a more complex system of VHI for higher-standard services. However, the elected social-democratic government is not supportive of private financing of the health system.

The future of VHI

No major changes to the VHI market are expected before elections to be held in 2016.

References

National Bank of Slovakia (2012) [website]. (http://www.nbs.sk/sk/titulna-stranka, accessed 22 November 2015).

WHO (2016). Global Health Expenditure Database (GHED) [online database]. Geneva, WHO (http://www.who.int/health-accounts/ghed/en/, accessed 5 April 2016).

29
Slovenia

Anja Milenkovic Kramer

Health system context

The health financing mix

In 2014, public spending accounted for 71.7% of total spending on health, while VHI and OOP payments accounted for 14.1% and 12.1% of total spending on health respectively, making Slovenia one of the three largest VHI markets in Europe (WHO, 2016).

Entitlement to publicly financed health care and gaps in coverage

Publicly financed health coverage is near universal and offers entitlement to a broad range of benefits. However, user charges are applied to almost all publicly financed health services, in the form of coinsurance, with coinsurance rates ranging from 5 to 90% of the service price (UL RS, 20/2010). Children are exempt from paying user charges (Health Care and Health Insurance Act, 1992; ZZVZZ, 1992).

Overview of the VHI market

Market origins, aims and role

VHI was introduced in 1993 to diversify sources of health financing and to keep public spending on health low. VHI has always played an explicitly *complementary* role, covering user charges for publicly financed health benefits. The comprehensive and near-universal cover provided by mandatory health insurance and VHI leaves little room for the development of other VHI products (Milenkovic Kramer, 2009).

Types of plan available

Complementary VHI plans cover user charges. Insurers are required to cover user charges for all publicly financed health services. Complementary VHI premiums are set at a flat rate and are the same for everyone covered by the same insurer. Adult dependants require their own policies (Stanovnik & Turk, 2009). Children are exempt from user charges and so do not require complementary VHI. There is a system of penalties in place for adults who do not purchase complementary VHI as soon as they become liable for user charges. For each complete year (12 months) of not having VHI, the penalty is equal to 3% of the premium. The maximum penalty is 80% of the premium (see Table 29.2).

Other VHI plans cover complementary and supplementary benefits that are not publicly financed, including: some services offered by private providers (specialist treatments, diagnostic tests and pain-reducing therapies); above-standard amenities in hospitals and health spas; more elaborate medical aids; medicines involving zero or 10% reimbursement only; above-standard dental care; cosmetic surgery; and cash benefits for sick leave, inpatient stays or nursing an adult family member or a preschool child (Adriatic Slovenica, 2012; Merkur, 2012; Triglav Health Insurance Company, 2012; Vzajemna, 2012).

Why do people buy VHI?

Complementary VHI plans covering user charges are purchased by almost everyone who is obliged to pay user charges. Some argue that such a high level of take-up indicates people's willingness to pay privately for health care (Josar & Toth, 2001; Toth, 2003). Others argue it is because of the high level of user charges required for most publicly financed health services (Keber, 2003; Ministry of Health, 2003). The introduction of penalties for late take-up of complementary cover in 2005 (see Table 29.2) is likely to have sustained the high take-up rate. No information is available on why people decide to buy other VHI products.

Who buys VHI?

Almost all premium income in the VHI market (99%) comes from complementary VHI covering user charges (Cotman, 2005; Keber, 2003). In 2010, user charges VHI plans covered 83.5% of the population aged over 18 (Adriatic Slovenica, 2010; STAT, 2011; Triglav Health Insurance Company, 2010; Vzajemna, 2010). The market for other forms of VHI is marginal and has not been subject to much analysis.

Who sells VHI?

When VHI was introduced in 1993, two entities sold complementary VHI plans covering user charges: Vzajemna (a mutual specializing in health) and Adriatic Slovenica (a commercial joint-stock company offering a range of insurance products). Vzajemna started selling VHI as an integral part of the Health Insurance Institute of Slovenia (HIIS), the statutory body responsible for purchasing publicly financed health coverage. In 1999, following amendments to the Health Care and Health Insurance Act, the HIIS separated its mandatory health insurance and VHI business, leading to the creation of Vzajemna, which was established as an independent, specialized, mutual health insurance company.

Two more recent entrants include Triglav (a limited liability company that started selling VHI in 2004 and specializes in health) and Merkur (a general insurer that entered the VHI market in 2007 but does not sell complementary cover of user charges and therefore plays a negligible role) (Table 29.1).

Table 29.1 *Market shares of VHI companies in Slovenia, 2010*

Company	Market share (%)
Vzajemna	58.55
Adriatic Slovenica	23.77
Triglav	17.66
Merkur	0.03

Sources: Adriatic Slovenica (2010); Merkur (2010); Triglav Health Insurance Company (2010); Vzajemna (2010).

Insurer relations with providers

Insurers offering complementary VHI for user charges simply reimburse user charges; there is no purchasing involved. For other VHI products, insurers may negotiate their own terms and prices with selected health care providers and reimburse them directly for services provided (Albreht et al., 2009; Stanovnik & Turk, 2009).

Public policy towards VHI

The development and regulation of the VHI market is presented chronologically in Table 29.2. Complementary VHI covering user charges is regulated by the Insurance

Table 29.2 *Development and regulation of VHI in Slovenia, 1992–2012*

1992	Health Care and Health Insurance Act (1992), Health Services Act (1992) and the Law on Pharmacies (1992) allow the introduction of private financing (VHI is introduced in 1993)
1999	Law Amending the Health Care and Health Insurance Act (1998) establishes Vzajemna as an independent legal entity that is completely separate from the Health Insurance Institute of Slovenia (HIIS)
2000	The Insurance Act (2000) declares that complementary VHI serves the public interest; risk equalization is allowed
2003	White Paper (2003) is published and a reform proposal by the Ministry of Health calls for the abolition of complementary VHI covering user charges
2004	The Insurance Act (2004) again announces the implementation of a risk adjustment mechanism. However, the mechanism was not implemented and risk-rated premiums continued to be allowed
2005	Law Amending the Health Care and Health Insurance Act (2005) introduces community-rated premiums for complementary VHI covering user charges, risk equalization in this part of the VHI market and penalties for late take-up of complementary VHI (for each 12 months of not having this cover, counting from the month when a person becomes liable for paying user charges, the premium increases by 3%, up to a maximum of 80%)
2005	High Court proceedings are initiated by Adriatic Slovenica (in October 2005) and Vzajemna (in December 2005) against the risk equalization scheme; Adriatic Slovenica argues that the scheme would result in higher average premiums and that would undermine competition by leading to a monopoly in the long run (Adriatic Slovenica, 2005); Vzajemna argues that the scheme does not account for differences in the health status of people insured by a particular company, putting companies on an unequal footing (Vzajemna, 2005); the court rules in the government's favour and confirms the legitimacy of the adopted risk equalization scheme
2006	Law Amending the Health Care and Health Insurance Act (2005) comes into force; in response to the introduction of community rating, VHI premiums rise by 18%; an additional 5% increase in premiums is attributed to rising health care costs (Smrekar, 2006)
2006	In June Vzajemna complains to the European Commission about the following shortcomings of complementary VHI covering user charges (Rednak & Smrekar, 2007): ▪ insurers offering complementary VHI are required to be included in the equalization scheme ▪ the Insurance Supervision Agency must be informed about any revision of terms for complementary VHI covering user charges; any increase in these premiums must be confirmed in writing by a certified actuary and can be done only under supervision of the Agency ▪ premiums for complementary VHI covering user charges must be equal for all subscribers of a particular insurer and contracts should not be shorter than one year ▪ insurers cannot cancel a complementary VHI contract unless the policyholder does not pay premiums ▪ revenue raised through complementary VHI can only be used for the implementation of this scheme; half of all profits generated must be used for implementing complementary VHI ▪ prior to entering the complementary VHI market, an insurer must receive written approval from the Minister of Health
2007	In March, the EC issues an official warning regarding Slovenia's health insurance legislation. The government had argued that complementary VHI covering user charges was, despite its voluntary nature, an integral part of the statutory health insurance scheme and therefore a matter of public interest justifying government intervention to protect the general interest. The EC rejects this, arguing that complementary VHI did not present a complete or partial alternative to the compulsory statutory health insurance scheme as it covered user charges and could not, on the basis of EU legislation, be regarded as part of the compulsory social security system (Rednak & Smrekar, 2007)
2011	Legislation on complementary VHI is not amended and the EC refers Slovenia to the ECJ (European Commission, 2011)
2011	The Ministry of Health's new reform proposal *Upgrading the health care system by 2020* calls for the abolition of user charges and the adoption of a newly defined, publicly financed benefits package (Ministry of Health, 2011)
2012	Act on Balancing Public Financing (2012) shifts costs from public to private funds and is followed by an increase of 13% in premiums for complementary VHI covering user charges
2012	The ECJ confirms that Slovenia's VHI legislation is not fully in line with non-life insurance directives; this ruling concerns the use of profits and systematic notification and prior approval, among other things; it does not concern risk equalization

Source: Author.

Supervision Agency (increases in premiums) and the Ministry of Health (market entry, approval of initial premiums, risk adjustment process). It does not benefit from any tax subsidies. The market for complementary VHI covering user charges is subject to relatively tight regulation. Some of these regulations have been found to breach EU rules, as discussed further on (ECJ, 2012). However, rules intended to promote efficiency and access to VHI have not been contested at all (community rating of premiums and penalties for late take-up of complementary cover) or have been contested but found to be in line with national and EU rules (the risk equalization scheme).

Debates and challenges

Public debate on VHI mainly focuses on issues such as the range of services included in the publicly financed benefits package; the high level of user charges for most of these services; the regressive impact on health system financing of community-rated VHI premiums (in contrast to income-related contributions for publicly financed health coverage); the shifting of costs from public to private sources achieved by increasing user charges for publicly financed health coverage and moving medicines from the positive list to intermediate and negative lists.

The first major development in the VHI market was the separation of compulsory health insurance and VHI schemes, which took place in 1999 according to the Law Amending the Health Care and Health Insurance Act (1998). The HIIS established a mutual insurer, Vzajemna, as a separate entity for providing voluntary health insurance. There were no further changes until 2003, when the Ministry of Health proposed abolishing VHI in favour of a new income-related contribution, to enhance solidarity in the system – an idea that was dropped following elections in 2004 (Ministry of Health, 2003).

In March 2006, a new set of reforms introduced tighter regulation of complementary VHI covering user charges, to promote access and affordability through the use of community-rated premiums, a risk equalization scheme and penalties for late take-up of complementary cover (Health Care and Health Insurance Act 2006). Adriatic Slovenica and Vzajemna challenged the risk equalization scheme in the Constitutional Court and, eventually, at the EU level, claiming that it distorted competition in the VHI market (Adriatic Slovenica, 2005; Rednak & Smrekar, 2007; Vzajemna, 2005). All disputes were rejected by the Constitutional Court and the risk equalization scheme remains in place (Constitutional Court, 2006).

The Health Care and Health Insurance Act (2006) introduced a number of controls on VHI business unrelated to ensuring access to VHI, including requiring health insurers from other countries to establish a branch office in Slovenia, controls over the use of profits, systematic notification of product changes and prior approval of premium increases. In 2011, the EC found these rules to be in breach of EU competition and free movement rules (specifically, the first and third non-life insurance directives) (European Commission, 2011). In response, the Ministry of Health planned to bring Slovenian regulation in line with EU rules, but reform efforts were halted due to early elections held in December 2011 and the Commission subsequently referred Slovenia to the ECJ (EU Court Rules, 2012; STA, 2011). In 2012, the ECJ found that Slovenia had failed to transpose the non-life insurance directives correctly (ECJ, 2012). This ruling does not apply to the risk equalization scheme.

The public–private mix in health financing and the issue of complementary VHI had not been seriously addressed before the publication, in 2011, of the government's programme *Upgrading the health care system by 2020*. The new reform proposed by the Ministry of Health envisaged the abolition of VHI covering user charges and other changes to the publicly financed benefits package (the latter had not been included in the 2003 proposal and were regarded as a significant innovation) (Tajnikar & Došenovic Bonca, 2011). The newly defined, publicly financed benefits package was to include essential health services accessible to all citizens within recommended waiting periods and free of charges, with VHI playing only a supplementary role (Ministry of Health, 2011). The December 2011 elections brought these reform efforts to a halt.

More recently, the financial and economic crisis has prompted several changes directly affecting VHI. The adoption of the Act on Balancing Public Finances (2012) increased user charges for some health services and medicines, shifting these costs to households and VHI. As a result, insurers immediately increased premiums for VHI covering user charges, which rose by an average of 13% in July 2012 (Dnevnik, 2012).

The future of VHI

Public debate, interventions by the EC, the shifting of costs from public to private sources and the issue of how best to regulate the market for complementary VHI covering user charges all point towards the need for some reform. Nevertheless, it is worth emphasizing the positive aspects of the role VHI plays. Although VHI premiums are regressive in comparison to the income-related contributions paid for publicly financed health coverage, placing a higher financial burden on poorer and larger households, the very high take-up of VHI covering user charges has meant that households are largely protected against the even more regressive and negative effects of OOP payments (Albreht et al., 2009). Given the current fiscal context and the potential for increased health spending in the future, private sources will continue to represent a vital source of health financing. So long as VHI remains accessible and affordable for all those who need it, it is preferable to OOP payments.

References

Adriatic Slovenica (2005). *Pobuda za oceno ustavnosti Zakona o spremembah in dopolnitvah zakona o zdravstvenem varstvu in zdravstvenem zavarovanju ZZVZZ, št. U-I-282/05-1, 10 October 2005 [Dispute put forward to Constitutional Court regarding the new Law on Health Care and Health Insurance Act, no. U-I-282/05-1, 10 October 2005]*. Ljubljana, Adriatic Slovenica.

Adriatic Slovenica (2010). *Annual Report 2010 and 2011*. Ljubljana, Adriatic Slovenica (http://www.as-skupina.si/financno-sredisce/letna-porocila, accessed 2 December 2015).

Adriatic Slovenica (2012) [website]. Ljubljana, Adriatic Slovenica (http://www.adriatic-slovenica.si, accessed 22 November 2015).

Albreht T et al. (2009). Slovenia: health system review. *Health Systems in Transition*, 11(3):1–168.

Constitutional Court (2006). *Odločba. Ocena ustavnosti in zakonitosti predpisov in drugih splošnih aktov [Decision. Assessment of the constitutionality and legality of regulations and other general acts]* (http://odlocitve.us-rs.si/sl/odlocitev/US25746?q=U-I-282%2F05, accessed 22 November 2015).

Cotman P (2005). *Slovenia, risk equalization scheme in the complementary health insurance*. Newsletter of the Association Internationale de la Mutualité (AIM) (extra issue). Brussels, AIM.

Dnevnik (2012). Dražje zavarovanje: Premije dopolnilnih zdravstvenih zavarovalnic od danes višje, [Insurance premium increase: premiums for complementary health insurance are higher from today]. *Dnevnik*, 1 July 2012.

ECJ (2012). Case C185/11 European Commission v Republic of Slovenia. Failure of a Member State to fulfil obligations – Direct insurance other than life assurance - Directives 73/239/EEC and 92/49/EEC – Incorrect and incomplete transposition. European Court Reports 2012 -00000 (http://eur-lex.europa.eu/legal-content/EN/TXT/?uri=CELEX:62011CJ0185, accessed 22 November 2015).

EU Court Rules (2012). *EU Court rules against Slovenia's top-up health insurance, 26.01.2012*. (https://english.sta.si/1719768/eu-court-rules-against-slovenias-top-up-health-insurance-adds, accessed 2 December 2015).

European Commission (2011). *Insurance: Slovenia referred to EU Court over complementary health insurance*. 16 February 2011. Brussels, European Commission (http://europa.eu/rapid/press-release_IP-11-181_en.htm?locale=en, accessed 2 December 2015).

Josar D, Toth M (2001). *Problematika dopolnilnih zdravstvenih zavarovanj in možnosti alternative [Problems of complementary health insurance and possible alternatives]*. 8 dnevi slovenskega zavarovalništva [8th Slovenian Insurance Days]. Portorož, Slovensko zavarovalno združenje [Slovenian Insurance Association].

Keber D. (2003). Utrjevanje vrednot in vzpodbujanje sprememb: Zdravstvena reforma 2003 [Strengthening values and encouraging changes: Health Reform 2003]. *Zdravstveni Vestnik*, 73:57–58.

Merkur (2010). *Annual Report 2010 and 2011*. Merkur Insurance Company. (http://www.merkur-zav.si/cms/beitrag/1009167/46643, accessed 2 December 2015).

Merkur (2012) [website]. Merkur Insurance Company (www.merkur-zav.si, accessed 22 November 2012).

Milenkovic Kramer A (2009). Slovenia. In: Thomson S, Mossialos E, eds. *Private health insurance in the European Union*. Final report prepared for the European Commission, Directorate General for Employment, Social Affairs and Equal Opportunities. London and Brussels, LSE Health and Social Care, London School of Economics and Political Science and European Commission:295–308.

Ministry of Health (2003). *Zdravstvena reforma. Pravičnost, dostopnost, kakovost, učinkovitost [White paper: Health Reform: justice, accessibility, quality, efficiency]*. Ljubljana, Ministry of Health.

Ministry of Health (2011). *Nadgradnja zdravstvenega sistema do leta 2020 [Upgrading the health care system by 2020]*. Ljubljana, Ministry of Health.

Rednak A, Smrekar T (2007). *Evropa žuga Sloveniji zaradi zdravstvenih zavarovanja [Europe is warning Slovenia on Health Insurance]*. Ljubljana, Finance.si.

STA (2011). Planet Siol.net [website] *Supporting the changes in health insurance*. (http://www.siol.net/novice/zdravje/2011/03/nadgradnjazdravstvenegasistemakonecrazprave.aspx, accessed 2 December 2015).

Stanovnik T, Turk E (2009). *Annual national report 2009 (pensions/health and long-term care): Slovenia*. On behalf of the European Commission DG Employment, Social Affairs and Equal Opportunities. Brussels, European Commission (http://www.socialprotection.eu/files_db/381/asisp_ANR09_Slovenia.pdf, accessed 22 November 2015).

STAT (2011). *Statistical yearbook 2011*. Ljubljana, Statistical Office of the Republic of Slovenia (http://www.stat.si/StatWeb/glavnanavigacija/podatki/publikacije/statisti%C4%8Dni-letopis?leto=2011, accessed 2 December 2015).

Tajnikar M, Došenovic Bonca P, (2011). Slovensko zavarovanje tretjič! Bomo zmogli narediti tudi skok ali bo tokrat ostalo le pri zaletu? [Slovenian insurance for the third time! Will we make the jump this time?]. *Delo Saturday supplement*, 4 June 2011.

Toth M (2003). *Zdravje, zdravstveno varstvo in zdravstveno zavarovanje [Health, health care, and health insurance]*. Ljubljana, Zavod za zdravstveno zavarovanje Slovenije.

Triglav Health Insurance Company (2010). *Annual Report 2010*. Koper, Triglav Health Insurance Company (http://www.zdravstvena.net/o-zavarovalnici/letna-porocila, accessed 2 December 2015).

Triglav Health Insurance Company (2012) [website]. Triglav Health Insurance Company (www.zdravstvena.net, accessed 22 November 2015)

UL RS, 20/2010 (2010). Sklep o spremembah Sklepa o določitvi odstotkov vrednosti zdravstvenih storitev, ki se zagotavljajo v obveznem zdravstvenem zavarovanju [Decision amending the decision on establishing percent of the value of health services covered by compulsory health insurance]. Official Gazette of the Republic of Slovenia no. 20/10] (https://www.uradni-list.si/1/content?id=96685#!/Sklep-o-spremembah-Sklepa-o-dolocitvi-odstotkov-vrednosti-zdravstvenih-storitev-ki-se-zagotavljajo-v-obveznem-zdravstvenem-zavarovanju, accessed 2 December 2015).

Vzajemna (2005). *Razširitev pobude za oceno ustavnosti določb ZZVZZ, št. U-I-277/05, 22 December 2005 [Dispute put forward to High Court regarding the new Health Care and Health Insurance Act no. U-I-277/05, 22 December 2005]*. Ljubljana, Vzajemna Mutual Health Insurance Company.

Vzajemna (2010). *Annual Report 2010*. Ljubljana, Vzajemna Mutual Health Insurance Company (https://www.vzajemna.si/sl/o-vzajemni/letna-porocila/, accessed 2 December 2015).

Vzajemna (2012) [website]. Ljubljana, Vzajemna Mutual Health Insurance Company d.v.z. (https://www.vzajemna.si, accessed 22 November 2015).

WHO (2016). Global Health Expenditure Database (GHED) [online database]. Geneva, WHO (http://www.who.int/health-accounts/ghed/en/, accessed 5 April 2016).

ZZVZZ (1992). *Zakon o zdravstvenem varstvu in zdravstvenem zavarovanju [Health Care and Health Insurance Act]*, Official Gazette of the Republic of Slovenia no. 9/92. Ljubljana, Government of Slovenia.

30
Spain

Joan Costa-i-Font

Health system context

The health financing mix

In 2014, public spending accounted for 70.9% of total spending on health, with OOP payments and VHI accounting for 24 and 4.4%, respectively (WHO, 2016). The public share has remained stable since 2000. Between 1981 and 2002, health competences within the national health system (*Sistema Nacional de la Salud*, SNS) were progressively devolved to the country's regions (known as autonomous communities).

Entitlement to publicly financed health care and gaps in coverage

Population coverage by the SNS is almost universal (99.5%) and guarantees quite a comprehensive benefits package to all citizens. Entitlement is independent of employment status and personal wealth (García-Armesto et al., 2010). Civil servants are entitled to choose to have their health care purchased by entities other than the SNS, such as the Mutual Fund for State Civil Servants, and around 2 million people opt for this alternative. They continue to pay taxes like everyone else and the SNS pays private insurers a capitation fee to cover their health care costs. Those with this form of private coverage are expected to use private providers only and receive a special health card, different from the SNS health card.

In 2010, new policies were put in place that reduced access to publicly financed health benefits: user charges were extended to more medicines, access to health care for adult migrants was reduced and the allocation of transfers from the central state to the regions was tightened, leading to spending cuts which have been more severe in some regions (for example, in Catalonia). The latter may have had an impact on the perception among the population of the quality of publicly financed health services and thus the desirability of VHI.

Overview of the VHI market

Market origins, aims and role

The role of VHI in Spain is mainly *supplementary*. It emerged during Franco's dictatorship (1939–1975), was available (as a privilege) to civil servants and developed with the emergence of mutual associations that covered the same goods and services as those covered by the underfunded publicly financed system. In 1986, a range of social insurance-type schemes was consolidated into a national tax-funded system (SNS). Since then, insurers have specialized in providing better quality elective treatment, offering faster access, enhanced consumer choice and better amenities.

Types of plan available

About 81% of all VHI policies in Spain are of the *benefits in kind* type (García-Armesto et al., 2010). Most policies provide faster access to elective treatment from a specific network of physicians and hospitals. Coverage may also include domiciliary care and dental care, depending on the policy purchased. Average premiums for a basic VHI policy range from €35 to €70 per month, depending on the insurer. Individuals with chronic conditions are excluded from VHI, as are those suffering from alcoholism and AIDS, among other things.

Just over half of all VHI policies are purchased through employer group plans (22% through the public administration and 35% through the private sector); the remaining 43% purchase individual policies (IDIS Foundation, 2013).

Why do people buy VHI?

VHI covers around 13% of the population, although this share varies widely across regions depending on household incomes and the availability of private health care provision (IDIS Foundation, 2013). The main reason for purchasing VHI may be the limited flexibility of the publicly financed system to respond to individual preferences regarding quality of care. VHI provides people with prepaid access to private providers and to above-standard amenities in public facilities.

Who buys VHI?

Group policies are concentrated among people working in large international corporations. Individual policies are usually bought by people with higher incomes, people who regard SNS care to be of lower quality than care covered by VHI plans and people who are slightly more risk averse

Figure 30.1 *Private health care expenditure (VHI and OOP) in Spain by region, 2012*

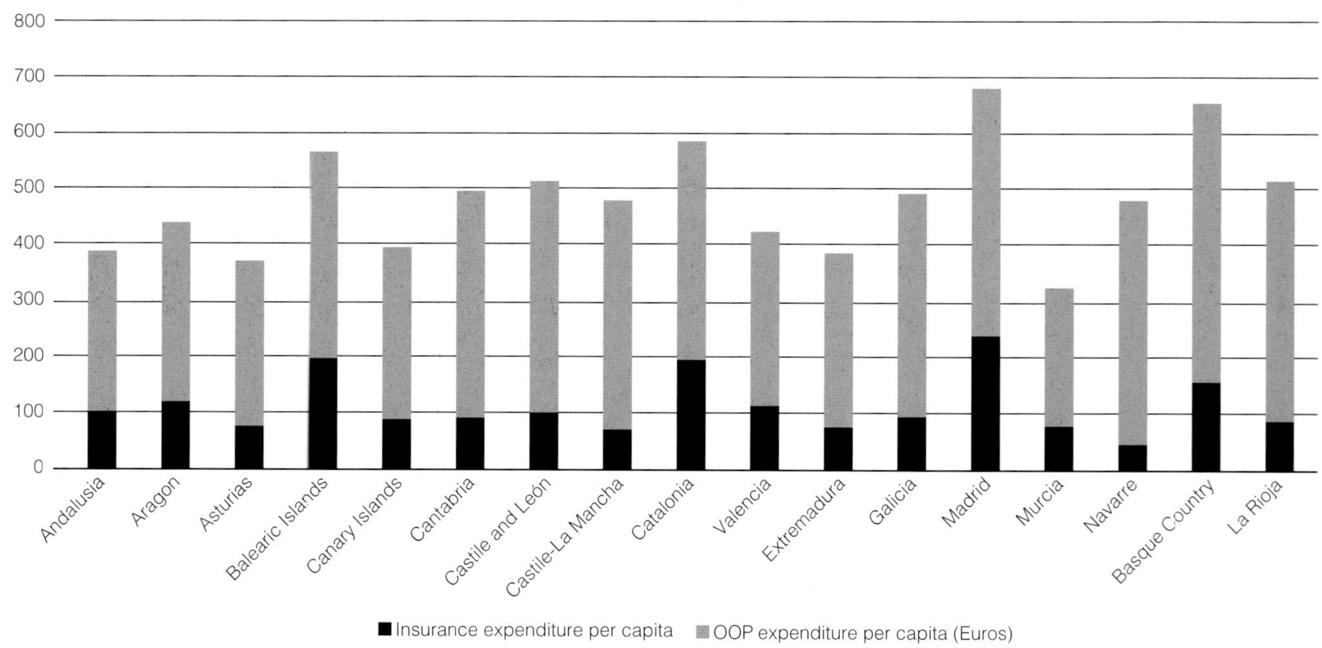

Source: IDIS Foundation (2013).

Note: Based on ICEA (2009–2012; 2013); INE (2013); MSPS (2013).

(Costa & Garcia, 2003). Expenditure on VHI varies across the regions and is the highest in Madrid, Catalonia, the Balearic Islands and the Basque Country (Figure 30.1).

Who sells VHI?

The major insurers offering VHI are commercial but there are also some non-profit-making mutual associations. The market is highly concentrated, with 10 companies accounting for 82% of the market (IDIS Foundation, 2013).

Insurer relations with providers

Providers are usually paid on a FFS basis and VHI subscribers generally have to pay user charges.

Public policy towards VHI

Spanish Insurance Law defines VHI (*seguro de asistencia sanitaria* in Spanish) as insurance that "provides the insured with outpatient, hospital and surgery care, with own medical staff whereby the insurer takes care of its own enrolees in exchange for a premium" (art. 105 of the Bill 50/80 of Insurance Contracts; Agencia Estatal, 1980). VHI benefits from tax subsidies. Until 1999, this was done via income tax relief. Since then VHI premiums can be deducted from corporate income tax only.

Debates and challenges

There are currently no debates about VHI. Take-up has continued to increase in spite of the economic crisis due to increased take-up by companies who purchase it for their employees as social benefits (and can thus benefit from tax advantages and lower premiums for corporate subscriptions). Corporate policies increased by 4% between 2009 and 2013, while the number of individual VHI subscribers fell by 14% (IDIS Foundation, 2013). The number of civil servants who opt to have their health care purchased by private insurers has remained stable (at around 2 million subscribers).

The future of VHI

Recent proposals from insurance industry advocates include the reintroduction of tax relief for individuals, but this is opposed by the government as it abolished this relief in 1999 when it was in power. A significant redefinition of the SNS benefits package, also put forward by the insurance industry, would allow insurers to offer more VHI products providing access to higher quality of care (a supplementary role) or to some types of care excluded from SNS cover (a complementary role). So far, however, no changes are planned.

References

Agencia Estatal (1980). *Boletín Oficial del Estado. Ley 50/1980, de 8 de octubre, de Contrato de Seguro. [Official State Bulletin. Art. 105 of the Bill 50/80 of Insurance Contracts]* (http://www.boe.es/buscar/doc.php?id=BOE-A-1980-22501, accessed 2 December 2015).

Costa J, Garcia J (2003). Demand for private health insurance: how important is the quality gap? *Health Economics*, 12(7):587–599.

García-Armesto S et al. (2010). Spain: health system review. *Health Systems in Transition*, 12(4):1–295.

ICEA (2009–2012). *Reports on private insurance 2009-2012. Investigación Cooperativa entre Entidades Aseguradoras y Fondos de Pensiones [Cooperative Research between Insurance Companies and Pension Funds]*. Madrid, ICEA.

ICEA (2013). *La eficiencia en el sector asegurador español? [Efficiency in the Spanish insurance sector?]. Investigación Cooperativa entre Entidades Aseguradoras y Fondos de Pensiones [Cooperative Research between Insurance Companies and Pension Funds]*. Madrid, ICEA (http://www.icea.es/es-es/investigacion/proyectos/paginas/proyectosfinalizados.aspx; accessed 22 November 2015).

IDIS Foundation (2013). *Análisis de situación 2013 [Private health care situation in Spain 2013]*. Madrid, IDIS Foundation (http://www.fundacionidis.com/wp-content/uploads/2013/03/AnalisisSituacion_2013.pdf; accessed 22 November 2015).

INE (2013). *Household budget surveys 2008–2011*. Madrid, Institute Nacional de Estadistica [National Institute of Statistics].

MSPS (2013). *Statistical data*. Madrid, Ministerio de sanidad y politicas sociales [Ministry of Health, Social Services and Equality].

WHO (2016). Global Health Expenditure Database (GHED) [online database]. Geneva, WHO (http://www.who.int/health-accounts/ghed/en/, accessed 5 April 2016).

31
Sweden

Caj Skoglund

Health system context

The health financing mix

In 2014, public spending accounted for 84% of total spending on health, with OOP payments and VHI accounting for 14.1 and 0.5%, respectively (WHO, 2016).

Entitlement to publicly financed health care and gaps in coverage

All residents are intended to have equal access to health care services under a largely decentralized system financed mainly through local taxes and some small user charges. Although quality of care and equity of access are good by international standards, long waiting times for elective care have been a cause of dissatisfaction for a number of years.

Overview of the VHI market

Market origins, aims and role

VHI plans are mainly *supplementary*, offering faster access to care in the private sector to services that are usually covered by the publicly financed system. Some VHI plans offer a small *complementary* element (between 1 and 3% of the premium), reimbursing user charges for publicly financed outpatient visits and prescription medicines.

Historically, the VHI market was typically restricted to top-level management and the number of people covered was very low (125 000 in 2001). Although the market has expanded in the last decade, with coverage growing especially among white-collar workers in private companies, less than 5% (2011) of the population has VHI coverage (author calculations based on data from Insurance Sweden (2013) and Statistics Sweden (2013)). The number of people with VHI more than doubled between 2006 and 2011 (Table 31.1). Employers purchasing VHI are most likely to be small or medium-sized companies in the private services sector.

Table 31.1 *Number of people covered by VHI in Sweden, 2006–2011*

Year	Number of people covered	Yearly increase (%)
2006	218 064	–
2007	294 783	35
2008	338 607	15
2009	386 185	14
2010	430 767	12
2011	464 909	8

Source: Insurance Sweden (2013).

The following factors have contributed to the growth of the VHI market: (1) concerns about the loss of productivity associated with sick leave while waiting for elective treatments; (2) increased marketing of VHI, partially because of more insurers joining the market; and (3) a growing number of employers, organizations and associations offering group plans in which employees or members can individually decide whether they want to join.

Types of plan available

VHI policies may be: group policies paid for by employers covering all or a limited number of employees on a mandatory basis; group policies based on a contract between the insurance company and an employer, organization or association, where employees can choose whether they want to join on an individual basis and pay their own premiums; and individual policies. Mandatory group policies dominate the VHI market (Table 31.2).

Table 31.2 *VHI policies in Sweden by percentage of insured people, 2010*

Type of VHI	Proportion of insured (%)
Group policies, mandatory participation	81
Group policies, individual voluntary participation	13
Individual policies	6

Source: Insurance Sweden (2013).

All VHI plans give the insured access to the following services: a telephone helpline staffed by registered nurses; elective care, including elective surgery for a number of conditions not requiring intensive care or more specialized treatment; and rehabilitation, for example, a maximum number of treatments by a physiotherapist (usually 10).

Why do people buy VHI?

The main reasons for purchasing VHI plans by *employers* is the prospect of shorter waiting times for employees and thus reduced sick leave absence. In some cases, providing VHI may also raise an employer's attractiveness to potential and current employees. Individuals may buy VHI on an individual or voluntary group basis for added security in case of needing elective care and, perhaps, as a status symbol.

Who buys VHI?

As shown in Table 31.2, most people with VHI are covered by group policies paid for by their employer. There is no information on the characteristics of individuals with VHI cover or on the characteristics of employers that offer VHI to their employees. There are signs that VHI coverage is expanding beyond the private services sector, for example, to the manufacturing industry. However, VHI is rarely offered to employees in the public sector.

Who sells VHI?

According to Insurance Sweden, 17 companies sell VHI (2013) (Insurance Sweden, 2013) and the number of insurers has been increasing. There is no information available regarding the market shares of different insurers.

Insurer relations with providers

Insurers contract with a network of private providers in Sweden and, in some cases, in other countries such as Denmark or Germany. The low profitability of VHI due to an increased number of claims in the last few years has made insurers more inclined to negotiate tariffs with providers to reduce costs. For the same reason, user charges have become a more common feature of VHI plans.

Public policy towards VHI

There are no VHI-specific regulations. Voluntary health insurers are, as all other insurers, under the supervision of the Swedish Financial Supervisory Authority. The law on genetic integrity (*lagen om genetisk integritet*) enacted in 2006 prohibited insurers from inquiring about the insured's genetic information (formalizing what had, in fact, already been practised previously through a voluntary agreement between insurers and the government).

VHI premiums are neither tax deductible for employers nor can they be deducted from taxable income by employees. On the other hand, the complementary part of the insurance premium (1–3% of the VHI premium) and VHI cover for dependants may be tax exempt for employers as well as deducted from personal taxable income by employees.

Debates and challenges

Despite its growth in the recent decade, the role of VHI in health financing remains marginal and VHI does not attract much public attention. One of the reasons for this low public interest may be the fact that although private insurers contract solely with private providers, the latter's incomes are mainly derived from contracts with county councils, not with insurers. The number of patients with VHI treated by private providers is in fact marginal compared to the total number of patients treated privately. Furthermore, there is no evidence that treating VHI patients contributes to longer waiting times for patients whose care is paid for by county councils.

If public providers were allowed to treat VHI patients, calls for legislation to ban such a practice would be expected. Presently, however, this scenario seems very unlikely. Because VHI-financed care is limited to private providers, a recent analysis of the VHI market commissioned in 2011 by the Swedish Association of Local Authorities and Regions concluded that VHI could not be seen as a threat to the principle of solidarity that underpins the health system (Skoglund, 2012).

A number of reforms at national and regional levels have aimed to reduce waiting times and sick leave absence. According to the waiting time guarantees introduced in 2005 by the county councils, no patient should have to wait more than 7 days for an appointment at a community health care centre, 90 days for an appointment with a specialist and 90 days for an operation or treatment. Since 2010, the guarantee has been included in the Health and Medical Service Act. Because of these measures, significant progress has been achieved in reducing waiting times. This has probably contributed to the slower growth of the VHI market in recent years.

The future of VHI

Based on the author's interviews with major insurers, it seems likely that the growth of the VHI market will continue, mainly fuelled by demand from small and medium-sized companies. However, growth is expected to be slower in comparison to the mid-2000s. Demand for VHI might increase more rapidly if the reduction in waiting times proves not to be sustainable (for example, if the county councils and regions are negatively affected by economic developments); VHI becomes an important factor in recruiting personnel in the context of an ageing workforce; or public sector employers decide to purchase VHI cover for their employees. Demand for VHI might decrease if current reforms to lower waiting times are successful in the end, thus undermining the rationale for VHI; VHI premiums rise and insurers impose more user charges to limit their liability; or the economic crisis makes private companies less keen to offer VHI to their employees. Overall, it seems unlikely that the development of VHI will have any noticeable consequences for the health system as a whole in the near future.

References

Insurance Sweden (2013) [website]. Information regarding VHI coverage and premiums. Stockholm, Insurance Sweden (http://www.svenskforsakring.se, accessed January 2013).

Skoglund C (2012) *Privata sjukvårdsförsäkringar i Sverige [Private health insurances in Sweden]*. Stockholm, Age Management i Sverige AB (AMSAB).

Statistics Sweden (2013). *Befolkningsstatistik [Population]*. Stockholm, Statistics Sweden (http://www.scb.se/Pages/Product____25785.aspx, accessed 22 November 2015).

WHO (2016). Global Health Expenditure Database (GHED) [online database]. Geneva, WHO (http://www.who.int/health-accounts/ghed/en/, accessed 5 April 2016).

32 Switzerland

Viktor von Wyl and Konstantin Beck

Health system context

The health financing mix

In 2014, public spending covered 66% of total spending on health, while OOP payments and VHI accounted for 26.8 and 7.4%, respectively (WHO, 2016). Public spending includes mandatory private health insurance under the Health Insurance Act (*Krankenversicherungsgesetz*), which is regarded by the authorities as a social insurance system (Federal Statistical Office, 2015).

Entitlement to publicly financed health care and gaps in coverage

The cornerstone of health financing is mandatory health insurance operated by private insurers on a non-profit-making basis. This is comprehensive, covering a broad range of essential interventions listed in a catalogue that is continuously updated by the health authorities, including alternative treatments such as acupuncture or homeopathy. The main exclusions are dental care and nursing home stays. Individuals are entitled to state-financed premium subsidies if their expenditure on mandatory coverage exceeds a certain percentage of taxable income and wealth (in 2009, 30% of population was eligible; Federal Office of Public Health, 2012). Inpatient care is jointly financed on an approximately 46–54% basis by mandatory coverage and direct transfers from the federal government and local government (cantons). Before 2011, subsidies for inpatient hospital care were only paid for hospital stays within the canton of residency, but this rule was abolished in a health reform in 2012.

Overview of the VHI market

Market origins, aims and role

The first law governing health insurance, introduced in 1911, left health insurance in the hands of private insurers. Although health insurance was voluntary, close to 100% of the population was covered by at least a basic health plan (in 1995). In 1996, health insurance was divided into mandatory and voluntary parts. Mandatory insurance covers expenses for essential treatments related to sickness, accidents and pregnancy. Since there are few major gaps in mandatory coverage, the role of VHI is primarily *supplementary*: people buy VHI to gain access to greater choice of hospital and a higher standard of amenities during hospital stays. There are also *complementary* VHI plans covering services excluded from mandatory coverage, such as dental care.

Types of plan available

The majority of VHI policies are hospital plans providing access to semi-private or private rooms in public and private hospitals or hospitals outside the canton of residency (depending on the level of coverage chosen). There are also dental plans and additional ambulatory care plans covering physiotherapy, prescription medicines not (yet) reimbursed under mandatory insurance, partial cover of glasses and contact lenses and some complementary and alternative therapies. Some VHI plans cover sick pay for self-employed individuals and companies.

Why do people buy VHI?

The main reason for buying supplementary hospital plans is to have free choice of physician in hospital and more privacy during hospital stays (double or single rooms). In 2010, approximately 60% of the mandatorily insured bought VHI, mainly in the form of supplementary cover for hospital stays (38% of total VHI premium volume in 2010) and cover for additional ambulatory treatments (29%) (Swiss Financial Market Supervisory Authority, 2010). Sick pay cover accounted for 30% of total VHI premium income. These figures do not seem to have changed significantly after the introduction of countrywide choice of hospital.

Who buys VHI?

According to a Swiss Health Survey (Federal Office of Public Health, 2007), VHI covers around 72% of the population, with higher take-up observed among older individuals (over 45 years old) and those with higher education. The share of individuals with VHI was lowest among young males between 25 and 34 years old (63%). Sick pay benefits are almost exclusively bought by companies (97% of contracts) as reinsurance, because employees are entitled by law to up to 6 months of continued pay in case of illness.

With the rising costs of mandatory insurance, fewer young and healthy individuals purchase VHI, leading to rising costs borne by the remaining older, sicker population with VHI. This has caused steep VHI premium increases in the last few years, which, combined with the expansion of mandatory insurance, explain the limited growth of the VHI market in the past five years (premium volume increased by an average of 1.8% per year; Federal Office of Private Insurance, 2007; Swiss Financial Market Supervisory Authority, 2008, 2009, 2010) in spite of high overall growth rates in health expenditure over the same time period (on average 3.5% per annum; Federal Office of Public Health, 2012).

Who sells VHI?

VHI is sold by insurers selling mandatory insurance and other private insurers whose main business is non-life insurance. Non-life insurers predominantly provide sick pay insurance. Although they could technically also offer other (supplementary) VHI products, this would require extensive negotiations with hospitals and physicians, which poses a high barrier to market entry. Both types of entity operate on a profit-making basis. By 2010, the number of entities selling VHI had fallen to 56 (from 99 in 2005) and 34 of them (61%) were also active in the mandatory insurance business.

Insurer relations with providers

Private insurers are usually not integrated with health care providers, although this is not explicitly prohibited under current regulations. Most ambulatory care is reimbursed on a FFS basis and inpatient hospital care through DRGs (SwissDRG). In principle, all fees can be negotiated on a case-by-case basis, but because of high transaction costs, negotiations mainly take place between groups of insurers and groups of hospitals.

Public policy towards VHI

In contrast to mandatory insurance, the VHI market is not subject to much regulation, although regulation on pricing and reserves has recently been reinforced. VHI does not benefit from any tax subsidy. For political reasons, there has been a tendency for mandatory coverage to expand at the expense of VHI coverage. Many major additions to the mandatory benefits package were introduced by popular referendum (for example, coverage of alternative medicines was shifted from VHI to mandatory insurance in 2009). Moreover, the list of medicines covered by mandatory insurance is continuously updated, and many medicines previously limited to VHI plans become eligible for mandatory reimbursement once they are considered standard, if they are deemed cost-effective.

Similarly, the health care reform of 2012 introduced nationwide hospital choice as part of mandatory insurance, which was one of the main reasons why people bought VHI hospital plans prior to the reform. The reform's intention was to promote competition among hospitals and to introduce a shift from a cost-based to a price-based remuneration system for inpatient hospital stays. The reform also included changes to hospital financing; cantons now cover a higher share of expenses (51–54%, as opposed to a 50–50 split before 2012), which – combined with the shift of some hospitalization costs from voluntary to mandatory insurance – has translated into lower premiums for some VHI hospital plans (but not for plans covering semi-private or private hospital stays). Together, these factors are likely to lead to stagnation or even to a contraction of the VHI market.

The development and regulation of the VHI market is shown in Table 32.1.

Table 32.1 *Development and regulation of the VHI market in Switzerland, 1911–2012*

Year	Policy
1911	First health insurance regulation: health insurance remains voluntary and operated by private insurers
1996	Major revision of health insurance regulation: health insurance is divided into mandatory and voluntary
2009	Referendum is passed to include specific alternative medicines in the mandatory benefits package (previously only covered by VHI)
2012	SwissDRG is introduced; free hospital choice in mandatory health insurance plans; redistribution of financing of hospital stays

Source: Authors.

Debates and challenges

Most political and public debates concern mandatory rather than voluntary coverage. Mandatory insurance and VHI (especially supplementary VHI plans) are heavily intertwined. For instance, hospitals and physicians work in the mandatory and VHI sectors and issue only one medical bill, leaving it up to the insurers to disentangle treatments and services covered by VHI from those covered by the mandatory benefits package. Waiting times are generally not an issue, so people with VHI do not receive preferential treatment in terms of faster access to care.

One recent discussion about VHI concerned subsidies for hospital stays. Before the 2012 reform, cantons tried to prevent people with VHI from benefiting from state financing for hospital stays, but a court ruling entitled all citizens to this, irrespective of their VHI cover. Other ongoing discussions about VHI concern a more stringent organizational separation of mandatory and voluntary coverage (supplementary VHI in particular), because many consumers fear that information from mandatory insurance (such as claim records) may systematically be used for risk selection by insurers active in both coverage markets. Changes in legislation to that effect have been passed in the parliament in March 2014. However, the implementation of these changes is only planned for 2017 and hence the implications for VHI are currently not clear.

With the introduction of free, nationwide hospital choice in mandatory insurance in 2012, VHI has lost one of its main selling points. Moreover, the new financing split for hospital stays – with a higher share now covered by the cantons – raised hopes among consumers that premiums for VHI hospital plans would fall. While premiums for basic VHI hospital plans have fallen since the reform, the long-term effects of the reform are still uncertain.

The future of VHI

The importance of VHI has steadily declined over time, especially since the latest health system reform in 2012. However, a referendum proposal on establishing a single, state-controlled system of mandatory insurance, replacing the current system of multiple, competing insurers, was overwhelmingly rejected by voters in September 2014. Had it been accepted, private insurers would still have been able to offer VHI, but would have faced much higher administrative costs due to significant losses in economies of scale; non-life insurers providing sick pay insurance would not have been affected.

References

Federal Office of Private Insurance (2007). *Zusätzliche Angaben zur Krankenversicherung (alle Krankenversicherer) [AS03N]*. Bern, Federal Office of Private Insurance (http://www.finma.ch/archiv/bpv/download/d/006_as03n_2007_de.xls, accessed 22 November 2015).

Federal Office of Public Health (2007). *Schweizerische Gesundheitsbefragung 2007; Krankenversicherung; Spitalversicherungsklasse*. Bern, Federal Office of Public Health (http://www.bag.admin.ch/themen/krankenversicherung/01156/02446/index.html?lang=de&download=NHzLpZig7t,lnp6I0NTU042l2Z6ln1acy4Zn4Z2qZpnO2Yuq2Z6gpJCJdIF,f2ym162dpYbUzd,Gpd6emK2Oz9aGodetmqaN19XI2IdvoaCUZ,s-, accessed 22 November 2015).

Federal Office of Public Health (2012). *Statistik der obligatorischen Krankenversicherung 2009*. Bern, Federal Office of Public Health.

Federal Statistical Office (2015). *Costs, financing – data, indicators*. Neuchâtel, Federal Statistical Office (http://www.bfs.admin.ch/bfs/portal/en/index/themen/14/05/blank/key/perspektive_der_direktzahler.html, accessed 22 November 2015).

Swiss Financial Market Supervisory Authority (2008). *Insurance market data, Electronic Tables, Table AS03N*. Bern, Swiss Financial Market Supervisory Authority (http://www.versichererreport.finma.ch/reportportal, accessed 22 November 2015).

Swiss Financial Market Supervisory Authority (2009). *Insurance market data, Electronic Tables, Table AS03N*. Bern, Swiss Financial Market Supervisory Authority (http://www.versichererreport.finma.ch/reportportal, accessed 22 November 2015).

Swiss Financial Market Supervisory Authority (2010). *Insurance market data, Electronic Tables, Table AS03N*. Bern, Swiss Financial Market Supervisory Authority (http://www.versichererreport.finma.ch/reportportal, accessed 22 November 2012).

WHO (2016). Global Health Expenditure Database (GHED) [online database]. Geneva, WHO (http://www.who.int/health-accounts/ghed/en/, accessed 5 April 2016).

33
Ukraine

Valery Lekhan

Health system context

The health financing mix

In 2014, public spending accounted for 50.8% of total spending on health, with OOP payments and VHI accounting for 46.2 and around 1%, respectively (WHO, 2016).

Entitlement to publicly financed health care and gaps in coverage

Formally, all Ukrainian citizens and foreign citizens and stateless persons permanently residing in Ukraine have the right to receive medical care in state-owned health facilities free of charge (Verkhovna Rada of Ukraine, 1996). The government has also listed a second group of services that do not threaten the life or the health of patients that may be provided to all citizens in return for user charges. Vulnerable population groups and people with specific, socially significant and serious diseases benefit from reduced price or free outpatient medicines. Overall, the government benefits package is not clearly defined, so in the presence of insufficient financing the boundary between free and non-free health care is blurred. Informal payments are an issue and access to health services is a problem. Survey data show that in 2012, 13.9% of households were not able to purchase essential medicines, 8.2% did not see a doctor when necessary and 3.9% did not obtain necessary inpatient treatment because of the costs involved (Ukrstat, 2012).

Overview of the VHI market

Market origins, aims and role

The introduction and development of VHI began with the introduction of the Insurance Law in 1996. VHI plays a *supplementary* role, providing people with greater choice of provider, a higher level of comfort in hospital and faster access to essential diagnostic and curative services. It also provides access to medicines and services that are included in the state benefits package; these should be publicly financed, but are not in practice due to the low level of public funding for the health system.

Types of plan available

VHI plans can be divided into different categories: VIP (treatment in private clinics of the highest level), Elite (lower-level clinics and coverage limits) and Classic or Standard plans (basic or partial cover in state-owned health care facilities). Most plans cover some spending on medicines and devices that are in theory covered by the state (Shpot, 2011).

Why do people buy VHI?

Although the VHI market has grown since 1996, the share of the population covered continues to be non-significant, largely due to the prohibitive cost of premiums, which makes VHI inaccessible for most people. According to different data sources, VHI covers between 1 and 1.5 million people (or 2.4–3.3% of the population) (Grishan, 2011; LSOU, 2012; Zagrebnoi, 2011). Employers buy VHI on behalf of their employees to promote staff loyalty and health mainly in sectors where the job market is competitive and there are shortages of qualified staff – for example, financial services, investment or legal firms and parts of the IT and telecommunications industry (INGO Ukraina, 2012; WHO, 2010).

Individual VHI policies are usually bought by people who have existing health problems to reduce OOP payments, to obtain a higher level of comfort in hospital or to avoid waiting lists for services where demand outstrips supply (Petrov, 2009).

Since the mid-1990s, quasi-VHI has been provided through nongovernmental, non-profit-making sickness funds. Sickness fund cover aims to lessen the burden of OOP payments, especially for medicines, and is bought by individuals and organizations (Lekhan, Rudiy & Richardson, 2010).

Who buys VHI?

More than 90% of people with VHI are corporate clients. Corporate policies account for up to 80% of VHI premium income (Sidorenko, 2011). Insurers usually differentiate the quality of VHI cover by category of employee, so top-level managers get the most expensive VIP policies (Lux), middle managers get the slightly cheaper Elite cover and regular workers get the standard, basic package at the Classic or Standard level or a more limited package of benefits. Take-up of individual VHI is concentrated among people with higher incomes.

Insurers generally exclude people aged over 60–70 years, people registered as severely disabled or those defined as high risk due to a pre-existing condition such as cancer, TB, diabetes, chronic kidney failure requiring dialysis, mental health issues, alcohol or drug addiction and HIV or AIDS.

Voluntary contributions to sickness funds are usually made by individuals and, to a much lesser extent (around 2% of total VHI premium revenue), by some private employers.

Who sells VHI?

Insurers selling VHI are general commercial entities, of which there are around 100 in total, but only around 20 interested in VHI (Yavorskaya, 2008). The market shares of the leading companies are shown in Table 33.1. Alongside insurers, there are also around 200 sickness funds. These are registered as charitable organizations and provide VHI on a non-profit-making basis. Their activities are regulated under the Laws on Citizens' Associations and Charity and Charitable Organizations.

The largest insurer in the VHI market is the general insurance company Neftagazstrakh (Ekonomichna pravda, 2011). Its main corporate client is the former State Administration of the Ukrainian Railways (Ukrzaliznitsya, recently converted into a public joint-stock company with 100% of the shares owned by the state), which covers the country's six state railways; 270 000 railway workers (82% of the total railway workforce) and 180 000 pensioners who used to work in the sector are covered by VHI. This insurer's VHI premiums are among the lowest, at UAH 600 or €54 (UAH 1 = €0.09 in 2011) per year in 2011. Moreover, due to the large number of people insured, the annual

Table 33.1 *Overview of VHI insurers in Ukraine, 2010*

Insurer (year of market entry)	Market share (%)		Annual cost of premium	Regulated by	Legal status
	Share of total number of insured	Share by value of total premium income (place in ranking)			
Neftagazstrakh (1995, VHI since 2003)	40	9.2 (2nd place)	Ukrainian hryvnia (UAH) 600 (€57)		
Ilychevskoe Insurance Society (1997, re-registered in 2005)	5.5	5.6 (5th place)	No data		
Providna (1995)	5	15.3 (1st place)	UAH 1200–6000 (€114–570)	Financial regulator Natskomfinuslug	Commercial
Oranta (1993)	4	1.6 (19th place)	UAH 7000–20 000 (€665–1900)		
Allianz (2005)	3	2.6 (11th place)	UAH 400–12 000 (€38–1140)		

Source: Specialized Internet project of Forinsurer magazine (http://www.forinsurer.com/) on health insurance in Ukraine, *Forinsurer: health insurance*, available online at http://med-insurance.com.ua.

Note: UAH 1=€0.095 (2010 avarage).

insured sum guaranteed is UAH 20 000 (€1800). The VHI premium is taken directly from railway workers' wages, but half of the amount is paid by the Ukrainian Railways Administration. The size of sums insured for different types of treatment is shown in Table 33.2.

The largest sickness fund is the Zhytomyr oblast Sickness Fund (registered in 2000). At the beginning of 2013, it had around 200 000 members (15.6% of the oblast's total population). Monthly contributions from members amounted to UAH 25 (€2.3 per month or €28 per year; UAH 1=0.092 in 2013). Fund members were guaranteed unlimited cover for medicines, irrespective of the price or the number of prescriptions, and cover for necessary laboratory or diagnostic tests as prescribed by a physician. In 2012, sickness fund revenues reached UAH 38.7 million (€3.7 million; UAH 1=0.096 in 2012).

Insurer relations with providers

Private insurers are not usually integrated with providers. Insurers can contract any registered and accredited medical facility (public or private) and prices are negotiated.

Public policy towards VHI

There is no VHI-specific regulation. VHI is regulated under the Law on Insurance (1996), which covers general conditions for insurance, and the Law on Financial Services and State Regulation of the Financial Services Market (2001), which is the general legal basis for providing financial services. The State Commission for the Regulation of the Financial Services Market (2003) issues licences for insurance activities.

Table 33.2 *Sums insured under VHI policies by the Neftagazstrakh insurance company, by clinical intervention, 2011*

Types of procedure covered	Intervention	Maximum sum insured per year
Hospitalization	Therapeutic treatment	UAH 800 (€72)
	Surgical treatment	UAH 1000–2000 (€90–180)
	Pregnancy and birth	UAH 700–1000 (€63–90)
	Anaesthesia	UAH 150–300 (€14–27)
	Intensive care	UAH 1200-5000 (€108–450)
	Different types of procedure (for example, stent, open heart surgery)	UAH 6000–16 000 (€540–1440)
Day care	Day care	UAH 400 (€36)
Different diagnostic procedures	CT, MRI, nuclear medical imaging (for example, PET)	UAH 600 (€54)
	Angiogram	UAH 1400 (€126)

Source: Website of Neftagazstrakh insurance company (http://ngs.biz.ua/); unpublished (internal) company materials..

Note: UAH 1=€0.09 (2011 avarage).

Debates and challenges

VHI is not widespread for several reasons. First, insurers are not always keen to engage in VHI activities, considering it to be too complex and unprofitable; the sums paid out in claims are considerably higher for VHI than they are for other kinds of insurance – up to 73% of total premiums collected (Gorun, 2010; Zagrebnoi, 2011). Second, employers are generally not interested in buying VHI for employees and their families, partly because there is no fiscal incentive for them to do so (Chubinskii, 2011). Third, the development of individual VHI is inhibited by the high cost of premiums relative to the population's generally low wages.

A government report entitled *Concept for the development of the insurance market by 2010* envisaged state support for the development of socially relevant types of insurance through the introduction of tax incentives (Government of Ukraine, 2005). A revised tax code adopted in 2010 proposed a range of tax incentives to increase demand for VHI, including giving businesses the right to reduce the level of social tax they paid on wages if they provided all their employees with VHI. However, these tax incentives were not included in the final version of the law.

Another issue under discussion is the establishment of a specialized health insurance company, but no decision has yet been taken.

Since the 1990s, there has been discussion about the introduction of a mandatory health insurance scheme with a clearly defined package of benefits, an increase in the volume of budgetary funding for health and a clearly defined role for VHI. However, although several draft laws have been put before parliament, consensus on this issue has not yet been achieved.

VHI has not had a significant impact on the way the health system operates because the vast majority of health care providers are not included in VHI plans. Medical care for most people with VHI cover is provided in the same state-owned facilities used by people without VHI, with the same medical technologies and often with the same level of amenities. Managers of state facilities tend to prioritize treatment of people with VHI because of the additional revenue they generate for the facility. However, doctors working in these facilities are not interested in treating people with VHI, who are less likely than others to make informal payments. In private facilities, where informal payments are absent, offering faster access to services is an explicit practice.

The contracting process generates substantial transaction costs for health care facilities and multiple insurers, as VHI plans vary widely in terms of what they cover and prices must be negotiated with each insurer. The introduction of a uniform pricing system would help lower transaction costs. Insurers would also like to see uniform clinical protocols applied in all health care facilities treating patients with VHI, to ensure good quality of care.

The future of VHI

Reducing the scope of the publicly financed benefits package would be a starting point for VHI market development, but could have serious implications for equitable access, equity in financing and financial protection for households. Changes to public coverage aside, without extensive tax incentives for individuals and businesses, the VHI market is likely to struggle to expand significantly. The difficult economic and political situation of the last few years has had a negative impact on the VHI market and the market for other types of insurance. Increasing nominal VHI revenue in the last two years is misleading; it reflects devaluation of the national currency, coupled with the fact that imported drugs account for the bulk of VHI costs, rather than an increase in the number of people with VHI. Experts note that the number of VHI subscribers, especially corporate ones, has in fact been declining. Prospects for further VHI market development are therefore regarded as being negative.

References

Chubinskii A (2011). When will the VHI market in Ukraine wake up? *MedFond.com*, 19 June 2011.

Ekonomichna pravda (2011). Effektivni rishennya. The number of policy holders in the Neftagazstrakh insurance company reaches 400,000 people. *Ekonomichna pravda*, 28 December 2011.

Gorun PM (2010). *Горун П.М. Проблеми та перспективи розвитку медичного страхування в Україні. Чернівці. Буковинська державна фінансова академія. Електронний документ [Problems and perspectives for the development of health insurance in*

Ukraine]. Chernikhiv, Rusnauka (http://www.rusnauka.com/4_SWMN_2010/Economics/56669.doc.htm, accessed 2 December 2015).

Government of Ukraine (2005). *Resolution on approving the concept for the development of the insurance market in Ukraine to the year 2010.* Stat. No. 369-r (23 August 2005). Kyiv, Government of Ukraine.

Grishan Y (2011). В Украине спрос на ДМС больше предложения. Украинский бизнес ресурс (UBR) Электронный документ [In Ukraine demand for VHI is a more Ukrainian proposal]. *UBR*, 13 July 2011.

INGO Ukraina (2012). *Добровільне медичне страхування: скільки коштує здоров'я персоналу? / ІНГО Україна. Електронний документ [Voluntary health insurance: how much is the health of the workforce worth?]* Kyiv, INGO (http://ingo.kiev.ua/ru/review/104-Добровільне медичне страхування: скільки коштує здоров'я персоналу?.html).

Lekhan V, Rudiy V, Richardson E (2010). Ukraine: health system review. *Health Systems in Transition*, 12(8):1–183.

LSOU (2012). *Analysis of insurance markets.* Kyiv, League of Insurance Organizations of Ukraine (LSOU) (http://uainsur.com/stats/analiz/, accessed 22 November 2015).

Petrov A (2009). "Бесплатная" украинская медицина или Добровольное медицинское страхование? Правильный выбор. PROSTOBANK.UA .Электронный документ ["Free" Ukrainian medicine or VHI? The right choice]. *Tristar*, 20 November 2009.

Shpot N (2011). *Voluntary health insurance in Ukraine: problems and prospects.* Lviv, The Ivan Franko National University of Lviv.

Sidorenko E (2011). Добровільне медичне страхування дорожчатиме / Ліга страхових організацій Україні Електронний документ [Voluntary health insurance will get more expensive]. *UBR*, 10 October 2011.

Ukrstat (2012) *Самооцінка населенням стану здоров'я та рівня доступності окремих видів медичної допомоги у 2012 році/ Державна служба статистики України. Статистичний збірник: Обстеження умов життя домогосподарств. Київ, 2013. – 149с. Электронный документ [Population's self- perceived health status and availability of selected types of medical aid. Data from the household survey conducted in October 2012].* Kyiv, State Statistics Service of Ukraine (http://www.ukrstat.gov.ua).

Verkhovna Rada of Ukraine (1996). Constitution of Ukraine. Kyiv, Verkhovna Rada of Ukraine (http://zakon3.rada.gov.ua/laws/show/254/96-%D0%B2%D1%80, accessed 3 December 2015).

WHO (2010). *Ukraine. National health accounts.* Geneva, WHO (http://www.who.int/nha/country/ukr.pdf, accessed 22 November 2015).

WHO (2016). Global Health Expenditure Database (GHED) [online database]. Geneva, WHO (http://www.who.int/health-accounts/ghed/en/, accessed 5 April 2016).

Yavorskaya TV (2008). *Яворська Т.В. Страхові послуги: Навч. посіб. /За заг. ред. д.е.н., проф. Реверчука С.К. – К.:Знання, 2008. – 350с [Insurance Services].* Kyiv, Znanie.

Zagrebnoi V (2011). ДМС продолжает оставаться одним из самых убыточных для страховщиков. Электронный документ [VHI continues to be one of the least profitable for insurers]. *Tristar*, 3 June 2011.

34
United Kingdom

Thomas Foubister and Erica Richardson

Health system context

The health financing mix

In 2014, public spending accounted for 83.1% of total spending on health, with OOP payments and VHI accounting for 9.7 and 3.4%, respectively (WHO, 2016). Public spending on health has dominated since the founding of the NHS in 1948 (Boyle, 2011).

Entitlement to publicly financed care and gaps in coverage

The NHS provides cover for a wide range of benefits to individuals ordinarily resident in the United Kingdom – overseas visitors and illegal immigrants are not normally entitled to receive NHS care, with some exceptions (emergency care, care to children and treatment for infectious diseases). The publicly financed benefits package, while comprehensive, is not clearly defined and there is a degree of variation across regions. User charges are applied to ophthalmic care, most dental care and outpatient prescriptions, as well as to certain products. There is a system of exemption from prescription charges for children, people aged 65 years and older, pregnant women, people with chronic illnesses and some lower-income groups. Scotland, Wales and Northern Ireland have abolished the prescription charge for medicines, but in England it remains in place, at pound sterling (GBP) 8.20 per prescription in 2015.

Overview of the VHI market

Market origins, aims and role

VHI plays a largely *supplementary* role, providing access to a range of benefits available through the NHS but with faster access, a choice of private provider (whether a private hospital or the private wing of an NHS hospital) and of specialist acting in a private capacity, and in a more comfortable care environment. VHI may also offer benefits not covered by the NHS, including cover for complementary and alternative therapies. High-cost and resource-intensive treatments are not covered by VHI, nor are they provided by the private provider sector. Similarly, private GP care is not generally covered.

A more recent development has been the establishment and growth of a complementary VHI market covering dental care. Cover for dental care by the NHS has diminished significantly over recent decades. User charges are high, and fewer and fewer dentists are providing NHS care. VHI for dental care takes the form of traditional indemnity insurance or, more commonly, a capitation plan with prepayment to the dental practice by the insurer. The capitation amount payable relates to the risk profile of the patient as determined by an initial assessment by the dentist and is adjusted over time. Around 5% of the population has VHI for dental care, not including those with supplementary VHI offering some level of dental cover (LaingBuisson, 2012).

VHI predates the NHS by a century or so. Insurance existed for primary care coverage, sometimes organized by doctors themselves, sometimes by workplaces or groups of workplaces, and sometimes by local communities. When NHI, providing cover for GP care to manual workers and to lower-earning non-manual workers, was introduced in 1911 (effective from 1912), existing VHI schemes continued much as before even if their role was diminished, providing cover for primary care to the dependants of workers covered by NHI and to others not eligible for NHI coverage, while also offering access to services not covered by NHI. VHI for hospital care was established early in the 20th century once advances in medical technology made hospital care desirable and, at the same time, expensive (Foubister, 2009).

The introduction of the NHS made VHI redundant as a means of assuring access to doctors or hospitals. The VHI market quickly adapted to this new environment to provide access to care for those who did not want to receive care through the NHS and cover for non-clinical quality perceived to be lacking in NHS care. Market development since then has continued in the same vein: adaptation to provide access to care without the perceived shortcomings of NHS care (whether comfort, timeliness or coverage of specific medicines), while seeking and developing new consumers willing to pay for this – in particular the group market, for whom what VHI offers is perceived to contribute to broader occupational health objectives.

The market for supplementary VHI remained relatively stable in terms of subscriber numbers following the introduction of the NHS, expanded rapidly from the mid-1970s to 1990, and has risen more slowly since then, the number of subscribers increasing from 3.5 million in 1992 to 4.3 million in 2009 (King's Fund, 2014). Between 2009 and 2012, numbers fell back to just over 4 million, probably because of the recession following the global financial crisis (LaingBuisson, 2014).

In 2011, supplementary VHI covered 10.9% of the population in the United Kingdom (a decline from 12.4% of the population in 2008). This figure includes cover provided by individual VHI, corporate VHI and self-insured medical expenses schemes (SIMES) or company self-insurance (often administered by external insurers). Some 2% of the population was covered by SIMES, leaving 8.9% covered by traditional VHI plans. Of this 8.9%, only 25% are covered by individual plans (some 2.23% of the population), the remainder being covered by corporate plans (LaingBuisson, 2012).

Types of plan available

VHI provides cover for treatment of acute conditions and is not designed to cover the cost of ongoing chronic care. Ongoing care will usually be covered for a limited time or up to a certain cost. VHI plans fall into three broad categories – comprehensive, standard and budget – and into a further category of what might be called restricted plans. These categories differ primarily in the range of services they cover, in price and in the extent of choice over provider (although this can also vary within categories and be reflected in price). Budget plans can include those that pay a cash sum to the policyholder if they use NHS care instead of their VHI policy or plans that provide cover only if NHS waiting times exceed a predetermined length. Restricted cover plans are those that focus on a very narrow range of services – for instance, cover for high-cost cancer medicines or cover for diagnostics – or on a particular condition or set of related conditions only.

Across categories, pre-existing conditions are not covered and premiums are risk rated for age, risk behaviours and other factors. Plans are renewable annually, but there is generally no new risk rating other than for age (though prices will rise to reflect medical inflation). Other factors affecting the price of the premium within categories are choice of the number of providers to which the policyholder has access and the level of user charges chosen. In the corporate market, premium pricing is based on experience rating, although exclusions may be applied on an individual basis, and again reflects the range of coverage desired and options relating to the number of providers covered and user charges.

Why do people buy VHI?

Individuals buy VHI to avoid potential waiting lists to see a specialist should they need to, have some choice over the specialist they see and to ensure more comfortable surroundings in the event of an inpatient stay. Companies purchase VHI cover for their employees as a fringe benefit or an extension of occupational health services.

Who buys VHI?

Sales of individual VHI have been in long-term decline relative to sales of corporate VHI. In the mid-1980s, the split was roughly half-and-half, but by 2012 individual policyholders accounted for only about a quarter of the market (LaingBuisson, 2014). With a further 2% of the population covered by SIMES, the ratio of corporate to individual cover is higher still.

Most policyholders are located in England, with lower rates of cover in Scotland, Wales and Northern Ireland (Boyle, 2011; Longley et al., 2012; O'Neill, McGregor & Merkur, 2012; Steel & Cylus, 2012). Cover is highest in the south-east of England, with 18.5% of the population there covered; Wales and Scotland had 8.5% covered and Northern Ireland 7% (figures for 2006; reported by LaingBuisson, 2012). Coverage is concentrated among wealthier groups.

Who sells VHI?

In the supplementary VHI market, market concentration as measured by share of premium income is high, with four insurers accounting for 87% of the market (LaingBuisson, 2014). Two insurers dominate, however, with 65% of the market between them – BUPA and AXA PPP Healthcare. The insurer with the third largest share, at 11%, is Aviva Insurance, while VitalityHealth (formerly PruHealth) comes fourth with about 10% (LaingBuisson, 2012). BUPA is the only health-specific insurer of the four, and the only non-profit-making insurer.

Insurer relations with providers

Service providers are paid directly by insurers according to set prices negotiated in advance. The policyholder must choose a provider from the list available to them under the plan they have selected. Insurers have fee schedules for specialists whom they reimburse directly or patients pay and then claim the money back. For specialists who charge more than the standard fee, the patient is expected to pay the difference. Insurers also operate lists of specialists from which the policyholder may choose. Insurers may have arrangements with treatment providers for case-based pricing and for pricing around standard care pathways, and may also use pre-authorization of care or other managed care-type techniques (LaingBuisson 2012).

Public policy towards VHI

Since the introduction of the NHS there has been no health policy interest in VHI and it has not been subject to regulation in respect of its role as a provider of access to health care. VHI is therefore regulated as a financial service only, with a focus on ensuring company solvency; there is also regulation of sales and administration. As with all insurance, premiums are subject to insurance premium tax, although this does not apply to SIMES. Corporate VHI is treated as a benefit in kind and subject to benefit in kind taxation and National Insurance Contributions.

The only significant policy intervention has been around tax relief. Tax relief on VHI premiums was introduced by the Conservative government in 1990 for people older than 60. It was argued that this would stimulate demand, make VHI more accessible to this age group and reduce pressure on the NHS. Tax relief was later withdrawn by the Labour government in 1997. A later study found the presence of tax relief to have had no effect on demand (Emmerson, Frayne & Goodman, 2001). It is likely that tax relief was effectively a subsidy to those who would have bought VHI anyway.

During the 1990s, the Office of Fair Trading launched two enquiries into the market for VHI prompted by concerns regarding possible consumer detriment arising from the complexity of the products being sold, difficulties in comparing products in terms of value for money and the use of moratorium underwriting (Foubister et al., 2006). In response, the insurance industry, through its self-regulatory body – the General Insurance Standards Council – and then the Association of British Insurers, introduced standards that sought to enhance clarity around VHI in its marketing and sales. Nevertheless, VHI remains a complex product and it is difficult for people to make cross-product comparisons based on value for money, especially given the vast proliferation of different products on the market.

Debates and challenges

Debate around VHI has tended to be low key because no government has sought to give it a formal role within the wider health system. What debate there has been has focused on two areas: first, concern about the possible adverse impact of VHI on the NHS; and second, concern about fairness in access to health services.

The adverse impact concern mainly relates to the use of doctors' time. VHI provides cover for the services of senior NHS doctors working in a private capacity. The worry here is that the time these doctors devote to private practice is time lost to the NHS, meaning greater waiting times for NHS patients or substitution of senior medical staff by less experienced junior medical staff (Yates, 1995). A related concern is the implicit subsidy provided by publicly funded medical education to VHI-funded private care. Doctors working in the private sector have been trained in publicly funded institutions, meaning the private sector does not have to invest in education. The NHS also serves as a backup when privately delivered care goes wrong, meaning the private sector does not have to invest in more resource-intensive types of care.

With regard to fairness, the issue is that VHI provides better access to health care for those able to pay – it allows people to access care more quickly, to choose their doctor and to choose the environment in which they receive care. Advantage in access goes against the principle underpinning the United Kingdom health system, which is that access should be based on need and not on ability to pay.

Concerns such as these have been countered by the argument that people are paying for VHI over and above their tax-related contributions to the NHS and, furthermore, that their use of VHI-funded care relieves pressure on the NHS, to the benefit of others. Even if this claim is valid, the benefit is unlikely to outweigh the doctors' time and public subsidy claims. However, there are no clear measures on any of these matters to allow a systematic weighing up of costs and benefits.

Challenges for the VHI market mainly relate to the high cost of VHI, which is expensive by international standards due to the size of the market and the level of specialist fees (King's Fund, 2014). Downward pressure on insurer margins is limited because VHI shows a low elasticity of demand (LaingBuisson, 2012). The diminishing individual market, both relative to the corporate market and in absolute numbers, may not pose too much of a challenge to the VHI market, however, as long as companies continue to see VHI as an attractive benefit for employees and as a contributor to occupational health. Another challenge may be the downward trend in the proportion of senior NHS specialists undertaking private practice – from around 70% in the 1990s to 59% in 2005 and 53% in 2009 (King's Fund, 2014). The workforce undertaking private practice is also ageing – in 2009, the British Medical Association reported that fewer than 10% of new NHS consultants (senior specialists) practised privately (King's Fund, 2014).

The future of VHI

It is likely that the VHI market will continue to take its cue from developments in the NHS, always looking to offer something over and above what the NHS can provide, even if much more limited in range. For example, it could play a role in providing cover to some overseas visitors if governments actively enforce regulations denying access to NHS care for people not ordinarily resident, and to students from outside the EU if policy discussion to limit access to NHS care for these people becomes a reality.

The single largest potential for an altered role for insurers in future is their involvement in administering new clinical commissioning groups – the new doctor-led agencies purchasing NHS care for geographical populations. These agencies have greater freedoms than the purchasing agencies they replaced, and with insurer involvement in NHS purchasing there is potential for insurers to seek to develop new ways for VHI and NHS-funded care to be combined.

References

Boyle S (2011). United Kingdom (England): health system review. *Health Systems in Transition*, 13(1):1–486.

Emmerson C, Frayne C, Goodman A (2001). Should private medical insurance be subsidised? *Health Care UK* 2001:49–65 (http://www.ifs.org.uk/docs/private_med.pdf, accessed 22 November 2015).

Foubister T (2009). The United Kingdom. In: Thomson S, Mossialos E, eds. *Private health insurance in the European Union*. Final report prepared for the European Commission, Directorate General for Employment, Social Affairs and Equal Opportunities. London and Brussels, LSE Health and Social Care, London School of Economics and Political Science and European Commission:315–328.

Foubister T et al. (2006). *Private medical insurance in the United Kingdom*. Copenhagen, WHO Regional Office for Europe on behalf of the European Observatory on Health Systems and Policies.

King's Fund (2014). *The UK private health market*. Commission on the Future of Health and Social Care in England. London, The King's Fund (http://www.kingsfund.org.uk/sites/files/kf/media/commission-appendix-uk-private-health-market.pdf, accessed 22 November 2015).

LaingBuisson (2012). Laing's healthcare market review 2011/12. London, LaingBuisson.

LaingBuisson (2014). Laing's healthcare market review 2013/14. London, LaingBuisson.

Longley M et al. (2012). United Kingdom (Wales): health system review. *Health Systems in Transition*, 14(11):1–84.

O'Neill C, McGregor P, Merkur S (2012). United Kingdom (Northern Ireland): health system review. *Health Systems in Transition*, 14(10):1–91.

Steel D, Cylus J (2012). United Kingdom (Scotland): health system review. *Health Systems in Transition*, 14(9):1–150.

WHO (2016). Global Health Expenditure Database (GHED) [online database]. Geneva, WHO (http://www.who.int/health-accounts/ghed/en/, accessed 5 April 2016).

Yates J (1995). *Private eye, heart and hip*. Edinburgh, Churchill Livingstone.